research
practice
for cultural studies

ann gray

research
practice
for cultural studies

ethnographic methods and lived cultures

SAGE Publications
Los Angeles • London • New Delhi • Singapore

First published 2003
Reprinted 2004, 2005, 2006, 2007

SAGE Publications Ltd
1 Oliver's Yard
55 City Road
London EC1Y 1SP

SAGE Publications Inc
2455 Teller Road
Thousand Oaks, California 91320

SAGE Publications India Pvt Ltd
B1/I 1 Mohan Cooperative Industrial Area
Mathura Road, New Delhi 110 044
India

SAGE Publications Asia-Pacific Pte Ltd
33 Pekin Street #02-01
Far East Square
Singapore 048763

British Library Cataloguing in Publication data

A catalogue record for this book is available from
the British Library

ISBN: 978-0-7619-5174-2 (hbk)
ISBN: 978-0-7619-5175-9 (pbk)

Library of Congress catalogue card number 2002102786

Printed and bound in Great Britain by
Athenaeum Press Ltd., Gateshead, Tyne & Wear

Contents

Acknowledgements

I would like to thank the many stimulating and challenging students who have spent time in the Department of Cultural Studies and Sociology at the University of Birmingham and whose questions convinced me of the need for a book like this. In writing the book I have drawn on the work of many wonderful and inspirational scholars – my thanks to them for providing so many rich examples. Thanks are also due to all my colleagues in the Department, but I am especially indebted to, Jan Campbell, Beth Edginton, Mark Erickson, Michael Green and Stuart Hanson with whom I have taught and whose support and friendship have been essential to the quality of my working and personal life. Frank Webster also provided much needed encouragement in the latter stages of writing.

Many friends have provided essential support, but I am especially grateful to Charlotte Brunsdon and Joke Hermes who listened to me, often fed me and who always made me feel better. I wish to thank Joke, especially, for reading the book in draft and for leaving Pieter, Sacha and Noah behind in order to spend a crucial weekend with me in September 2001. Finally, my thanks to Nick Gray who, as ever, is generous with his time, energy, love and respect.

Ann Gray

Since writing this book the Department of Cultural Studies and Sociology at Birmingham has been subject to abrupt closure with devastating effects on staff and students. I would like to offer this book as a modest testimony to the work carried out at Birmingham in cultural studies by staff and students from the early days of the CCCS to the present.

AG

for *Nick*

Introduction

My aim in writing this book is to enable students and researchers within the broad field of cultural studies to approach the study of some aspect of the social world. This might be a small-scale project, an assessment for a module, for example, a final year dissertation or a more ambitious master's dissertation or doctoral thesis. There is a need to grasp the intellectual dimensions of the chosen topic and the available methods, but there are many more fundamental questions that should be asked. What exactly are we trying to do? What is research itself? How do we generate a research topic? Where might you position yourself as a researcher and generator of a study? The questions are the same for us all and immediately present themselves as we embark on an exploration of some aspect of cultural processes.

An important part of the project of this book is to work through an understanding of what constitutes cultural studies itself. It is the case that cultural studies means different things to different people within the academy, and any attempt to produce an account of what cultural studies is, or to plot its history and development is bound to be selective. The label itself is used within departments of English, modern languages, sociology and communication and media studies. It is also used as a 'catch-all' title for degree programmes that combine different elements of the humanities and social sciences. My approach to definitions here, which will be discussed further in Chapter 1, is to insist that cultural studies is an interdisciplinary and open field of enquiry which is in constant development and, in its institutional form in the academy, will take on different complexions depending on that context. However, I want to argue that one of the key characteristics of cultural studies is that of understanding culture as constitutive of and constituted by 'the lived', that is the material, social and symbolic practices of everyday life. This focus can most obviously be traced back, in the British case, to Raymond Williams work in the late 1950s and early 1960s. His works, *Culture and Society* (1958) and *The Long Revolution* (1961) were concerned, among other things, to wrench 'culture' from its artistic and literary ties and insist that 'culture is ordinary'. This was to understand culture in its more anthropological sense as the product of the social interactions of everyday life. Williams was concerned to democratise culture and, in a sense, to universalise it as that which is present in all forms of social life. It was, perhaps, the democratising potential of Williams' formulation, along with a sense of the politics of culture that focused cultural studies on 'lived experience'. Thus, many of the scholars, from different intellectual backgrounds, who have worked in the field in the past and present have recognised the importance of the empirical study of ways in which 'the cultural' is constituted by and is constitutive of 'the social' in and through the practice of everyday life. One of the contentions of this book is that these studies have been, and remain important sites for the continuation of complex and dynamic ways of thinking about culture and the cultural within the field.

The book has three main but related aims. First, to give a critical selective account of ethnographic methods which have been used within cultural studies. Throughout the book I will constantly refer to the importance of locating oneself, as intellectual, researcher and writer, thus, I must acknowledge my own location in the Department of Cultural Studies and Sociology at the University of Birmingham, the successor of the Centre for Contemporary Cultural Studies (CCCS). Indeed, the early part of this book addresses the work carried out by scholars at the CCCS in the period 1960-80 which, arguably, saw the emergence of a particular version of cultural studies. However, my construction of this version of cultural studies is not to identify, nor claim it as the originating point of cultural studies, but to indicate how the field took on certain contours through different engagements with methods and methodologies. This will suggest that there is a core within the field which has been engaged in the attempt to study 'life-worlds' of groups, users, consumers, agents and that, in doing this, cultural studies has developed a particular set of qualitative methods which have often been described as ethnographic.

Second, the book will offer guidance on how to approach research. From the initial question to its final written form(s). And finally, it will encourage the reader researcher to reflect on epistemological questions, that is, how we know what we know and the relationship between the knower and the known, proposing, as Beverley Skeggs has argued that 'there is no such thing as a disinterested knower' (1997: 27). While these threads are woven through the whole text, it will be possible for readers to use the book in different ways. For example, those students who are about to attempt a piece of research can dive straight in to Chapter 4 and follow through to Chapter 9. I hope, however, that while it should be a useful book for solving research problems, it will also intrigue the reader into a curiosity about the broader historical context of cultural studies and the deeper epistemological questions which research engenders.

This, in part, is a 'how to' book which I have been moved to write because, as a teacher of research methods to undergraduate and postgraduate cultural studies students, there is no such text to which I can direct students. Cultural studies is now the subject of degrees and as such is assessing and examining students on their learning and skills. While many writers insist that cultural studies is not a discipline as such, there exists some, albeit implicit, agreement about its existence as a teachable and assessable field of study. Books like this and others such as readers or text books (e.g. During, 1993; Gray and McGuigan, 1993, 1995; Barker, 2000) are all in the business of defining what they mean by cultural studies, its histories and its 'best practice'. This is a tension, then, throughout this book, a tension acknowledged by Larry Grossberg when he confesses: 'Those of us working in "cultural studies" find ourselves caught between the need to define and defend its specificity and the desire to refuse to close off the ongoing history of cultural studies by any such act of definition. This is, it must be said, a real dilemma' (1996a: 179).

Indeed, in thinking about the structure of this book and when writing initial drafts, I was constantly moving between the 'how to' prescription and a desire to resist 'pinning down' the field or to provide any set or guaranteed research procedures. In order to work with this ambivalence and to keep faith with this project I recalled the countless conversations I have had with students over the years about research methods. The questions they asked then, such as, 'But how did you go about analysing your interview material?' and 'Well, how many interviews should I do?' or 'Are five (or ten or twenty) interviews sufficient?' served to remind me of the absence of texts which address methods within the context of an interdisciplinary field such as cultural studies. But these questions are also indicative of commonly held attitudes to research methods. My response to such questions, much to the frustration of the students, is to say 'Well, it depends on what you are trying to do' before encouraging them to articulate the actual aims of their project. Their questions come, I believe, from misunderstandings about the nature of inquiry, the relationship between the methods of empirical research and the main questions or focus of the research area under study. Thus, I am not setting out to prescribe particular sets of methods or develop a cultural studies method, rather this book is an investigation of methods which I address in relation to what a cultural studies project might want to do within a theoretical framework and in identifying its 'knowable subject'.

One of the inherent dangers in concentrating on empirical studies and those which explore the social world of lived experience is to imply that this is the 'real' or the only 'acceptable' version of cultural studies. I do not want to suggest that, nor do I want students go away from this book with the idea that an investigation of the empirical world of, say, consumers and their uses of cultural forms, is a necessary part of cultural studies. There are many examples of wonderful work that would be included in the field of inquiry which does not address lived practice. Furthermore, in examining 'ethnographic methods' I do not wish to claim that this will give access through some notion of authenticity, to some 'real' truth and therefore that empirical work is the only kind of investigation that is worth doing. This view, based on doubtful notions of 'the authentic', will be questioned throughout the book. On the other hand, however, perhaps we do need to question the legitimacy and authority claimed for theoretical work and the focus on textual analysis. Why does the academic community invest so much power in these intellectual practices often to the detriment of other accounts or versions of the world? This is to suggest that we should reflect on the shaping of research in which the theoretical framework is the dominant narrative. I would insist that all research and scholarly work should begin by justifying the very object of its study, whether this is theoretical, textual or empirical. It is not sufficient to take this as a given even if (or because) we have powerful institutional backing which supports us in our silence.

What is method?

It is important to understand what is meant by the terms method and methodology. These are terms that are often used interchangeably, but they refer to very different dimensions of research and scholarly inquiry. Putting it simply, method refers to those different techniques of research which any researcher employs in order to construct data and interrogate its sources, while methodology describes the overall epistemological approach adopted by the study. There are important philosophical and political issues to be raised in relation to an understanding of epistemology which pedagogically are often kept apart from the more 'practical' issues of method. I will argue that these issues are integral to the research process and this has informed the structure of this book. Suffice it to say at this point that our choice of methods says a lot about our approach to what is to be known and ways of knowing the world.

It is certainly the case that all disciplines have, to a greater or lesser degree, agreed sets of methodologies for the pursuance of their research or investigation. It is interesting to note to what extent these methodologies are implicit or, alternatively, made explicit within the field. In the humanities, for example, the approach to method is not so developed or debated, although in areas such as critical art history this has formed an important strand within the fields of film, cultural and visual studies (e.g. Tagg, 1988). In the social sciences the opposite is the case as there is a long history of writing on methodology, with, perhaps, a tendency to an over-rigid version of research methods. The prescriptive approach to methods often found in methodology text books and on some research methods courses implies that, once understood and mastered, methods can then be applied to any number of research topics and questions. This is to understand methods as a set of 'generic' skills rather than as procedures which should be considered to be integral to the research topic, its problematic and its site of investigation. While there are clearly things to be known about techniques of, say, carrying out interviews, or how to think about selecting a sample, these are not 'rules' set in tablets of stone. Nor are they simply 'tools' to be taken up and tried. Rather, they must themselves be generated through the development of the project. Questions of method, therefore, cannot be settled and resolved in the early stages, but will recur throughout the research engendering questions, not only about the 'what' of the research, but also about the 'how' of it. This reflexive approach to research is appropriate for studies that seek to explore the complexities of social and cultural processes, meanings and practices.

Since doing my own study of the use of the VCR (Gray, 1992) and in developing my current study of 'enterprise cultures' (Gray, 2001), questions of method and methodology have fascinated me. I am well aware that this fascination and enthusiasm are not shared and are often thought of as downright weird. In part this can be accounted for by the rather dry and abstract ways in which methods have been written about and taught, which are far from exciting. The reasons for this, in my view, are that, in many cases, methods are divorced from the stuff of research and students can be forgiven for being less than enthusiastic about these texts. My enthusiasms were caught and given expression in a book to which I have returned since those days. C. Wright Mills' *The Sociological Imagination* (1959) which I recommend most warmly to students embarking on any form of social or cultural research. He was deeply resistant to the fixing of methods and insisted, rather on the importance in understanding the 'craft' involved in intellectual work. He insisted on a rigorous approach and that 'respect for materials, clarity about objectives and a sense of the high drama and stakes of intellectual life' were what made for work of value. The concluding chapter of *The Sociological Imagination*, 'On Intellectual Craftsmanship' is an inspirational read and no less relevant than it must have been when it was written in the 1950s.

Cultural studies, methodology and methods

Cultural studies has become notorious for, among other things, its neglect of considerations of method and methodology (e.g. Tudor, 1999) and, in some ways this book is an attempt to respond to this flaw. However, in looking at the often innovative research methods which have been adopted by scholars, I regard this methodological eclecticism to be a strength within the field and evidence of the energy and dynamic nature of much of which we would describe as cultural studies. It is a malleable and ever-changing field. The subjects, the theoretical developments and politics of new work are often cited as examples of these dynamics. However, I would suggest that the methodological strategies adopted by scholars, in order to explore new research agendas, are as interesting a part of the development and shaping of cultural studies as those more obvious features.

When I was developing my own research project and trying to put Wright Mills' advice into practice, two of the most interesting texts I read came from the CCCS and both talked about method. Paul Willis whose work over many years has problematised questions of methods in cultural studies, refers to the element of 'surprise' in research. He also speaks of the importance of listening to people, of respecting their accounts, and of the necessity to attend to sensuous human experience. This appealed to my, admittedly, idealistic approach to research and intellectual work in general. It also put real flesh on the bones of methodological questions. In a similar vein, Angela McRobbie's 'The politics of feminist research: between talk, text and action' (1982) talks about the politics of feminist research as that which negotiates between intellectual developments, empirical work and the wider 'grass roots' feminist politics. Here were authors advocating a spirit of inventiveness and insisting that methods are and must be 'strategic'. They, and other researchers, encouraged me to allow my area of research and the questions I wanted to explore to develop my approach and not to feel tied to a certain set of methods. In spite of the intellectual support afforded by such authors, some of the most challenging and difficult parts of my research involved issues relating to method. They threatened the continuation of my research more than once and caused me to sink into depths of despair. It is during that process of thinking and working out our methods, formulating strategies and clarifying our position that interesting questions and dilemmas arise. In addition, there is a myriad of unsettling obstacles, disappointments and surprises that can confront us in our research encounters in our chosen location. Thus, while wishing to encourage inventiveness, you will need to be aware of the choices of method and approach explored in this book and of what the consequences are of making particular choices in order to make the most of your research topic and to produce good work.

Outline of the book

This book draws on a number of studies, in addition to my own, in order to demonstrate particular methods and approaches. These have been selected because they exemplify particular research strategies and approaches, but also because all the authors reflect on their research methods and, in most cases, the politics of research. Many have engaged with 'cultural studies' from different intellectual backgrounds, e.g. social and cultural anthropology, psychology, communication and media studies, sociology and gender studies. All are interesting critical researchers, but I have found that I have constantly returned to the work of two scholars, Beverley Skeggs and Les Back. The reason for their appearance at different stages in the book, is that they both problematise ethnographic research methods while insisting that they are of value in generating knowledge. They both speak of their positions and roles as researchers, the politics of their work, their own identities and reflect on the ways in which they have presented their work in written forms. One way of developing good researcher practice is to read others' work and I recommend that you read the full versions of some of the research examples that I give throughout the book.

The research examples also plot a trajectory, or a narrative, of the study of 'lived cultures' across cultural studies and, as I suggest in Chapter 3, present us with key characters or 'figures on the landscape' of cultural studies. These figures begin as the classed and gendered subjects of early studies at the CCCS, to the more multiple, diverse, de-centred and dispersed 'identities' of more recent work. This trajectory can be mapped onto broader theoretical developments across the humanities and social sciences, especially the impact of post-structuralisms, but also onto the internationalisation of cultural studies. In many ways, in writing this book, I have attempted to respond to Angela McRobbie's suggestion that:

> [It] is necessary that we somehow move away from the binary opposition which still haunts cultural studies, that is, the distinction between text and lived experience, between media and reality, between culture and society. What is now required is a methodology, a new paradigm for conceptualising identity-in-culture, an ethnographic approach which takes as its starting point the relational interactive quality of everyday life and which brings a renewed rigor to this kind of work by integrating into it a keen sense of history and contingency. (1992: 730)

I see this binary between the text and the social as a methodological issue and one which this book will attempt to move beyond by suggesting different ways in which we can mobilise and explore the figure of an 'identity-in-culture', to which McRobbie refers, in all its complexity through qualitative or ethnographic investigation.

The book is divided into two parts: Part I, 'Ethnographic Methods' and Part II, 'The Research Process'.

Chapter 1, 'Grasping Lived Cultures' looks at how cultural studies has drawn on methods developed in sociology and anthropology with particular reference to the 'problem' of the text for both these more established disciplines. Critiques of ethnography, especially in relation to the construction of 'the other' are addressed, before moving towards developments in both sociology and anthropology that have themselves been influenced by cultural studies. Here the importance of reflexivity and the development of a modest epistemology are explored.

Chapter 2, 'Articulating Experience' focuses on the concept of experience as a key category in cultural studies work. It asks how we can use this problematic category in our research raising epistemological questions to which its use gives rise.

Chapter 3, 'Imagined Communities: The Spectacular and the Ordinary' presents work developed at the CCCS as a 'cultural studies case study' and looks at how particular kinds of topics, issues and questions emerge in this particular context. Drawing on the notion of 'imagined communities', it identifies 'figures on the landscape' of this early work before tracking later and more dispersed developments in researching 'lived cultures'. It is the contention of this book that research and intellectual work in cultural studies are highly contextual and this chapter includes two 'communities' which are often notable for their absence in research. The communities of the powerful, hardly ever examined by cultural studies, and the academic community itself as a significant but usually hidden shaping force in our work.

Chapter 4, 'A Question of Research' concludes Part I of the book in discussing how we begin to focus on a research topic and what might be at stake in doing this. Questions of epistemology, validity and the ethics and politics of research are included here as important questions to be posed, if not answered, at this stage in your research.

Part II, while bearing in mind questions of epistemology, contains more practical and detailed chapters on various stages of the research process.

Chapter 5, 'Locating Instances and Generating Material' covers what might conventionally be called 'data gathering'. Here we address this notion through a cultural studies lens before looking at participant observation and interviewing as key strategies in gathering research material. Sampling and issues of power and difference are also discussed here.

Chapter 6, 'I Want to Tell You a Story' introduces the increasing significance of autobiography in cultural studies, and in other approaches to research. Its emphasis is on 'storying' as it draws on work using autobiography, testimony, life-story and memory while also discussing the role of the 'autobiography' of researcher or cultural critic in research.

Chapter 7, 'Tying in the Texts' goes to the crux of much cultural studies work when it asks how we might 'tie in the text' to our studies of lived cultures. We first of all think about what we mean by 'the text' in an increasingly saturated textual world before looking briefly at the different approaches to texts upon which cultural studies has drawn. The second half of the chapter is devoted to some excellent examples of research which have created rich studies of the textual and the lived, from female romance readers, families watching television in New Delhi, fans and Trekkies to new kinds of audiences for 'reality TV' shows such as *Big Brother*.

Chapter 8, 'Strategies and Tactics in Analysis' addresses the important questions of analysis of data, often the process least written about in finished research publications. It looks at different analytical approaches that have been used in cultural studies projects and offers very practical suggestions for analytical procedures.

Chapter 9, 'Writing' deals with the problems associated with writing. The book follows other 'methods' texts which always save writing for the last chapter. Its position here should not indicate that writing is the last stage in the research process. Indeed, the earlier chapters all emphasise the importance of writing as a continuous process and useful 'thinking tool' in the development of research and, more broadly, our intellectual trajectories. Why not buck the tradition and read this one first?

Chapter 10, 'Sources of Knowledge and Ways of Knowing' as the concluding chapter returns to broader issues within research into lived cultures.

It suggests, drawing on the exploration of research examples included in the book, that in order to respond to social change through an address to the experience of everyday life, we need to work on theories of subjectivity and identity and to ask what the consequences are of Ang's insistence on the 'radical contextualisation' of research. In order to do this I return to questions of appropriate evaluative criteria for cultural studies work. This chapter also indicates new research into 'diasporic cultures' which suggests ways forward in continuing to produce relevant, provisional, modest and contingent studies which have shaped the field.

As researchers starting work in the twenty-first century, you are doing so in a period of uncertainty, both globally and epistemologically, in which social change is rapid and in which methods and methodologies themselves are in a certain amount of turmoil. Claims to 'truth' and 'the real' are questioned across the humanities and social sciences to the extent that 'social science and ethnography have become one version of reality amongst many' (Denzin, 1997: 45).

Lest this context of 'uncertainty' and 'provisionality' places us in a quicksand of anxiety, let me suggest ways of raising some questions which will help us ground our research practice. These are in relation to the politics of knowledge. This is to suggest that politics operate at a number of levels and are always an important element in what we do and research is no exception. We need to be aware of what it is to begin to know and to claim the right to produce knowledge, what is involved in this and what is the nature of our relationship to knowledge. My approach throughout the book means to keep these issues in mind, they run like threads through any attempt to understand the world and it is as well to acknowledge them and deal with them. Questions such as 'how am I entitled to call this knowledge?' and 'what gives me the right to investigate people's lives?' have a habit of entering your mind during the process of your research, and usually when you have the least reserves to cope. Probably when you are knocking on someone's door asking for an interview, or knee-deep in interview transcripts wondering how to make a start on your analysis, or even when you can't quite seem to get started on formulating a research topic.

One of the most important factors in all the different stages of your research is to feel centred and confident in what you are doing. This is usually best achieved by stepping back, by re-thinking your purposes and reasons for wanting to do the project in the first place and by asking yourself exactly why you became interested in this phenomenon. Research has a nasty habit of running away with you and can do so at any stage, from reading masses of theoretical texts and earlier related research projects, to analysis of your data and writing. You will need to develop strategies for coping and continually (re)building your confidence. This book, if it achieves its aim, will encourage you to find a position of strength within your intellectual work. It will not always be comfortable and should be challenging. There already exists wonderful work which has been produced by people like you who have brought to cultural studies important new questions about the cultural world, about power and agency, about inequalities and dismissal of the so-called trivial. Keep on bringing new questions to your study and you will find the space to explore these within the constantly emerging field of inquiry known as 'cultural studies'.

Part I

ETHNOGRAPHIC METHODS

<table>
<tr><td>o n e</td><td>Grasping Lived Cultures</td></tr>
</table>

If at the end of the twentieth century ... one were inventing a method of enquiry by which to grasp the complexity of social life, one might wish to invent something like the social anthropologist's ethnographic practice. (Strathern, 1999)

'What is cultural studies?' This is a question with which, as students and researchers within cultural studies, you will no doubt be familiar. It is one that is just as likely to be posed by curious friends and family as in the many weighty articles in books and journals that have attempted to provide answers. The very necessity of this question and the generation of lively debates and disagreements as to what constitutes cultural studies are indicative of some of the key characteristics which have shaped this book. These are the lack of clear-cut boundaries and disciplinary certainty that suggests a 'field of inquiry' rather than a fixed and stable discipline. As such, what can variously be described as 'cultural studies' will take on different contours and raise specific topics, issues and questions in different locations which, in turn, will be shaped by intellectual paradigms as well as national cultural contexts. Indeed, the debates and discussions that inform the different manifestations of cultural studies produce different emphases, foregrounding different aspects of culture. However, the many undergraduate and postgraduate programmes in cultural studies simply must, through selection and often simplification, produce one version of cultural studies for their curriculum. The point is that what might constitute this field of inquiry is open for discussion and tentative. What I consider to be important is to think about how we can make sense of the ways in which culture is produced in and through everyday living, what Raymond Williams called 'lived cultures', the focus of this book (Williams, 1981: 11). Meaghan Morris recently posed what, especially in relation to research methods, I think is a productive question. She asks, 'What does cultural studies *do?*' (my emphasis). Put this way, the question demands a different kind of response, one which requires more practical and substantive examples in order to demonstrate the concerns of the field. To begin to answer her own question, Morris draws on Henri Lefebvre and his notion of the 'critique of everyday life' which she suggests is at the heart of cultural studies (Lefebvre, 1990): 'an investigation of particular ways of using "culture", of what is available as culture to people inhabiting particular social contexts, and of people's ways of making culture' (Morris, 1997: 43). This formulation provides some markers for identifying the concerns of cultural studies as a field of enquiry and it specifically points to that aspect which is central to this book: the cultures of everyday life. In addition, it insists on the materiality of culture. Here culture is not a free-floating set of ideas or beliefs, nor is it exemplified only by a canon of great works of art or literature. The meanings, processes and artefacts of culture are produced, distributed and consumed within particular material circumstances. In other words, texts and practices are both products of and constitutive of the social world. This is made up of a whole range of organisations, from, for example, institutions of the media and other cultural producers, the family, education and various agencies of civil society to everyday practices within specific social groups. Therefore, any attempt to understand culture and cultural processes must take account of this always complex set of material conditions. Questions of power and access are also contained in Morris's formulation. Thus, to ask who has access to specific and legitimised forms of culture and who is excluded is to raise questions about the determinants and dynamics of inclusion and exclusion. There are powerful forces which shape cultural processes and products. Cultural studies, however, acknowledges that people can and do engage actively in their uses of cultural artefacts in making sense of their own and others' lives.

Thus, Morris' formulation is already suggestive of the terrain of cultural studies concerns. Culture is understood as being actively produced through complex processes. It is broadly the production of meaning, or 'signifying practice' that happens at every level of the social and at every moment within cultural processes. This leads to questions about how and in what ways human beings make culture, why and to what end. How culture and the cultural shapes social relations and, more broadly, how culture takes its place in instigating or resisting social change. In order to begin to investigate these complex sets of relationships which are present in cultural processes we require a variety of methods ranging from textual analysis, observation, different ways of gathering knowledge and information from individuals and groups, such as diaries, different kinds of interviews and participant observation. Morris puts great emphasis on 'lived experience' in her formulation and this will be the focus of this book. However, 'texts' which includes written texts, e.g. literature, the press, but also visual, e.g. film, photography, advertising, aural, e.g. music, radio, and other kinds of symbolic artefacts, e.g. fashion, will clearly feature in our field of research. Thus it is important to identify some of the key issues in relation to texts and lived experience, and indeed, the consumers of those texts.

In the late 1950s, Raymond Williams wrote tellingly of the highly selective nature of the literary canon, which works were included and which excluded, and called into question the way in which the academy approached the text (Williams, 1958). Alongside the canon of literary texts were methods of analysis that privileged the text and sought to identify the inherent meanings within the text. Building on Williams's insights, those working within the emerging field of cultural studies looked for methods of analysing texts which did not necessarily follow the existing approaches from, mainly, literary studies. Such scholars brought different kinds of questions to the text. They were not interested in finding the inherent meaning within the text but in the significance of different elements of the text in constructing what could be a multiplicity of meanings. In addition to this they were critical of evaluation which was implicit in the very selection of the texts for study. Of importance here was the work of structuralist Roland Barthes (1977) and that of the formalists, such as Propp (1968), which provided the necessary concepts for more 'scientific' modes of textual analysis. This was to look at how the text worked through different elements such as narrative structure; character function; cultural codification, etc. and what kind of 'reality' the text constructed. In addition, Roland Barthes' collection *Mythologies* (1972) expanded the very notion of 'the text' to such activities as a wrestling match, consumer goods such as cars and children's toys and the images and language of advertising, and exposing the ideological nature of the text. Barthes' work informed much of the early work on textual analysis, especially the analysis of advertisements, visual texts and popular fiction. It provided a way of departing from the evaluative study of texts and placing them within their social, cultural and political contexts. Barthes' work and that of his followers 'read' texts within a perceived cultural and ideological context, but it was not obvious how to figure out the relationship between the text and its social context and, in particular how readers interpreted the text. As Angela McRobbie (1992) observes, there is still a distinction within cultural studies between 'text and lived experience'. I now want to look at why this distinction might still maintain.

The social and the textual

The perceived division between the social and the textual can be seen more generally within the structures of the academy. Broadly speaking, it can be defined as the split between the social sciences and the humanities. It assumes different objects of study and has developed particular concepts and methods. The divide has created much friction within the emerging field of cultural studies, spanning both disciplines, and many have insisted that 'true' cultural studies must go beyond an analysis of the text itself. They argue that texts must be understood within particular material conditions. These are usually identified in terms of a 'circuit' made up of the different stages of production, text and reader. The analysis of texts themselves, no matter how sophisticated the framework, nor how broadly a text might be defined, they argue, is of limited use in understanding the circulation of culture and the production of meaning. In other words, the text must be seen as both a product of particular social, cultural and historical conditions and as an agent in circulation. Richard Johnson, who succeeded Stuart Hall as director of the CCCS, presents a more subtle argument in suggesting that it is important to clarify how 'the textual' is understood. He cites scholars who have investigated bodies of literature for their broadly discursive practices in the engendering, for example, of imperialism (Said, 1978) and suggests that the re-evaluation of bodies of texts, or genres such as this are involved 'not so much in the literary text itself, but more in the "larger social text"' (Johnson, 1997: 465), that is the discourses of power which operated in constructing those texts, which becomes the object of study. In considering the status of 'the textual' in cultural studies it is useful to quote Stuart Hall: 'To me, cultural studies is impossible without retaining the moment of the symbolic; with the textual, language, subjectivity and representation forming the key matrix' (Hall, 1996: 403, quoted in Johnson, 1997: 464). Thus, for Johnson and Hall the textual is a crucial element in cultural studies, but as they suggest, it is the expanded notion of the textual which informs such research.

By way of example, let us consider a cultural form like the soap opera. Produced by television and some radio broadcasting organisations, structured through particular generic conventions, transmitted via television and radio and watched or listened to by large numbers of people. The text itself can be subject to analysis and in relation to national identity, race, class, gender and sexuality. But, is that where the soap opera text ends? What about the many auxiliary texts which accrue around a popular soap opera; the tabloid press, the gossip magazines, other television genres, for example, the chat show, books and the more ephemeral yet significant chat and gossip conducted between fans or casual followers of the serial? Everyday chat about television, and especially long-running serials, provides important social currency, and here we move into how the consumption of soap opera, and other popular forms, construct identity, a sense of self and relationship to others. This simple example should alert us to the dangers of marking dividing lines between the text and the social.

Thus, we can concur with Johnson when he questions the split between the social and the textual insisting that it is a 'phoney' division. Furthermore, he insists that the social is textual and the division does not serve cultural studies' intent which is to tap into cultural structures and formations, through and via evoking responses to questions, discussions, conversations, as well as observations. But it is the case that the academic study of texts, cultural artefacts and the ways in which they are used and understood, have been marked out for particular study and for the purposes of analysis. For most of us, however, popular media forms, and other 'texts' are entwined in our everyday lives, they provide a shared social and cultural currency and their images, catch-phrases and characters often settle into the sediment of popular memory. Furthermore, we draw on the rich resources of narrative, image, style which circulate within the symbolic worlds of media in thinking about ourselves, who we are and who we might become.

This emphasis on the 'lived' and the 'social' in the development of cultural studies in the late 1960s and 1970s, clearly required a range of methods which would enable the researchers to explore specific practices and contexts within which cultural texts and artefacts were produced and consumed. These developments will be addressed in Chapter 3, but for now I want to look at what existing methods were available to researchers in the 1970s who were attempting to ask new questions of new social phenomena such as youth subcultures, popular culture and the media. Two relevant disciplinary areas were sociology and anthropology. In this period, sociology itself had begun to move towards more qualitative and interpretive methods and the notion of 'lived cultures' proposed by Williams was suggestive of an anthropological approach. It will be useful to explore briefly some of the key distinctions between sociology, anthropology and cultural studies.

Sociology, anthropology and cultural studies: different questions, different methods

It is perhaps when looking at methods and methodologies that we can shed the most light on the differences between, and within disciplinary areas. Cultural studies has appropriated a range of methods from different disciplines, for example, textual analysis, historiography and historical analysis and psychoanalysis and drawn upon them as and when they are appropriate to its object of study. When specifically seeking to investigate the social practices of lived cultures it has drawn from methods developed within sociology and anthropology. Thus we can identify a range of methods that sociology labels 'qualitative' and which anthropology labels 'ethnographic'. In adopting and sometimes adapting research methods more associated with other disciplines, projects carried out under the umbrella of cultural studies have been the subject of critique from both sociological and anthropological perspectives. At this stage a brief examination of the nature of the critiques can effectively reveal what is distinctive about the cultural studies approach to the cultures of everyday life and the necessary adaptation of existing methods. The criticisms inevitably point to absences and shortcomings and can be categorised as follows:

1   Scale and breadth. The most common critique from sociology is that the studies focus on specific examples, they draw on a limited number of respondents and are therefore inadequate in representativeness and generalisability, two key criteria of validity in sociological research.

2   Depth and duration. The dominant critique from anthropology is that cultural studies research tends not to immerse itself in the cultural or social site or the worlds of their respondents. There is little attempt, they argue, to provide broad context over time of the subjects and their cultural practices.

According to the thrust of these critiques, research carried out in the name of cultural studies is neither sufficiently broad nor sufficiently 'in-depth' to satisfy certain established criteria. The assumption here is that cultural studies conceptualises the subject, the social world and even the cultural in ways which are commensurate with the sociological and anthropological approaches. The methods employed by cultural studies researchers have certainly been shaped and influenced by the demands of existing approaches and this book will explore how they engaged with and were critical of them. But for now, I want to over-simplify the implications of the sociological and anthropological critiques in order to make my point about the distinctiveness of the cultural studies approach.

Scale and breadth

It is important to think about what is produced through adopting different kinds of methods. Survey methods, drawing on large samples, can usefully reveal social patterns or overall trends. For example, through large data sets we can establish how many people go to football matches, or how many people watch *EastEnders*. Surveys could go further and identify which social classes go to football and watch *EastEnders*, and to some extent, the reasons they give for doing this. Thus a sociological project using these kinds of methods is preoccupied with the study of 'population' (Johnson, 1997). While it can ask an infinite range of critical and analytical questions about this phenomenon and develop theories, concepts and categories for understanding, via a whole range of methods, quantitative and qualitative, it will, in the main, be seeking to produce some representative and generalisable results which can shed light on the movements, formation, dimensions, changes in that broader population. It is the case that empirical studies using qualitative methods, such as in-depth interviews, while eliciting deeper accounts from respondents, tend to be seen as adjuncts, or preliminary to the necessary larger-scale study. But what surveys cannot do is to explore the questions which are important for cultural studies, such as, the reasons for investments in such texts and/or practices, what meanings they have for people in their everyday lives, and the significance of how they account for this engagement. Furthermore, cultural studies would seek to explore how these practices might relate to identity, to a sense of self and to social relations, questions that a larger sample would not necessarily deliver.

Depth and duration

Anthropologists insist that work carried out by cultural studies in its ethnographic mode does not engage sufficiently with the subjects of their research. This requires us to think about the value, and indeed the practicalities of 'immersion' in the ways of life of our subjects. This assumption about 'proper ethnographies' is redolent of the by now much criticised intrepid anthropologist exploring a hitherto unknown 'field' and 'culture' in a specific place and time. But, quite apart from matters of intrusion involved in long-term 'observation' the kinds of contemporary cultures we are interested in are those which, to a greater or lesser extent, we inhabit ourselves. Thus, we are already to a certain extent, participant observers in our studies. But, more fundamentally, John Fiske (1996) suggests that the critics are somehow missing the aims of the researchers who are, he insists, primarily 'interested in meaning making'. I would concur, but go further and suggest that what cultural studies work attempts to do is to explore meaning in relation to the construction of social and cultural identity. These questions about the nature of the relationship between identity and subjectivity and lived cultures have primarily been carried out in relation to an understanding of the interpretation, consumption and use of 'texts'. Arguably, this requires periods of intense investigation into meaning production, rather than extended periods of observation. Extended time spent with groups as participant observers would not necessarily be any more productive than listening to people in close conversational interviews. In fact, extending the range of descriptive accounts might be the only possible achievement here. The production of rich descriptive accounts of social and cultural practices is valuable, but we must always ask what the epistemological value of this data might be. Perhaps the use of more innovative methods, employing conceptual and analytical frameworks, might be more effective for our investigations and more appropriate to the subjects of study

For cultural studies, the key questions are about meaning and the significance of the cultural at every level of the social and cultural processes. For these explorations we need flexible research methods. Marilyn Strathern, an anthropologist, argues that social scientists generally approach their subject of study with the 'deliberate selection through coupling specific methods with the expectation of specific types of data' and a strong argument for method which links to the theoretical perspective of the study. While this is an accepted and rigorous approach to method, it does present some problems for the kinds of questions and insights the researcher might be interested in, and particularly if we are concerned to 'tap into' cultural and social formations and processes through a range of different methods. The point here is that there are relevant elements to those formations that we cannot know at the outset. It is therefore extremely difficult to predict the kinds of routes and avenues through which our research might lead. We need some flexibility in our methods which will enable us to, in Strathern's (1999) terms, be 'dazzled' and in Willis's (1980) terms, be 'surprised' by our research. This approach to method acknowledges the dynamic nature of cultural and social processes and of meaning production, and has the potential to respond to complex ways in which individuals, or agents, or subjects, inhabit their specific formations, identities and subjectivities. As the sociologists Glaser and Strauss, among others, have argued, the tendency of even the most open-ended qualitative methods within sociology is to freeze the different aspects of the subject of research in the deployment of rather rigid and fixed categories, if not in the data-gathering stage, then certainly, and more likely, at the point of analysis (Glaser and Strauss, 1967).

While examples of cultural studies research have been found lacking when certain criteria are applied, there is no doubt that many of the small-scale explorations were interventions in fields such as youth studies, media and communication studies, and were suggestive of new directions which have shaped further developments, especially in relation to cultural power and the politics of class, gender and race. Examples of such studies will be critically assessed in more detail in Chapter 3 and throughout the rest of this book. It is clear that methodologically the study of 'lived cultures' within cultural studies are situated somewhere between a sociological approach and ethnographic approaches associated with anthropology. While this presents particular sets of issues at the level of method, I now want to discuss two problem areas which are pertinent to all such approaches, those of the politics and epistemology of empirical research.

Issue 1: Constructing the 'other' - surveillance and display

There is a rich seam of criticism that is concerned with looking at the role which ethnographic and sociological investigation has played in constructing that which it claims to describe. Ethnographic practice and research have a long and various history. They can be traced back to early travel writing, to anthropologists attempting to 'write down' cultures before they disappear and in order to establish the discipline of anthropology. This has been seen as an operation of power with the ethnographer fixing his or her gaze on different cultures and rendering them visible, through published work, for the gaze of his or her community of readers. In this process anthropologists tended to present groups as 'other' and 'exotic' emphasising the difference between 'them' (the primitive) and 'us' (the civilised). Edward Said, referred to earlier in this chapter, argues that anthropology is one of the many western practices (in addition to literature and art) in which the West fixes its 'imperial' eye on the oriental other and in so doing defines both the West and the non-West (Said: 1978). In addition to Said's fine work, a number of scholars have demonstrated the presence of discourses of colonialism in cultural artefacts, including travel writing, fiction, fine art and 'ethnic' collectors and museum exhibitions. Michel de Certeau, speaking of the development of the discipline of anthropology, notes the gap between the anthropologist as docile and grateful for the hospitality of the host culture and the anthropologist as author of the written monograph. The latter reveals the institutional affiliations (scientific and social) and the profit (intellectual, professional, financial, etc.) for which this hospitality is objectively the means. Thus, he says, the Bororos of Brazil sink slowly into their collective death, and Lévi-Strauss, the world-famous anthropologist, takes his seat in the French Academy.

While these are examples of ethnography's past complicity in the exercise of colonial power, we can look in the West and identify similar mechanisms of power and particularly those of visibility and surveillance in the history of ethnographic and social investigation, especially in relation to urbanisation.

How the Other Half Lives is the title of a visual study of the poor of the newly urbanised New York carried out by Jacob Riis in 1890. The title and Riis's aims alert us to two of the most telling criticisms of ethnographic research practice. The 'other half' indicates a division in society between 'us' and 'them', those members of 'the other half' being people not like us. Second, the focus on the poor and disadvantaged who were produced as 'the other' and, some would argue, aestheticised as 'exotics' and constructed as such across a number of social and cultural texts. Although these paradigms have themselves been questioned and are more indicative of work done in early anthropology, sociology and documentary photography, these tendencies still linger. We can see their traces in, for example, the predominance of working-class or lower income groups which are the focus of much research within cultural studies. Andrew Tolson suggests: 'exotic cultural types [continue to be] discovered in the working-class communities of large industrial cities' (1990: 112). He has argued that these investigatory practices have a long history. He traces it through a number of important institutional sites developing and taking hold in the mid-nineteenth century. Tolson refers to Henry Mayhew, a journalist who began to publish his own survey of urban poverty and conditions of labour in the *London Morning Chronicle*, subsequently publishing his book *London Labour and the London Poor* in 1851, identifying what would appear to be a sub-culture, an urban sub-culture. Through the work of such 'social investigators' as Mayhew and Riis, it is possible to trace the visibility of sub-cultures, of the working class and the poor in the public domain to the formation of a particular sociological perspective in the mid-nineteenth century. Tolson calls this perspective the 'sociological gaze' which, while often a mechanism for social intervention of a reformist nature, nevertheless renders 'others' visible through various symbolic and textual constructions. This historical dimension to the formation of a potentially powerful 'gaze' should alert us to some of the poignant issues and problems that prevail in thinking about researching 'others'. Putting it bluntly, it is potentially exploitative in nature. As researchers we are in the business of winning the trust and confidence of our respondents whom we then encourage to speak openly to us about their lives, their routines, their feelings. This can include revelations of a most intimate nature and the telling of stories previously untold. We then attempt to represent the material gathered from our respondents usually within particular written forms that are intended for circulation within specific reading communities. Thus, the political and ethical considerations of what we do and how we do it should be foremost in our minds, and will be returned to throughout this book.

Issue 2: Access to truth - the dangers of empiricism

The ethnographic method can often seem deceptively simple. In part this is because it is rather similar to our common-sense and everyday approach to living in the social world. We operate by abiding by structures and routines, we make sense of the world through observation, picking up clues based on our social and cultural competence, through relating to others via conversation and discussion. This can result in a non-reflexive and naïve approach to the accounts people give of their lives, or the observations which researchers note down. Description is piled upon description with ranges of voices coming through the written text, standing there as evidence of the authentic experience or account of way of life. The ethnographer was there at that very moment, and the ethnographic text goes to great pains to persuade us of that.

However, this characteristic of ethnography can be useful. According to some of the early statements from the Centre for Contemporary Cultural Studies (CCCS), their interest in 'ethnography' was, in part, driven by what could be described as a weakness in the ethnographic enterprise, i.e. perhaps in its naïvité, its 'strength against theoretical reductionism' (Hall et al., 1980: 74). It is tempting for academics to work towards ever more sophisticated theoretical accounts of how the world is, but good empirical work can call into question some of these theoretical assumptions. However, as we shall see in Chapter 3, it is clear from this that the CCCS researchers during the 1960s and 1970s were addressing analytical and theoretical questions which went beyond an interest in providing descriptions or of documenting 'experience' for its own sake, or for its own guarantee.

Theories of language were especially crucial in challenging 'claims to the real', to facts and to the 'truth'. Far from a neutral means whereby people communicated with one another, theories of language emphasised the social and ideological function of language. Language, and how it is used, are arbitrary; it operates as a system, rather than being linked to the objects it describes, and its use relies on shared social and cultural convention. As such, it cannot be thought of as a neutral conduit through which descriptions, explanations, versions of the social world can be demonstrated. This post-structural turn in the social sciences and humanities has a strong legacy across different disciplinary fields and systems of thought. Thus, an acknowledgement of the constructed nature of knowledge through social processes has had a profound effect on epistemological thinking and the whole notion of 'truth' or, put more accurately, claims to truth. A key term here is representation. Most obviously these insights have had an impact on the ways in which we understand visual representation. Photography is a particularly good example. The photograph has a long history of signifying 'truth', often being invested with the status of 'evidence' in areas such as the legal system, the press and broadcast media. More recent debates which relate to such notions indicate the constructed nature, even of those cultural documents which make the strongest claim to truth and direct access to the real world 'out there'. The documentary photograph is the product of selection, i.e. what gets into the frame and why. The developing process is far from neutral and is subject to a range of increasingly sophisticated manipulative techniques. And, of course, meanings are not self-evident, but depend on the context within which they are displayed or exhibited, for example, in a newspaper or on a gallery wall and what linguistic text accompanies them. All these elements play their part in anchoring meaning, which is far from fixed or predictable. This brief diversion into visual representation suggest that different 'truth' claims or of access to the 'real' have been put into question. The products of research can also be questioned as to what their claims to truth are and on what grounds they are making that claim. Perhaps at the centre of ethnographic practice is the recognition that, as Myrdal (1969) suggests: 'ethnography involves a series of experiments with truth that can never be completed conclusively'. As researchers, we can never capture the 'whole truth' of any aspect of the social and cultural, rather we can, from our specific vantage point, produce a version of the truth, but one which we present modestly for others to consider.

Reflexivity, provisionality and modesty

The far-reaching critique of representation indicated above has also influenced anthropology. Marcus and Fischer (1986) note the emergence of interpretive anthropology which they use as a description which covers 'a diverse set of reflections upon both the practice of ethnography and the concept of culture'. The metaphor of culture as text established by Clifford Geertz (1973) opened the doors to debates about the moments of interpretation at all stages in the ethnographic project. These were followed by important work, notably by Clifford and Marcus, which examined the ethnographic text as construction. To return to the notion of 'vantage point' in ethnographic practice, this emphasises the centrality of the researcher to the research process and invites a far-reaching acknowledgement of that presence. It is this potential for reflexivity which makes ethnographic methods so useful for the exploration and investigation of cultural processes and the production of meaning. Reflexivity requires some explanation, but again it is useful to think it through in relation to our broader epistemological position. A reflexive approach is one that questions the theoretical and other assumptions of the project. Furthermore, it actively interrogates its research categories (e.g. gender, class, ethnicity, etc.) in the light of the data being generated. Thus, by paying close attention to social actors, to cultural and social processes, some of the more extravagant claims of theoretical work can be questioned and investigated. A reflexive process, then, allows the project to grow and particular avenues to be pursued. It is open and genuinely exploratory. In a good ethnographic project the researcher can be said to be entering into a range of dialogues. First, those with the subjects of her or his research. Here the dialogues, through conversational interviews and less formal conversations present the possibility of open work. Second, the dialogue you can have with different theoretical perspectives or frameworks, through your research data. Third, of course, the dialogue you can have with your colleagues in discussing your work and, finally, the dialogues you can enter into when writing or presenting your work, usually in the form of written texts. At every stage in the process then, you have the possibility of reflecting on what you are doing, what kinds of knowledges are being produced, which concepts are too rigid and which frameworks hide more than they reveal. These are extremely important and useful epistemological questions which, if you are able to ask them of your own work, then you have achieved a flexible and reflexive approach to your study.

Imagine that you are an ethnographic researcher into music festivals. You live and work in the UK so have visited Glastonbury and spoken to, listened to, observed, photographed people involved in that event. Think then of 'scraps' of different kinds of data: a black and white photograph, a hand-bill, a voice telling you a story, an observer's account of an event, an analysis of a musical text or performance, a list of sponsors of the event, a description of the space, the noise, the smells, the atmosphere. As a researcher you would find yourself dealing with a great amount of such material, and there are no clear or hard and fast rules as to what you might do with the data. These fragments of data can be combined and juxtaposed in a variety of ways, they may be multiple reflections of one event and as such are changeable and fluid. Rather like a kaleidoscope, using our various data, we can produce complex patterns of frequently changing shapes and colours. This suggests that there is no one 'truth' or true story of the event, but many perspectives on the event. Thus our first epistemological observation is: that social and symbolic worlds are to be known not through some prescribed, fixed and 'logical' method (as proposed by the natural sciences, for example), but they are to be discovered by attending to many levels of practice through which meaning is generated, within particular social and cultural settings. Furthermore, what happens within these worlds is not predictable: we cannot know beforehand what we are going to discover. This is in marked contrast with the positivist approach to knowledge. Knowledge and ways of knowing the world are much less certain than the positivist model suggests and now even the natural sciences are acknowledging that we are playing some kind of trick (mainly on ourselves) when we believe in this kind of 'science'.

There is still, however, a spectre of 'the real' and 'the authentic' hovering over ethnographies. Somehow, there is the suggestion that by listening to and describing what people do in particular contexts, we are getting nearer to the 'truth' than, say, through the analysis of texts or any form of document. Les Back's very useful discussion on methodology in his *New Ethnicities and Urban Culture*, says:

> [M]y intention here is not to present ethnography as the privileged arbiter of 'what is really happening on the streets', neither is it to characterise these new developments in cultural theory as removed or empirically uninformed ... [I]t means embracing a contingent and modest epistemology that attempts to achieve rigorous forms of reporting alongside a reflexive consciousness of the codes, textual moves and rhetoric integral to the process of writing ethnography. (1996: 5)

Here Back speaks of the limits of ethnography, of the dangers in claiming too much on the basis of our access to the social worlds of 'others' and indicates the importance of reflecting on the written versions of our research.

In a similar vein, Purnima Mankekar, a cultural anthropologist, describes her work as that which 'explores the potential of ethnography as an *evocative* genre of cultural analysis that aims to represent specific structures of feeling' (1999: 49, original emphasis).

Notions of 'evocation' and the rather vague term 'structures of feeling' are more suggestive of works of imagination or fiction than of social research, but perhaps this approach is more appropriate for the kinds of phenomena that ethnographers wish to examine; human beings and the meanings they make of and invest in their daily lives.

I hope it is clear by now that the ethnographic approach, while presenting problems and difficulties, also raises exciting questions that are some of the most pressing in the current intellectual climate. Elspeth Probyn suggests that:

> Given these [postmodern] intellectual conditions, it is hardly surprising that there has been, of late, a great deal of interest in ethnography's 'problems' ... certain problematics seem to appear more pressing from its perspective, questions about the (im)possibility of representing others; the increasingly unstable construction of the white male as expert; the eclipse of science as a ruling metanarrative. In short, questions about where one can speak from, to whom one speaks, and why one speaks at all seem to be more immediately articulated within ethnography than elsewhere. (1993: 61)

These are questions about the politics of research and about how and in what ways we can represent other people in our research. Who are we as researchers, not only to grasp the right to intervene in other people's lives, but to use their words and experiences, freely given, to form the basis of our dissertations, theses and books? But Probyn's are also epistemological questions about how we see ourselves as knowledge producers in relation to our chosen subjects of study and how we find a speaking position within that research.

It is arguably the case that the interests and concerns of certain branches of anthropology are converging with those of cultural studies, especially the notion of the constructed nature of the cultural. Akhil Gupta and James Ferguson suggest that the notion of the cultural as construct and something which is in process has severely challenged the anthropological assumption that 'culture' is somehow to be found in particular and specific settings, bounded within groups located and linked to space and place. These assumptions are now being challenged and researchers are pointing out that culture itself is part of a process and not a given and that it is not a fixed and observable entity to be found by immersion in a group or milieu. Questions of cultural identity and difference are being spatialised in new ways in the context of flows of global capital and migration, and can no longer be seen as fixed and located to a specific time and place. And, as Gupta and Ferguson point out, this acknowledges that 'all associations of place, people, and culture are social and historical creations to be explained, not given natural facts. This is as true for the classical style of "peoples and cultures" ethnography as it is for the perhaps more culturally chaotic present' (1997: 4). Clearly, the nature of the culturally chaotic present would include transnational flows of peoples, cultures and economies, global communications and sense-making practices, the complexity of which makes our challenge of 'grasping lived cultures' far more challenging than attention to an assumed fixed and bounded community of culture. However, Gupta and Ferguson insist that ethnography will still remain an important set of methods and that anthropology connects to the field of enquiry of cultural studies. Thus, the reading of texts, cultural products and public representations can complement the emphasis on daily routines and lived experience more associated with anthropology. What is exciting about these shifts is that they offer great potential for new combinations of theoretical and methodological approaches which can produce theoretically reflexive but strongly grounded empirical work which conceptualises culture and subjectivity as in process and flux. This is the kind of approach we need in cultural studies.

I have attempted in this chapter to introduce ethnography by relating it both to its usefulness for cultural studies and by outlining some of the main criticisms of its practice and politics as an intellectual project. This is to indicate the debate between the sociologically, textually and the ethnographically minded about the contested area of 'lived cultures'. My main point here is that implicit in its range of methods is its epistemology, that the world is to be discovered and that knowledge and 'truth' are always provisional and contingent. In the following chapter I will explore one of the key and important concepts within ethnography, cultural studies and especially in addressing lived cultures, that of 'experience'.

| t w o | **Articulating Experience** |

The lived is only another word, if you like, for experience: but we have
to find a word for that. (Williams, 1979: 168)

The previous chapter refers to the importance of 'experience' in the early
development of cultural studies. This chapter, in beginning to outline the
project of cultural studies, is part of the larger argument of the book which is
that research practice defines cultural studies. Thus, the central role which
'experience' has played in that development can be seen in the agendas of the
research projects themselves, the 'biographies' of the individual and collective
researchers as well as, more obviously, in the 'data' drawn from their respondents. I now want to examine this concept more fully and the ways in which
it has been used for the potential it can still offer our research. It is, like all
deceptively simple concepts, highly problematic. It attracts with notions of
obviousness and simplicity, of authenticity and a democratic ethos. Like all
concepts, it is open to contestation and the understanding of 'experience' and
its status has certainly undergone changes in the development of cultural
studies. My aim is to demonstrate, following Probyn, that experience is a useful political and critical category and not simply a repository of authenticity
nor of 'common sense and ideology'. Furthermore, I agree with her insistence that it is an important epistemological category and that it can function
as a 'way of knowing' both our own and others' 'ways of being'. In other
words, we need to theorise 'experience'. Theory is often considered to be difficult, abstract and something which we need to tackle as part of our curriculum. I want to make a distinction between Theory (with a capital T) and
theorising which is a practice and an integral part of good research. In order
to use experience in this way, the notion of 'articulation' is a useful one.
Experience can be understood as a discursive 'site of articulation' upon and
through which subjectivities and identities are shaped and constructed. This
involves both how we are positioned in the world and how we reflexively find

our place in the world. Thus, experience is not an authentic and original source of our being, but part of the process through which we articulate a sense of identity.

By way of example I will draw on Stuart Hall or, more accurately a doubled self of Stuart Hall. That is, Stuart Hall the author and cultural theorist and Stuart Hall as one who inhabits a range of identities and who has experienced particular events in his life. Hall has expressed this 'doubledness' in a number of articles and through interviews. In his article entitled 'Minimal Selves' (Hall, 1987) which he refers to as 'adjectival notes' he speaks of his own 'background', growing up in Jamaica, his family and his relationship to them, the broader social and cultural context of his home country and how he came to leave that setting as a migrant to Britain. Questions of his own fluid identity/ies are introduced in this short piece. We are familiar with the idea of people telling us about their background and family, but Hall is reflecting on his personal history and how it made him who he is. This is achieved not straightforwardly, but through particular formations and often painful encounters with hostile realities. He reflects on theories of identity through his own experience and says: 'But my experience now is that what the discourse of postmodernism has produced is not something new but a kind of recognition of where identity always was at' (Hall, in Gray and McGuigan, 1993: 134). Hall is performing an interesting double move here. In reflecting on his knowledge drawn from experience, his way of being (ontology) through a theoretical formulation – of postmodern identity – he is producing knowledge (epistemology). His experience thus is taken beyond his own individual account, which he locates historically, into a more theorised and therefore general notion of constructions of (post)modern identity.

Williams also spoke of the usefulness of experience in similar ways: 'An acknowledgement of the ontological aspect of one's experience is necessary if one is to locate 'those specific and definable moments when very new work produces a sudden shock of recognition' (1979: 164).

But Hall's recognition can tell us even more about the necessity of acknowledging 'experience'. He speaks from 'the margins'. His experience, as one of migration from Jamaica to England, endowed him with identity characteristics of which he was previously unaware; in becoming a migrant he knew, for the first time, what it meant to be black. He experienced fragmentation and marginalisation which are often spoken of as the key elements in the modern experience of migration. The fact that postmodern theories have only just caught up with these lived experiences reveals much about the positions of Western theorists and the consequences of ignoring lived experience of the marginal which are easily undervalued or discounted.

Thus, attention to the lived, to how individuals account for their lives and how they position themselves in relation to their experience can produce new knowledges and the 'shock of recognition' of which Williams speaks. This work is essential if cultural studies is to remain a dynamic field of inquiry and avoid becoming a conventional discipline.

It is the case that in early cultural studies and feminist research, experience – especially of marginalised groups, for example, youth, young women and girls – was treated as authentic and valued for its own sake. We can see that in breaking new ground in research, in introducing new and hitherto silenced voices into research, the drive to reveal those statements or expressions of experience is paramount. However, as Elspeth Probyn suggests in relation to feminist theory: '[they] either verify the experiential for its own sake, or reject its potential out of hand' (1993: 5). Rejecting its potential out of hand is one remedy. This is simply to say that the dangers of the 'authentic account' are too great and should be mistrusted as the foundations of any knowledge at all. In her reassessment of Raymond Williams's work, Elspeth Probyn finds 'experience' to be a central category and for her a major source of inspiration in his work. She says, 'I want to focus on experience as a keyword, and map the productive tension that Williams constructs between the ontological and the epistemological' (1993: 18). I agree with Probyn that experience remains a rich and fruitful category for our research and she draws on Raymond Williams's formulations to suggest three analytical possiblities, or ways forward for retaining and mobilising the experience of 'others', but also our own experience in social and cultural analysis. However, it is important to be clear that what Williams was seeking to examine was the nature of what was for him the 'indissolubility of ... the continuous social-material process'. This was made up of politics, art, economics, and family organisation as elements of the whole, but his point was that these are inextricably linked in lived experience. Williams was clearly seeking to qualify the then dominant Marxist model of the determination of the economic and mode of production on the rest of the social whole. What is interesting, and caused him considerable trouble at the time, is that he drew on his own experience to impel his theorisation. His three analytical propositions are:

1 Experience can be overwhelming and work to conceal the connections between the different structures.

2 Experience itself speaks of the composition of the social formation.

3 The critic's own experience can impel the analysis of his or her differentiated relations to levels of the social formation. (adapted from Probyn, 1993)

The first two of these three propositions are helpful in thinking about ways in which we might use experience analytically and critically in our research when attending to experience of others. The third proposition introduces the experience of the critic, or researcher, as a useful and usable dimension in our theoretical and analytical work. Thus, as researchers, our own experience of everyday life and culture is regarded not as a hindrance or something which might sway or bias our research, but something which should be acknowledged and employed in our intellectual work.

It will be helpful to develop these three propositions in turn in order to get some purchase on the ways in which experience might function in our research projects.

1   Experience can be overwhelming and work to conceal the relationship between the different structures. This is a warning against the tendency for experience, and its obviousness, to be a repository for common sense and ideology. In this way experience can, for example, suggest a sense of a unique and active human agent who exercises free will and choice in their everyday lives. This is a highly persuasive and often successful ideology of the individual in Western societies and cultures which erases the operations and limitations of the structures. Williams puts it thus:

[I]in certain epochs it is precisely experience in its weakest form which appears to block any realization of the unity of this process, concealing the connections between the different structures - not to speak of the unnoticed relationships of combination and subordination, disparity and unevenness, residue and emergence, which lend their particular nature to these connections. (1978: 138)

2   Experience itself speaks of the composition of the social formation. In other words, as Probyn puts it, 'while experience describes the everyday or "way of life", it is also *key to analysing the relations that construct that reality*' (1993: 18, my emphasis). Experience, then, is expressed and articulated through language. How we account for ourselves, how we 'tell our story' or present ourselves to others speak of our place within a particular social and historical context. As individuals, then, we are not the authentic source of accounts of our experience, but rather mediators of our positions within the social and cultural worlds we inhabit. When we elicit accounts from others, therefore, we are putting into play a repertoire of knowledges, positions, discourses and codes through which the 'individual' articulates or expresses their 'own' experience. Williams insisted on the importance of valuing what we experience in our everyday lives, not simply because it produces a richer understanding of human life and the social, but also because analyses that emphasise only the economic and the political ignore the stuff of social life that, in itself, is constitutive of the social. He argues that his experience tells him that this is so. '[M]en' and societies are not confined to relationships of power, property and production' (Williams, 1978: 138). Williams was responding to the intellectual climate of his day where the public, masculine, domain was understood to be of significance, while the private and intimate world of the domestic was kept in the margins of intellectual life.

3   The critic's own experience can impel the analysis of his or her differentiated relations to levels of the social formation. As researchers and scholars we are part of that world in which we are interested. Put simply, we experience the world as social beings which can often provide our starting points for 'theorising' the world. Before I began studying for a higher degree, I mused while taking the 'bus into my office job in town why and how it was that thousands of people were making that similar routine journey. A pretty low-flying empirical observation, it is true, but it marked the beginning of my intellectual curiosity about the social and my search for explanations. As I began to learn, read and think I turned to theories of economics, labour, the family and gender in order to analyse my lived experience, which indicated what Williams called 'the indissolubility' of the social. For Probyn, there is a danger of 'the lived' becoming simply 'another mantra, another abstract nod' in academic work. In order to put real flesh on the bones of the lived, critics and scholars need to put their experiences 'in the terrain of the theoretical' (1993: 21).

What Williams offers, emphasised by Probyn, is a way of conceptualising experience which lifts it out of its romantic authenticity and into a rich source and resource for students and researchers of lived cultures. He does this by insisting that we can produce knowledge and ways of knowing by being aware of our own subjectivity and experience and acknowledging the experience of others as valuable both ontologically and epistemologically.

In what follows I will discuss the different ways in which experience has been used and the problems encountered within cultural studies. So, what happens when experience is used in such a way that it might overwhelm and conceal the connections between the different structures?

The documenting of 'experience'

Early researchers in cultural studies insisted upon the democratising potential of opening up narrowly defined knowledge fields to different accounts. Thus accounts were sought of 'lived experience', based upon knowledges and literal experience. How and in what ways did people account for and express the experience of living within particular sets of circumstances, particularly those limited and constrained by adverse social and cultural factors? This approach can be divined in the early cultural studies research, particularly studies of youth sub-cultures. Here researchers wanted to investigate and explore the 'real' worlds of working-class youth asking questions such as: what was it like to live in that particular set of socio-economic circumstances? How did class and the changing cultures of working-class life affect that generation? What sense were young people able to make of their existence? What meanings did they invest in their worlds of work and leisure? To see the world from the point of view of these actors or agents was the main and driving force behind these studies. Methodologically they drew upon qualitative techniques, mainly participant observation and interviews with the actors involved, in order to produce rich and full accounts of these lives and social worlds. 'Telling it like it is' and allowing for the subaltern's (of British and US societies) to have a voice were familiar claims made by and for this approach and this strand of study.

Equivalent studies within feminist sociology and cultural studies sought to reveal the isolation of women within prescribed domestic lives and of the entrapment of the 'feminine career' (Gavron, 1968; Comer, 1984). This work explored different aspects of women's lives and experience, for example, their encounters with the medical profession, how 'housewives' used radio and television, aspects of women's leisure, acquisition of femininity by working-class girls, etc. (McRobbie, 1978; Hobson, 1981; Graham, 1984; Deem, 1986). All these studies were empirically based and used, more or less directly, expressions of women's experience in generating data. The importance of attending to women's experience was considered to be a political imperative of much feminist research. Feminist research of this period can, then, be characterised as being made up of a rich variety of interventionist projects driven by the need to pay attention to and document women's lived experience.

We can see here, across these disciplinary areas, what can be described as a democratic impulse motivating researchers whose aim was to document 'hidden' lives and worlds, to 'tell different stories' and reveal different accounts. This mode of research was often politically informed, many of its practitioners were beneficiaries of a broadening of educational opportunity who brought aspects of their own backgrounds and experience to their scholarship, and all were working against the grain of the constraints of traditional disciplinary paradigms.

This testimony remains important and can still have a powerful force when used strategically and politically. An example of recent work is Clare Alexander's study of young Asian males in which she draws on their own accounts of their lives and cultural practices to counteract the emerging stereotype of the 'Asian Gang' seen, in the UK popular and broadsheet press, as the new threat to urban and inner city stability (Alexander, 2000). There is every point to gathering these accounts from the agents involved for who will do this in ways which might be to their advantage but social and cultural researchers?

It is the case, however, that this 'documentary' or 'empirical' mode has a number of serious limitations which the earlier studies manifest. These limitations can, in part, be traced to the core of the enterprise: the highly problematic category of 'experience'. Joan Scott, a historian, usefully discusses the status of experience in historiography. Here experience is the authenticating source, what she describes as the descriptive evidence of 'the already there' (Scott, 1992). Thus, in a similar way to cultural studies and feminist work, the project is one of rendering visible hitherto hidden lives and unacknowledged experiences. However, Scott is critical of the metaphor of visibility itself, implying as it does, the possibility of a direct, unmediated apprehension of a world of transparent and knowable objects. She argues that, within history, the accumulation of more evidential accounts based on this approach merely provides an enlargement of the existing picture.

This has broader consequences in the extent to which it is possible for the mainstream disciplinary practices to accommodate this body of work. For, while the rich documenting of people's lives and experiences broadens the picture, this data can simply by 'bolted on' to existing work more or less unproblematically. These accounts, then, become another aspect of the field of study, rather than presenting a radical challenge to the theoretical and methodological assumptions of that field. A set of more radical questions need to be asked, such as: why have *these* accounts been rendered invisible? What is it about the established methodologies which hierarchise particular ways of knowing? Is it possible, using existing and 'legitimate' theoretical approaches, to, in Spivak's (1987) words, 'make visible the assignment of subject positions'? For Spivak, theories and methods should be called into question unless they enable us to: 'understand the operations of the complex and changing discursive and material processes by which identities are ascribed, resisted or embraced, and which processes themselves are unremarked, indeed achieve their effect because they aren't noticed' (ibid.: 214).

In his second proposition, Williams suggests that 'experience speaks of the social' and this insight provides us with a useful way of thinking about experience and meeting some of Spivak's demands.

Articulating experience

It is now important to find ways of thinking about how to relate experience, of others and our own, to those organising structures of the social. Again, Probyn is useful when she states, 'at an ontological level, experience speaks of a disjuncture between the articulated and the lived aspects of the social and, at an epistemological level, experience impels an analysis of the relations formulated between the articulated and the lived' (1993: 22). This requires a lighter touch than those studies which reduced experience to 'economics' or 'patriarchy' as if there could be one primary explanation for the limited scope of the social and cultural life of particular groups. This is to put the theoretical cart before the empirical horse, or to do a certain amount of violence to the research data. To say, for example, that I, as a woman, am totally determined by my position in patriarchal society is to overlook the myriad of encounters, activities and practices in which my gendered identity shifts into the foreground and background. For example, in my work at the university I can feel positioned as 'a woman' in, say, meetings of mainly male committees, but, while still clearly gendered female, during my teaching, discussions with students and colleagues, I feel that my gender is much less significant. Gender regimes are different within the family, friendships, hetero- and homosexual relationships, and so on.

The main methodological problem is to find an analytical mechanism which can catch the subtlety of lived experience and how that is expressed through language and action or performance. This mechanism would need to acknowledge the dynamic processes of lived cultures while not losing sight of those forces which shape the trajectories, the life choices and the mundanity of the everyday.

Articulation is a useful way of thinking about both the complexity of contemporary societies and cultures and what it is like to inhabit them as a social subject. Developed by Laclau and elaborated by Stuart Hall for cultural studies, it provides an anti-essentialist and anti-reductionist method of complicating the relationship between individual action (subjectivity) and the broader social (determining) structure. The role of experience here is for Hall the ground upon which different and sometimes contradictory discourses are unified (Hall, 1996).

'Experience', then, is the ground for engagement with and the manifestation of the moments of 'unification' where the elements are somehow brought together. The value of the concept is that it avoids a deterministic and mechanical model in which powerful social structures and ideologies shape who we are. Rather, it enables an exploration of the relationships between subjects and different, if powerful, discursive elements. In the more deterministic models of 'individual' and 'society' there is little space for the active human agent as one who can operate within particular contexts and through which specific articulations of subjectivity and identity can be constructed. This is also to acknowledge that the subject does not somehow reside within a particular context, taking what comes, as it were, but is actively producing that context. Here we have a number of possibilities for conceptualising the role and articulation of experience within our research.

Much early work in the development of cultural studies drew on notions of the subject and assumed specific social categories of 'belonging' with class and gender as 'primary' subject positions. The concept of articulation opens up the possibility of understanding the flux of postmodern societies and postmodern experience. The concept which has emerged from this re-working of the agency/structure relationship is that of 'identity'.

The question of identity

In 1992 a collection of papers from a conference called 'Cultural Studies Now and in the Future' held at the University of Illinois was published as *Cultural Studies* (Grossberg et al., 1992). Angela McRobbie notes that the theme of 'identity' runs through the collection. Similarly, in another volume, Paul Gilroy writes: 'It took me a long time to appreciate how the founding texts of my own encounter with English cultural studies could be seen to converge around the thematics of identity' (Curran et al., 1996: 44).

But what, McRobbie asks, is meant by 'identity'? Stuart Hall suggests that we understand identity, not as the clue to the essential core of our being, but rather that experience is 'the ground for engagement: the manifestation of the moments of "unification" where the elements are somehow brought together'. Hall suggests that the subject is related to 'discursive formations' through a process of articulation. The subject, then inhabits different and various positions in relation to the available discourses in constructing and having his or her identity constructed for her or him.

McRobbie reflects on the significance of the concept for cultural studies:

> Identity could be seen as dragging cultural studies into the 1990s by acting as a kind of guide to how people see themselves, not as class subjects, not as psychoanalytic subjects, not as subjects of ideology, not as textual subjects, but as active agents whose sense of self is projected onto and expressed in an expansive range of cultural practices, including texts, images, and commodities. (1992: 730)

McRobbie makes a further observation that, although increasingly theoretically sophisticated notions of identities are discussed and figured within cultural studies, there are few actual ethnographies or encounters with social and cultural identities in the making. That is, research which explores the reflexive construction of identity. How do we construct our sense of self and our own identities? What kinds of discourses do we access, e.g. music, fashion, language, and what forms of expression does this take, e.g. style, embodiment and the narratives we tell ourselves and others?

The final proposition which Williams offers requires us to reflect on our own position within our research.

Where do we speak from?

For me the notion of experience can be related to what Donna Haraway describes as standpoint epistemology or the notion of speaking from a particular vantage point. This is to say that we cannot speak from nowhere, but from where we are positioned, socially, culturally and politically. Haraway is one of a number of feminists who have insisted on the acknowledgement of this fact (Harding, 1986, 1987; Haraway, 1990). Too many theorists and intellectuals, they argue, appear to speak from nowhere, to be disembodied arbiters of truth and knowledge. From a feminist perspective, this has not only produced masculinist (biased) theories and knowledge, but it discounts and devalues knowledge which might come from a particular and specific lived experience. For Liz Stanley, this has also been a way of 'disowning' responsibility, of not being accountable for the ways in which your knowledge is produced (Stanley, 1990). And, finally, it is possible to adopt the pseudo-objective position of the intellectual, above the humdrum banalities of reality, unquestioned and unquestionably in possession of 'the truth'.

Haraway claims that our ontological positioning, our experience of being, can privilege certain kinds of knowledges. Stuart Hall 'knows' what it is to be marginalised as a migrant and as 'black' and that, she would claim, gives him a particular privileged insight into the process of power and discrimination which, for example, a 'white' resident of England would not. Let us reverse the positions above and insist that the white resident intellectual always acknowledges their position in relation to their intellectual work, so how does that social positioning speak through their theories? Is it acknowledged as a speaking position at all? Or simply, as Dyer has argued in relation to 'whiteness' (1997), an absent position, perhaps thought of as the obvious and natural position of an intellectual.

A critique and challenge to the unlocated (and unlocatable) intellectual can be made through the insistence on experience as a constitutive element in individual selves and how that may have directed the questions placed on a research agenda and practice. It is, perhaps, not surprising that feminist scholars have argued for the significance of experience and have been the first to locate themselves in relation to their research and in politicising their intellectual practice in general. For example, the philosopher, Sandra Harding, is one of a number of feminists who have drawn attention to the centrality of methodology in considering a feminist social science. She takes women's experience as a starting point and argues that: 'Once we undertake to use women's experience as a resource to generate scientific problems, hypotheses, and evidence, to design research for women, and to place the researcher in the same critical plane as the research subject, traditional epistemological assumptions can no longer be made' (1987: 181).

This, then, gives rise to a feminist agenda for, in this case, social science, which asks questions about who can be 'knowers' and what can be known; what is considered to be 'legitimate' knowledge?; what is the nature of objectivity?; what is the appropriate relationship between researcher and her/his subjects?; what is the purpose of the pursuit of knowledge? (Harding, 1987: 181). To paraphrase: 'who can know what about whom, by what means and to what purpose?' It is then necessary to think about how 'experience' is used, what status it is given and the modes of interpretation employed.

Learning through articulation

The difficulties involved in the use of the category are clear and legion. However, it is the very recalcitrance of 'experience' which is, in my view, the strongest argument for its retention. This is in some ways to return to its potential for 'surprise', but not as some naïve and innocent expression of the authentic event or knowledge expressed by the individual who is then understood as the locus of agency. Rather, as representations and expressions of direct personal participation in or observation of events; accumulated knowledge of the world in particular sets of circumstances; what it is like to live in these circumstances and the personal feelings and emotions which are engendered. This, then, is to suggest that the first step forward is to understand 'experience' as a non-unified category which can be mobilised in a number of ways, for different purposes and with different epistemological outcomes. These variant categories, and the 'data' which different methods will generate, are challenging, unwieldy and possibly intractable, but there is a need to acknowledge the nature of experience, its status, what is being drawn from this source in terms of analysis and interpretation and how it relates to methodology and the methods employed in any study.

It was suggested in the previous chapter that by opening up our studies to different accounts and ways of being in the world our more abstract theories can be challenged and questioned. This necessitates attendance to the cultures of everyday life, but with a sophisticated understanding of the nature and status of experience, subjectivity and identity.

Thus, research is always a combination of theorising and a search for the most appropriate and productive methods for our research topic. Our key theoretical terms, as they have emerged through this chapter are those of experience, subjectivity and identity which can be understood as articulating through 'lived cultures'. The following chapter will look at the ways in which these elements have been mobilised within the development of this significant dimension of cultural studies.

three	**Imagined Communities: The Spectacular and the Ordinary**

The aim of this chapter is to examine the emergence of particular topics and subjects of study. It asks why certain groups have been studied in cultural studies work into 'lived cultures', how have they been produced as ethnographic 'others' and how do the researchers involved account for this, if at all? If, as I have argued in the previous chapter, theory, experience and method are integral to our research practice, then we need to understand how these layers have worked together in specific research examples. I also want to think about how they are embedded in developing the wider field of cultural studies. In order to explore these questions we must take a historical perspective and dig down into the early development of cultural studies. Any attempt to construct a history involves selection and will be but one version of a number of possible (hi)stories which could be told on the same topic. In the first part of this chapter I offer an account of the emergence of particular groups for study, or figures on the landscape, as they were identified through the work of the CCCS. My story centres on the processes of intellectual self-understanding through critical engagement with theory and politics which in turn defined others as research subjects. These will be examined through the articulation of methods, politics, experience and their theoretical underpinnings. Thus I will examine the articulation of experience of both researchers and researched and how the experience of the researched has been used by researchers, for what purpose and to what end. I hope to explore the sensibilities of a cultural studies research practice which engaged with what was important, even crucial to other people's self-understanding and how the experience of particular groups, or 'others' were produced by the researcher/intellectuals as 'imagined' communities. I should make it clear here that, although this term comes from Benedict Anderson's notion of 'imagined communities' constructed through shared engagement with the press, I am using it to define particular groups which were produced as 'research communities' in the early work of the CCCS. I will identify some of the main characters on this landscape which was to become cultural studies, but before I do I want to look at the formations of the researchers themselves and their identities who in turn constructed particular research 'others'. These are (1) the 'scholarship boys and girls'. I have used this as a broad term which indicates that at the time of the formation of the CCCS in the late 1960s, a generation of scholars from less privileged social backgrounds entered higher education for the first time; (2) the second group are the feminists who challenged androcentric intellectual practice, theory and method and the focus on class as the key social category; (3) the third group of scholars formed a collective of black intellectuals who contested the implicit whiteness of the work which systematically excluded black history and experience; and, finally, (4) the post-Marxists, post-structuralists and queer theorists, who were interested in fun, resistance, pleasure, consumption and sexuality. The aim in identifying and briefly introducing these groups is to suggest that fields of enquiry develop through the experience which researchers brought to their intellectual work and produced 'figures on the landscape' of cultural studies.

CCCS

My own location at Birmingham is obviously important here, more for the influence of the early work of the Centre on my own work and intellectual trajectory than what Birmingham is now. As an undergraduate in the early 1980s, I found the work coming from the CCCS to be the most exciting, challenging and relevant academic work I had read. The collection on *Working Class Culture* which insisted that culture was to be understood as belonging to all, and not just a privileged few, and the *Uses of Literacy* in which Richard Hoggart writes of his own childhood in Leeds, my own home town, connected with my own experience. In 1963 Richard Hoggart, the then Professor of English at the University of Birmingham, established the Centre for Contemporary Cultural Studies because he felt that the existing disciplines of English and Sociology were inadequate for the study of contemporary culture. It brought together academic staff from English and eventually research fellows and post-graduates who then worked on identifying the very terrain of their studies. They brought their own experiences and backgrounds to the academy, were critical of conventional work and began to define what they felt needed to be done in order to gain legitimacy for a new approach to questions of culture. Within the rapidly changing society of the British post-war period, these scholars were critical of existing disciplinary frameworks which excluded significant aspects of these changes and the straitjackets of existing theories and analytical methods. In addition, as the Centre developed, its members sought to connect with cultural politics outside of the academy. Thus, envisaging cultural studies as a politics and as a potential strategy for intervention was important in this early formation. Also, its members were interested in questioning the pedagogic conventions of the academy and the conventions of individualistic academic ways of working. This is to indicate some of the complex intellectual, institutional and political factors which contributed to and constructed the specific concerns with objects and subjects of study which, in short, shaped their research. In looking at the CCCS, we are able to identify a 'cultural studies case study' if that is not too cumbersome a term, and examine its dimensions and developments. I offer this, then not as a claim to be writing the 'real' history of the 'origins' of cultural studies, but as a concrete example of one particular formation which can be identified as 'doing cultural studies'.

Early questions

First, drawing on earlier work by Williams and Hoggart himself, the definition of culture itself was problematised, made necessary because of societal changes, such as the development of mass media, the expansion of higher education, etc. but also as a challenge to the then dominant ideas of high culture. This developed into a material definition of culture as constructed within social relations, institutions and ways of life, and as such always subject to power. Second, a continuing engagement with and critique of existing disciplines, especially those of English and Sociology, contesting the limitations of the disciplines, their modes of analysis and their theories. Third, there is evidence of grappling with theory and exploring theoretical developments across a range of existing disciplines and re-examining sociological concepts, especially class and later gender, 'race' and ethnicity. And finally there is attention to the very objects for study, especially the media and popular culture, subjects which were absent from the curricula and were treated with general disdain within the academy. The development of ethnographic approaches also demonstrated the concern with the everyday. Culture, if it is to be understood in its broadest sense, is not just the property of the powerful and elite, but is produced through interactions and encounters within daily life. Here the notion of 'lived cultures' is critical. This group of researchers (Hall et al., 1980), working with ethnographic methods asked how this recognition of culture as lived could be mobilised within research. Who they chose to study and the subjects of their enquiry are revealing of the actual social, historical conditions, concerns and preoccupations of the wider society, but also their theoretical and political concerns, for example, youth and youth sub-cultures, working-class cultures, young working-class women. In their methods they were concerned to understand the processes of the making and using of culture and what this meant to the agents involved, which, for a particular generation of researchers were 'the lads'.

Youth sub-cultures and 'the lads': 'Marxism's heroes'

A particularly intense and spectacular cluster of studies (Jefferson, 1976; Willis, 1977; Hebdige, 1979) focused on working-class youth as figures constructed, or imagined as a 'community' by these researchers. They were interested in ideology and its relationship to the particular forms or manifestations of spectacular youth sub-cultures. They were theoretically informed by engagements with Marxism, e.g., Althusser's concept of ideology as material practice, Gramsci's concept of hegemony as a moving and negotiated equilibrium and, for Hebdige, Barthes' semiotics, and were methodologically influenced by existing studies from the Chicago School, especially Whyte's *Street Corner Society*, a study of Italian youth in Boston. (Whyte, 1943) The problematic of the Birmingham studies was the conflicts and ambiguities between the dominant culture, the 'parent' culture, youth and the rise of leisure and commercial culture. Their key category was 'class' and youth appeared to be emblematic of the shifting nature of class within the post-war context. Youth cultures were seen as sub-cultures in subordinate relation to both the dominant and parent cultures and as 'folk devils' or 'deviants' in the wider society. Another powerful discourse within British society at the time was one of the disappearance of class and class division, justified largely in relation to increasing affluence and access to consumer goods. Researchers at the CCCS argued against this grain of social consensus, suggesting that working-class youth occupied an uneasy position in relation to changes in contemporary society and they sought to demonstrate that class remained a powerful and resilient social division in spite of the affluent society of the 1960s. Studies therefore suggested that the outward expressions of youth sub-cultures, music, dress, styles, etc. manifested a 'symbolic resistance' to the more powerful orders in society. The notion of resistance was crucial to the sub-culture researchers as youth was awarded some agency and cultural production in their efforts to resolve the tensions experienced through their positioning within the contradictory cultural structures. Gramsci's theory of hegemony offered a way of understanding the relationships as one of negotiation and consent, as an equilibrium of power relations constantly in flux. The methods used in order to explore sub-cultures ranged from participant observation, interviews and subjecting the cultural artefacts of the groups, such as style, dress, mannerisms and music, to semiotic analysis.

Stanley Cohen, in his critical review of the work on youth sub-cultures (1997) identifies 'new theories' of sub-culture, in contrast to those of urban sociology, for example, that of the Chicago School. He distinguishes three levels of analysis present in the CCCS studies. He calls these levels structure, culture and biography and it is worth expanding on these in order to get a clearer sense of the youth (sub)cultural studies projects. Drawing on Cohen:

- Structure refers to those dimensions of society which are beyond the control of the participants, usually referring to structures of power within society and across class and gender. Implicit here is the notion that people's lives, their opportunities and limitations, are shaped to a greater or lesser extent by their position within the social structure. While individuals do have agency nevertheless this is contained within particular constraints about which they have no choice.

• Culture refers to meanings, traditions, cultural practices, demeanour and language which are seen to be responses to the structural conditions. Thus the different kinds of youth sub-cultures represent a specific symbolic form.

• Biography refers to the personal trajectories through which culture and structure are experienced. More specifically what the sub-culture is and what it means to its participants. (adapted from Cohen, 1997: 150.)

Cohen suggests that:

Much of the new work of British post-war youth cultures is a teasing out of the relationships between these three levels. And all of this work is more or less informed by the Marxist categorisation of structure, culture and biography as the determinate conditions ('being born into a world not of your own choosing') to which the sub-culture is one of the possible working-class responses ('making your own history'). (ibid.: 151)

Cohen is critical of many of the sub-culture studies in terms of their method:

The method used in most of this work detracts us from answering the more traditional, but surely not altogether trivial sociological questions about the different patterns of involvement. Why should some individuals exposed to the same pressures respond one way rather than another or with different degrees of commitment? (ibid.: 161)

One of the strategies of the sub-culture theories is to start from the position of an already established and self-identified social group, in order to examine the interplay of structure, culture and biography. Cohen takes issue with this and finds that studies which take their focus more broadly, i.e. school, neighbourhood, work, come up with a more complex and 'looser relationship' between class and style (ibid.: 161).

This is a clear example of the difference between what sociologists might want to ask about youth cultures and what cultural studies researchers were interested in. A sociologist would want to ask of sub-cultural affiliations, 'Why some people and not others?' in order to get some sense of a broader picture of class culture. Researchers in cultural studies observed the emergence of these sub-cultures and asked, 'Why have these groups emerged, and by what processes do they produce their identity, meanings and culture?' They were concerned to 'tap into' those already defined groups to understand the processes and the connections across the different levels of analysis, and in particular how cultures are produced within and through material circumstances, rather than why particular individuals invested in those identities.

The intensity of the studies allowed researchers to make connections between structure, culture and biography, but not to make more generalised statements about broader society and culture. I do not intend to defend the youth sub-culture studies against all criticism, because Cohen certainly has a point in relation to the highly selective focus they took, but to emphasise the strong political and theoretical agenda the researchers had, and through which they formulated their research.

With Cohen's critique in mind, it is worth looking more closely at the study by Paul Willis of the schooling of working-class young males entitled *Learning to Labour: How Working Class Kids Get Working Class Jobs* (1981). In this study he addresses questions of method, and seeks to make more generalised claims based upon his research. While Willis' aim is clear in the title of his study, he was interested in what actually occurred in the classroom and, especially, what schooling and education meant to young men within this socio-economic category. Willis started from a quantifiable fact, i.e. that working-class kids ended up in particular occupations but wanted to know how that reproduction came about. His was a study of a 'micro' world, that of a school, but it was set within a 'macro' understanding of the broader social context. His theoretical framework was clearly Marxist, but also influenced by Althusser's notion of the role of ideology in the reproduction of existing (capitalist) social structures. In his Introduction to the American edition, Willis himself expresses his approach: 'I was concentrating on certain cultural and symbolic processes within a relatively discrete "cultural form", focused mainly in the school' (1981). Willis suggests using the term 'cultural ethnography' to describe his methodology, as distinct, perhaps, from ethnography 'proper' but he insists that his is not an holistic attempt to grasp the entire life-worlds of the agents, rather, to take a close look at very specific processes contained within specific setting.

As we have noted, the scholars at the CCCS were concerned to develop a materialist understanding of culture. That is, culture produced by individuals as active agents, but not in conditions of their own choosing. In this way culture can be seen, according to Willis, as a response to particular (oppressive) structural conditions, and, paradoxically, the reproduction of class structure via education.

Ordinary women: white, working-class, female

The next figures on our landscape are indicative of the interests of a group of feminist scholars. Angela McRobbie criticised the youth sub-culture studies for the absence of a discussion about their personal interests and motivations in research, and also what she argued was their gender blindness. To begin with the category 'youth' is rendered unproblematically masculine in their studies as they pay no attention to young working-class women even though they are often referred to by their respondents. They ignore the sexist statements of their respondents which reveal, according to McRobbie, their oppressive male attitudes to women and how certain definitions of working-class masculinity are related to an often aggressive form of heterosexuality. Likewise, Hebdige, although centrally interested in style and resistance to dominant cultures, is blind to the implications this might have for young women and fails to ask why these routes of resistance were generally not available to women at the time. McRobbie's critique reminds us that both our choice of frameworks and our politics can blind us to elements of meaning within the data gathered which might, in spite of the radical credentials and aims of the researchers, simply reproduce gendered forms of oppression. As the sub-cultural studies were focusing on spectacular youth sub-cultures, style as resistance, etc., feminist work in cultural studies sought to understand the 'structure, culture, biography' dynamic in relation to the unseen, domestic worlds of women.

The authors of *Women Take Issue* (Women's Studies Group, 1978), a collection of papers published by the Women's Group at the CCCS is evidence of the introduction of feminist concerns into the work of the Centre. From the introduction to the collection it is clear that this was not an easy task and involved intellectual and political struggles in order to render women and gender visible categories within cultural studies in particular and the academy in general. This work was undertaken in the 1970s which saw the emergence of the Women's Liberation Movement and a strong grass-roots feminism which clearly influenced the group but presented some problems in locating the 'politics' of their feminist work. The group were concerned to find ways of being 'intellectual' feminists while maintaining a commitment to political intervention. This was not an easy task, added to which, the environment of the CCCS was not conducive to feminist work. 'We found it extremely difficult to participate in CCCS groups and felt, without being able to articulate it, that it was a case of the masculine domination of both intellectual work and the environment in which it was being carried out' (Women's Studies Group, 1978: 11).

In addition to papers which examined aspects of early feminist work, e.g. the notion of 'the personal', psychoanalysis, sexuality and subjectivity, feminism's relationship to Marxist theories and textual work, on, e.g. women's magazines and romance, this collection also included two papers based upon empirical work with women. Dorothy Hobson describes how isolated housewives used radio and other media to counteract their feelings of isolation and loneliness. She was interested in the significance of everyday experience in the construction and reconstruction of gendered lives. The methods she adopted were conversational interviews with women in their homes and, in a later project, viewing the then popular soap opera, *Crossroads* with her respondents. Angela McRobbie's paper 'Working class girls and the culture of feminity' was based on a five-month study of young female members of a local youth club in which she 'wanted to look at the culture of these working class girls, at their 'peculiar and distinctive way of life' (Women's Studies Group,

1978: 96). She wanted to address notions of working-class culture and femininity and in particular the lived experience of teenage girls. McRobbie talked to teenage girls between 13 and 16 about their lives under the headings of 'school', 'family' and 'leisure'. She used a mixture of methods including questionnaires, observation, interviews, informal discussions and asked the girls concerned to keep a diary. Her respondents were female subjects, inhabiting femininity and expecting and aspiring to embark upon the 'feminine career' of marriage and family.

Indeed, 'the housewife' and the ordinary, or working-class woman, become characters on the landscape of cultural studies work and arguably have become constructed within the academy as "feminism's other"' (Brunsdon, 1993; 2000). But above all the feminist researchers insisted on gender as an important category for analysis and understanding of practices of text and consumption. In addition they raised questions of the pleasures of popular texts and in particular the enthusiasms of female audiences for those genres which were understood to be directed at them.

The question for early feminist work at CCCS was how girls became women and, in particular, how they came to inhabit femininity. As popular texts were considered to be important in the circulation of particular meanings, researchers began to analyse both the texts themselves in order to identify the ideological workings of, say, comics and magazines addressed to young women. It is clear from a number of accounts of the CCCS (Brunsdon, 1996; Hall, 1992) that the dynamics of development were often in contestation. This can produce versions of the 'history' of cultural studies as a series of interventions, or struggles to be heard. While this carries dangers of producing a narrow and highly selective version of what cultural studies is, it seems clear, if only from their research examples and topics, that the scholars at CCCS were constantly working with theoretical developments but always in relation to the socio-economic and political context of their work. The context of their work, while most obviously within a university, was also as inhabitants of the broader society and culture. The necessity to ground studies was paramount and also the contestations, of which feminism was one.

Black intellectuals and the empire strikes back

In 1978 the results of a collective CCCS study *Policing the Crisis: Mugging, the State and Law and Order* was published (Hall et al., 1978). This was an analysis of the moral panic which developed around the figure of the mugger. This was a conjunctural analysis which took a particular moment in British political history as a flash-point in the politics of race and the ways in which forms of representations and legal discourses of power and control were mobilised to control the perceived 'threat' to the dominant white society. The Race and Politics group at the CCCS continued this work, and their publication *The Empire Strikes Back: Race and Racism in 70s Britain* criticised the

British left for ignoring the role in which slavery had played in the development of capitalism and the 'making and remaking of the working class'.(CCCS, 1982: 7). Two essays in this collection by Hazel Carby and Pratibha Parmar also locate racism in relation to patriarchy and thus posed a challenge to 'white' feminism.

Researchers at the Centre worked with empirical methods that prioritised the grounding or concretising of political and theoretical imperatives in specific social and historical contexts. But also, and largely as a result of the interventions by researchers with particular agendas, the simple (Marxist) model of power relations which the sub-culture studies and some of the feminist work had posited was challenged as was the neglect of black history in cultural studies and questions of race and racism. Thus, while identities became more complex, the figures on the landscape also became less certain and clear-cut in the CCCS work. However we write the story of CCCS and however contested it is, I would argue that these contingent, exploratory and provisional studies provided the engine house from which many studies developed. These take us beyond 'Birmingham' and eventually into wider international context. But I want now to look at how the study of lived cultures was developed. The interest in popular culture, and especially the texts of 'the media', television, magazines and popular literature fuelled an interest in the ways in which people interpreted and used these texts. The concept of ideology and the perceived 'power' of the commercial media and popular forms raised questions of how and to what extent popular texts were influencing those who consumed these texts in every increasing and evermore enthusiastic users.

The 'active audience'

The unsettling of Marxist frameworks, especially by feminists and the disruptions within feminism itself around the category 'woman' and the work of black scholars in thinking about forms of oppression based on class, gender *and* race, questioned all certainties which the *grand narrative* of Marxism had provided thus far. The theoretical challenges also came from developments which emphasised the significance of pleasures in, especially, popular culture and the capacity which groups had to resist the dominant forms within society.

An interest in mass communication has been quite central to cultural studies work since the 1960s when Richard Hoggart addressed the developments of a commercial culture which, in his terms, was threatening to engulf a more authentic lived working-class culture and traditions. The production of media texts by powerful institutions, often part of the state apparatus, was an important focus of attention and also, because cultural studies was interested in lived culture, how these products were engaged by 'the people'. The emphasis then shifted to the exploration and understanding of some version of readerships, audiences, users, consumers. Studies of audiences for popular forms represent a significant strand in cultural studies, especially through the 1980s.

Dorothy Hobson had addressed the domestic world of broadcast media use and consumption. Her emphasis was on women audiences for popular forms. At the same time, Charlotte Brunsdon and David Morley carried out work into the construction and consumption of the then popular television magazine programme, *Nationwide* which will be discussed in Chapter 7.

Attempts to explore the everyday and lived cultures focused on media use and largely in the domestic context. Morley's project, Family Television, explored the ways in which texts and genres of television were taken up by, enjoyed by, disliked by different members of households within and alongside their domestic routines. Through his investigation of television within the general dynamics of family life, Morley wanted to pursue the notion of specific genres appealing to specific 'publics', who would possess the appropriate cultural competences demanded by the particular genre. Morley's methods were extended, tape-recorded interviews with members of the household during which he asked them about their viewing practices, their likes and dislikes and the ways in which household members negotiated television viewing. Morley's analysis of his interviews suggested that gender was a key organising element in households which dynamics were those of relationships of power.

Fans: poachers and cultural nomads

We now move from our very 'British' landscape to the different landscapes which have emerged from the mid-1980s in cultural studies. For example, this decade saw the development of American Cultural Studies, emerging, in part, out of American Studies. A significant text here is Janice Radway's important study of romance readers which will be discussed later. But also work has emerged from different regions in the fields of media studies, informed by the cultural studies approach, with an increased interest in audiences, the politics of pleasure and 'fans'. In this work there is a disappearance at times of the difference between the researcher and the researched, for example, Ien Ang identified herself as a fan in her study *Watching Dallas*.

Scholars have argued that taking 'fans' seriously can tell us a lot about the significance of 'the popular', thus, Lawrence Grossberg notes that the notion of 'the fan' implies a particular relationship to culture, and furthermore that this kind of relationship only exists in relation to the popular. He refers to this kind of engagement as 'mattering maps' which is indicative of how much popular forms matter to their fans creating 'affective alliances' (Lewis, 1992: 59).

> It is in their affective lives that fans constantly struggle to care about something, and to find the energy to survive, to find the passion necessary to imagine and enact their own projects and possibilities. Particular apparatuses may also provide the space within which dominant relations of power can be

challenged, resisted, evaded or ignored. (Grossberg, 1992: 59)

This is to acknowledge the ways in which affective alliances can organise the emotional and narrative lives and identities of 'fans', but also as a vestige of resistance in an increasingly overpowering world. A major proponent of the actively engaging subject is John Fiske who has worked in British, Australian and American academic institutions. His work has been the subject of much criticism largely because he was seen to be celebrating the ability which people had to read and make use of popular forms.

> This popular discrimination involves the selection of texts or stars that offer fans opportunities to make meanings of their social identities and social experiences that are self-interested and functional. Those may at times be translated into empowered social behavior ... but at other times may remain at the level of a compensatory fantasy that actually precludes any social action. (Fiske, 1992: 35)

Fiske's more extravagant claims for the potential of popular culture to empower subjects incensed many critics who saw this as a departure from any social critique or focus on the power relations inherent in the circulation of popular forms. However, we can see in the quote above that Fiske qualifies this more extreme version of the empowered consumer of popular culture. Perhaps what we can most usefully take from Grossberg and Fiske in this instance is the unpredictability of the ways in which people use popular culture and that our theories and analytical models should retain the equivalent flexibility.

The work of Michel de Certeau was suggestive in relation to reconceptualising the audience and their relationship to texts. Henry Jenkins used his ideas of 'poachers' and 'nomads' as useful metaphors for developing an understanding of the ways in which enthusiasts or 'fans' of particular genres or programmes actively used them for their own ends. Thus, the notion of a more fluid, unfixed and de-centred community of readers and viewers was posited. Also, questions of identity and subjectivity were foregrounded. Previous conceptualisations of audiences had assumed a fixed subject and new theories of the subject put these assumptions into question.

Henry Jenkins has carried out some work to identify fan groups (for a particular programme, performer, musical style, film genre) who inhabit an imagined community which is likely to be dispersed and connected, not within locatable and bounded space or community, but through a variety and number of mediated practices: media text, fanzines and websites. Jenkins argues that in order to understand the 'fan' we must:

> focus on media fandom as a discursive logic that knits together interests across textual and generic boundaries. While some fans remain exclusively committed to a single show or star, many others use individual series as points of entry

into a broader fan community, linking to an intertextual network composed of many programmes, films, books, comics, and other popular materials. (1992: 40)

'To focus on any one media product – be it *Star Trek* or "Material Girl" – is to miss the larger cultural context within which that material gets embedded as it is integrated back into the life of the individual fan' (ibid.: 41). Thus, the studies of investments which fans make in popular culture takes us back to the importance of how these practices relate more broadly to the cultures of everyday life.

As Jenkins suggests, many of the traditionally assumed boundaries, such as that between producer and consumer and between commercial and creative products, are broken down. 'Fandom here becomes a participatory culture which transforms the experience of media consumption into the production of new texts, indeed of a new culture and a new community' (ibid.: 46). And, we might add, the boundaries of researcher and researched as they share their pleasures in the consumption of popular texts.

Those scholars who have studied fans and fan cultures have looked at the appeal of specific genres or texts for individuals. To be a 'fan' is to have extraordinary recognitions and identifications with aspects of popular culture. The insights gained here, especially into the construction of subjectivities are very interesting indeed and reveal the complex processes of such identifications. They take us into the realm of fantasy, desire and give us some understanding of the role of the popular in giving us a sense of who we are, or who we might be. Clearly this is the language of psychoanalysis, an approach which cultural studies has always found problematic. It is interesting, therefore to relate this to arguments put forward by Valerie Walkerdine, a critical psychologist who herself has worked on popular culture, especially in relation to children and young women. She is concerned to reach an 'understanding of the relation of the popular to the production of subjectivity ... [M]y concern is to analyse practices in order to understand how subjects are produced within them' (Walkerdine, 1997: 122). For her, the popular is dispersed across our lives: the catch phrases from a popular television show, a popular song we sing as we work, the naming of our pets after 'famous' pets, etc. She wants to understand the popular and subjectivity in this way. As she insists, 'it would certainly make no sense to describe this as "audience research". (ibid.: 122). Walkerdine's work moves us to explore 'the complex intersection of social and psychic' (ibid.: 168) which would take us beyond the binaries of dominated and resistant but also give us some conceptual purchase on the more complex processes of identity and subjectivity. This social psychic dimension remains an intriguing if undeveloped strand within cultural studies. Indeed, the (re)conceptualisation of the notion of the 'social audience' into fans, nomads and poachers is of enormous significance and the subject of much debate. Some argue that this is a slide into individualism, that it ditches any notion of the political and evacuates any possibility of social critique. The implications for these developments will emerge in the following chapters.

The way we were? Reasons for choices: constructing a 'community'

We have looked at some of the 'communities' which collective research projects have constructed, and how they have produced particular figures and recognisable tropes on the landscape which, in turn, have become part of the shared knowledge of cultural studies. But, in identifying the related figures of the researchers as constructors of these figures we can begin to ask how the researcher relates to these groups constructed as 'communities' within their research. For example, if the researcher shares the background of her informants, what is the nature of these points of connection? How have the connections between the lived experience of the researcher and those of her respondents been understood as both political and academic issues? The question is, where do these differences matter and, crucially, how are they dealt with methodologically? I spoke in the previous chapter of the dangers inherent in the 'democratic impulse', where experience threatens to overwhelm and hide or even erase the relationships of oppression and power. This suggests the first way of understanding the relationship between the researcher and the subjects of their study. That is as a champion, celebrating the hitherto hidden heroes (and heroines) of the everyday. In validating their experience and ways of life, there is a danger of valorising their accounts and acting as their spokesperson within the academic community. The second form of relationship is that of being 'one of them'. Here a researcher might choose to explore, as Henry Jenkins did, his or her own 'fan' community or an academic researcher who shares her or his respondent's background or social identity is obviously in certain ways a 'member' of the same group. Whether as a champion or as one of them, the researcher can be compromised into being much less critical of their practices, views and daily lives. Also it can close the eyes to a sense of the broader context of the research. Here it is appropriate to heed Williams's warnings about the overwhelming nature of experience, where contradictions and connections are rendered invisible, as in, for example, the gender blindness of the youth studies noted by McRobbie.

Les Back (1993) discusses his own location in his research and argues against what he calls the use of 'credentialism' in justifying one's choice or selection of research area. He grew up in a white working-class neighbourhood on a council estate outside of London. During the 1970s he became aware of racism and the rise of the British National Front party amongst his peers. This experience, plus his relationship with black friends was formative. As he puts it:

This combination of experiences informed my decision when it came to choosing a doctoral research project. At the time I felt quite genuinely that I wanted to try and conduct anthropology within areas about which I had close experiential knowledge. As a result, I decided to do fieldwork within the working-class areas that surrounded the college where I had been an under-graduate. This was little over 10 miles from the place I had lived as a child. (1993: 221-2)

Back is very frank about his subsequent embarrassment in acknowledging that, as he puts it, 'I used my working-class origins as a way of gaining credit for this research and thus fictitiously dissolving the division between self and other' (ibid.: 222). While he did have background knowledge and experience which informed his research, he now insists that 'it was simply farcical to pretend that I had remained what I once was. In a sense I possessed a language and operated intellectual models that were simultaneously my possessions and yet not mine' (ibid.: 222). Back reminds us that however much we can identify with our respondents and, in some cases, have shared their experience, as academic researchers we have the resources of the university, a theoretical and intellectual language and conceptual thinking, all of which makes us not the persons we used to be.

He gives an example of a moment during his fieldwork which shocked him into the realisation of these tensions and difficulties:

I remember one night walking home through the estate to the flat where I was living. I recognised the jacket and frame of my brother ahead of me with his face turned away (my family regularly visited during the time I was doing fieldwork). I rushed up behind him. The man turned and faced me; it was not my brother. At the time I felt a profound discomfort. That man could quite easily *have been* my brother. Yet here I was turning people like him into 'objects' of anthropological study and in the process of constructing the 'other', I was also starkly defining my 'self' as alien and separate. The experience left me with serious doubts about the personal consequences of conducting research of this nature, and for me these issues remain unresolved. (ibid.: 223)

These conflictual positions of the researcher and their chosen subject of study are often what sparks the investment in the project itself. Mark Pursehouse who carried out research with and into readers of the popular British tabloid the *Sun* speaks of himself as a postgraduate in cultural studies, but also as sharing a common background with his reader respondents. 'In many ways this project on the *Sun* is a product not of long-entrenched [political] convictions but of the clashes between some of these "academic identities" and other "races", other experiences, wider relations, which have formed and continue to be lived as significant elements of my existence' (Pursehouse, 1989: 27). Or, as he put it, 'I could easily have been a *Sun* reader.' His respondents were friends who were readers of the *Sun* and these established relationships meant that his respondents were willing to speak to him openly about their reading practices. Pursehouse's study is one which walks a path between spaces and communities but he, like Back, is willing to examine the often contradictory relations engendered through 'researching in your own backyard'.

Wendy Hollway, a social psychologist who explored the construction of gendered subjectivities, also selected people she knew as her participants. She adopted a grounded theory approach, in which theory and method can be brought together and selected friends who were the most likely to reflect on their own subjectivities and identities and who were, in her words, prone to 'self-analysis'. They were used to questioning their situation, themselves and their relationships, they were curious about themselves and their own lives. They were reflexive and used to 'doing' interview work/identity work on themselves. Hollway explains it thus: 'Because participants gave me complex dynamic, multiple and contradictory accounts of themselves and their experience, it was possible to develop a theory of multiple and contradictory subjectivity ... I sought participants and developed methods which would be adequate to the theoretical framework' (1989: 18).

In my own study, although I did not know my participants, I drew attention to certain 'recognitions' I felt as women told me about their lives, their expectations, etc. because of my own earlier experience. These recognitions maintained, although I was now in possession of frameworks for understanding those experiences, the ways of life and their accounts. Thus, useful knowledge can enrich the quality of the data being especially productive during the interview itself. In this way the dialogue is more dynamic and points can be picked up and developed which might otherwise be overlooked.

Absences: the powerful, or 'researching up'

We can see, from the earliest cultural studies projects, that concern and interest in the less powerful have been afforded priority. This can be explained with reference to the marginalised or powerless groups to which the researchers wished to 'give a voice' or at least to demand that the field be expanded to include the everyday understandings and passions of 'ordinary people'. The emphasis of cultural studies thus far on popular forms, especially commercially produced texts disseminated through television, popular cinema, music and those identified sub-cultures has also taken researchers into specific groups and not others. However, this ignores crucially important groups – cultural producers, consumers of middle or so-called 'high' culture, policy-makers – who in different ways shape and form the cultural landscape. Some of the difficulties encountered by researchers can be outlined in an effort to explain the difficulties. One most obvious one is that of access. Researchers have embarked on projects which require access to, say, a television organisation, only to be refused access. Large commercial organisations are both suspicious of researchers and, understandably, protective of their time. There are, however, some notable exceptions. Hobson spent time with the producers of

Crossroads (Hobson, 1982) and David Buckingham gained access to the producers of the popular soap opera, *EastEnders* (Buckingham, 1987) as did Irene Meijer (2001). These have been useful studies in understanding the practices and processes of cultural production. Schlesinger's important study of the BBC news production (1978) more ambitiously identified 'corporate ideology' present in the working practices, the customs and traditions in reproducing a very particular approach to news and news production. Similarly, Liesbet van Zoonen has looked at the masculinity of news production and journalism in her studies of media professionals (van Zoonen, 1998). More recently, Georgina Bourne has carried out an 'ethnography' of the BBC which, in her earliest statements of work in progress, promises to suggest nuanced ways of understanding media creativities and cultural intermediaries than has hitherto been the case (Bourne, 2000).

Questions of access, then, are often, but not always, barriers to 'studying up', but there are other reasons for the difficulty. Janice Radway attempted to study editors of the Book of the Month Club but found it impossible largely because of the class privilege of her readers. When finding women to talk to me about their VCR use, I found it very difficult to make contact with and persuade middle-class women to speak to me and, when they did, they asked searching questions about my research. This information was offered to all my respondents, but those with more social and cultural capital pushed me further in accounting for myself and my work. The way in which the 'tables were turned' here in terms of power relations of researcher and respondent reveal much about the dynamics of interviewing and social research which will be explored in further chapters.

Being an academic

The conflicts often painfully experienced when researchers like Back and Pursehouse research their own 'communities' is often combined with another set of conflicts in identity. Identities are also constructed within the academic community itself. As many students and young scholars have experienced, there is a largely unwritten code within the academy, not only around areas of expertise, but as to who may count as an 'expert' in the first place. This always leaves room for self-doubt and feelings of inadequacy. Pursehouse and Walkerdine have spoken of their unease and difficulty in finding a position within the academy. Pursehouse, who was from a working-class background and politically committed, encountered 'people occupying forms of cultural elitism or exclusivity in ways that were very different from my experiences of local peer group sub-cultures' (1989: 28). Similarly, Walkerdine speaks of her anger at encountering academics on the political left who were studying working-class culture. Many of the people she met at university had led 'interesting' lives which included early political commitment and interest. For Walkerdine this was indicative of the kinds of choices and opportunities afforded to the middle classes, or those with high cultural capital, unlike herself:

I came from the class which these people were supposed to be interested in, but there was nothing exotic about my former life. Indeed, I felt that none of the markers of anything interesting were present at all. I dreamt of glamour, read comics, listened to pop music, worked hard at school and my father died early. I couldn't find in my history any of the exotic sub-cultural resistance that cultural studies wanted to find. (Walkerdine, 1997: 19)

These disclosures are important for a number of reasons. They are indicative of the contradictions within much of cultural studies work where politically committed researchers are keen to attend to hitherto ignored or demeaned aspects of working-class life and how a young postgraduate might feel coming from those very backgrounds with different experiences of what life was like. It reveals the romanticism of work on sub-cultures perhaps more poignantly than the written research itself does. These scholars are speaking and writing from a standpoint which reveals the academy as a closely bounded community and one which constructs its research subjects/objects as 'other'. I have seen these conflicting identities and commitments in many students and consider that class difference continues to be a painful and often hidden experience in relation to academic work in Britain, if not elsewhere. Researchers like Pursehouse, Walkerdine and others referred to throughout this book have been important in revealing these kinds of conflicts and differences in identity which their participation in the academic community have provoked.

Are 'we' academic voyeurs?

In acknowledging 'the academy' as a still powerful site of knowledge production, we might then question our rights as researchers to subject others to scrutiny, whether through observation or by eliciting information from long tape-recorded conversations. Is it not true that we are extracting data from those who are generous with their time and willing to co-operate with us that will largely be to our benefit? The subjects of our study can rarely claim or see such benefits. In whose interests, therefore, is the research being done is a perfectly legitimate question to ask. The issue of constructing audiences, users, consumers, sub-cultural groups as ethnographic 'others' must be carefully considered. In a number of respects, there is an unacceptable exchange, positioning the academic as voyeur. In a now famous piece which is an account of her observations of a working-class family's viewing of the film *Rocky* (Walkerdine, 1986), Walkerdine argues that psychoanalysis provided the 'best tool kit available' to understand the 'investments and meanings, as well as the relation of my fantasies to those of the film and to those of Mr Cole (father)' (1997: 55). She thus, insists that the subjectivity (or role as based on her own experience) of the researcher should be examined within the research process itself which can then specify the locations from which particular interpretations are produced. For a psychologist like Walkerdine, the central source of both the viewing of the film and her interpretations is the unconscious. This, then, is where, she argues, we should look if we are to understand the drives, fantasies and desires involved in the engagement with popular culture *and* the 'bourgeoise' academic researchers' fascination with working-class pleasures and uses of popular culture.

These are extremely important questions for cultural studies and especially for ethnographic or empirical work (see Chapter 7 for a fuller discussion of these implications). Walkerdine's piece on *Rocky* has become a *cause célèbre*, and the target of much criticism. She insists that, by including an analysis of her own psycho-subjectivity within the research, she is taking a radical step to genuinely expose the subjectivity of the researcher in the interpretive process. Critics have decried this attempt as being 'autobiography' (Lull, 1990) as an example of the 'small industry' and as 'the "me" generation lives on' (Probyn, 1993: 10). Walkerdine suggests that these extreme reactions against her methods are revealing fantasies of Marxist and post-Marxist intellectual assumptions about the masses which she views as 'dodgy'. These, she argues, 'have more to do with the hopes, fears and disappointment of the researchers than with the subjectivity of the subjects of the research.' (Walkerdine, 1997: 58). Walkerdine, however, remains 'deeply committed to empirical work' (ibid.: 60). In a reflection on 'Video Replay' she states that she criticised:

> what I still see as the voyeurism of a social science that wants to get inside the living rooms of the working class to produce a truth about them and gets a voyeuristic thrill out of the 'oh, are they *really* like that!' feeling - a desire to know the truth mixes with less salubrious sentiments. (ibid.: 67)

Your community

And finally in this chapter I want to remind you of your position within the academy, whether as an undergraduate or postgraduate. C. Wright Mills (1959) said: 'I do not know the full social conditions of the best intellectual workmanship, but certainly surrounding oneself by a circle of people who will listen and talk – and at times they have to be imaginary characters – is one of them.'

Discussing your work with others is an extremely important part of its development. It is often in the process of explaining what you are doing to a friend or colleague that the focus becomes clearer. Talk is a significant practice and a necessary element in intellectual work. This is a recognition that, again in the words of Wright Mills: 'you cannot split your work from your life – you must use both for enrichment of the other'. Allow yourself, in other words, to be absorbed by your research. Make certain that you are open to new ideas and insights. Get into the habit of expressing and articulating the new ideas, however vague. They are your own and unless you work them up and give them shape they will disappear from view.

Many university departments have lively postgraduate research communities, even if promotional versions exceed the actuality. However, you might be isolated within your institution, especially if your research topic is unfamiliar or of no interest to those around you. If this is the case you need to find ways of contacting scholars who are working in your area. This can be done through researching websites, attending conferences, keeping up with reading, especially journal articles and making contact. If you have access to the Internet, e-mail is a wonderful device for this. During your period of research for your doctorate you can build yourself a community of scholars who will not necessarily be based in the same institution. In my own and others' experience, it is most likely that your support group will be very widespread and invaluable in the development of your work and in producing 'new' communities of scholars and research topics so vital to the growth of cultural studies.

The following chapter takes us into more practical research issues and the process of identifying and developing your own research topic.

four	A Question of Research

There is an implicit assumption within colleges and universities that we all know what we mean when we refer to 'research'. What this broadly describes is the exploration of some phenomenon in a systematic and rigorous way and there are many different kinds of research activities that are becoming increasingly important in contemporary societies. Most generally, research forms the basis of much of the production of what passes for knowledge in our modern societies, that is what we might call administrative or bureaucratic knowledge, for example, government statistics, census and social trends, but this would also include media, especially broadcasting and the press. Research is also an activity engaged in by academics whose key activity is to further intellectual development within their particular field of study and is becoming increasingly significant as a 'measurable' commodity. Students across a range of disciplines are also required to carry out research as part of their assessment on undergraduate and postgraduate degrees. However it is described and whatever its outcome, research is above all a practice. It takes place within specific institutional and professional contexts and is always the product of social relations. Although many students and academics work as 'individual researchers' nevertheless, they are part of a university department where they have colleagues, research teams and supervisors. I have written elsewhere of the importance of the institutional context in shaping research, for example, access to particular kinds of knowledge, the encouragement of some theories over others, or the denial of certain kinds of methods (Gray, 1995). Clearly, this material and social setting can often have quite profound effects on the shaping and development of research. This is to emphasise that, although research and its products are often thought of as esoteric, they are the processes and products of a profoundly material practice and engage with material aspects of the social and the cultural. Furthermore, like all human practices, there are different ways of doing it. The process of research, that is, how research develops, takes shape, the kinds of decisions made about particular methods or theories and so on, are rarely revealed in the written version of the research, but when carrying out research we encounter moments of uncertainty, points at which we have to make decisions about how to proceed, select a particular mode of analysis or decide on the exclusion of a particular avenue of enquiry. The process and the moves made, the choices we settle for and perhaps the compromises which are necessary, should be rendered visible. Not necessarily in the written version, although this aspect is developed in Chapter 9, but essentially to ourselves. We need to be honest and thorough in revealing and being able to justify our choices.

Increasingly, cultural, media and communication studies degree programmes incorporate practical research skills into their courses and modules. Thus students' research skills will be developed and, eventually, assessed. This can be through small projects on individual courses, undergraduate or Master's dissertations or much larger projects for Doctorates. Students pursuing any or all of these research activities will be required to formulate a topic, to think about how to investigate that topic and to be able to justify the choice of methods and procedures. This chapter will discuss ways to proceed.

First, it is worth attending to what the text books refer to as the 'ideal' research model:

> Literature review - Topic - Data gathering - Analysis - Writing up

This model suggests that the research is carried out through particular and discrete phases starting from the literature review and ending with the writing-up in the form of a report or research monograph. This is regularly disputed as only an 'ideal' model and it is generally accepted that actual research rarely proceeds so neatly. It is, of course, useful to have indicators of the different kinds of activity involved in carrying out a research project, but in the event the different stages are, at the very least, overlapping. When, for example, might reading stop? And when might writing begin? These two extremes of the research timetable are activities that should, and in practice do, continue throughout the project. Indeed, both activities are important in reflecting on and, possibly, re-thinking approaches in the light of new or newly discovered work. Writing, although often referred to as 'writing up' in the final phase of a project should never be left until the very last stage. Writing should be part of the research process. Writing helps to clarify ideas that will remain vague unless they are thought through on the page. Writing, however, can take very different forms and it is worth experimenting with different kinds of writing throughout the project. A research journal, for example, could include descriptions of particular events or incidents relevant to the topic; a discussion of a key text or debate; analysis of a visual text; and, importantly, more personal reflections on the progress of the research.

Where and how to begin?

I suggest that the best way of thinking about research is to envisage it as a series of questions. The art of formulating a manageable research project is therefore to identify key questions appropriate to specific theoretical and intellectual concerns and those aspects of the world that might be explored empirically.

The first thing to consider is the immediate academic context within which the research is placed. For example, undergraduates, might be carrying out a research project for assessment on a particular course or module. Therefore, they will be working within certain parameters, e.g. the topic of the course, the theoretical and methodological framework and the particular kinds of skills which they have been encouraged to develop. The tutor will be looking to assess the grasp of a topic and its substance, the theoretical approach and student's ability, through collection and analysis of data, documents or visual texts, to apply what they have learnt to some concrete example. This should be the initial framework for thinking through and generating a research question. It is not a good idea, for example, for specific course or module assessments, to launch into some area which has not been covered on the syllabus as this could involve vast amounts of background reading in order to become familiar with the topic. Choosing as the starting point an area which has already been covered and one that is of particular interest is a much better strategy. Thus, course-work is the first key resource. The other important factor is the amount of time available for each assignment. This requires careful planning and organisation. Although this may seem irksome, it is a very valuable exercise and extremely good experience for future projects both in and outside the university.

In the case of more independent projects such as dissertations or doctoral theses, defining the context of the topic is an important initial activity. Thus, what is often described as 'reviewing the literature' is a key first stage in research. The aim in doing this is to place your own work within an existing research context, for example, the kinds of theories which have underpinned the key writers in the chosen field and the methodological questions they raise. It is also important to look for examples of specific research that will inform the development of the research topic. Through doing this search and intensive reading, gaps and lacunae in existing research can be identified which your project will seek to fill. The important thing to bear in mind is that you will not be 'parachuting' into the unknown, but aiming your landing position within an established terrain. Thus, you will be orienting your own study in relation to existing work and taking that work as a stepping off point for designing your project.

Using the library and other information resources is obviously important here. For most projects it is simply not sufficient to use only the texts or references which have been presented on reading lists. Students will be expected to demonstrate wider relevant reading but the breadth of this reading will depend on the size of the research project. While the object of this exercise is to explore what has been written about the chosen area, it is important to be very precise about the parameters of your topic. With sophisticated information search technologies it is easy to become overloaded with references many of which will be of no use at all. Having identified the topic and the component subject parts, or key words these can be analysed to find as many *relevant* research terms as possible. It is also important to set some notion of limits on the search, for example: how far back is it necessary to go? Are you interested only in your national context, or does your topic extend to other regions? What kinds of material are relevant to your project? These are likely to be some combination of books, journal articles, reports, theses and resources found on the Internet.

Deciding on a topic/living the problem

In one of the most welcome recent developments in the writing of research, and following feminist interventions, some researchers are owning (up to) their reasons for pursuing specific research topics. Often this involves a declaration of interest (anathema to more conventional research) and an admission of partiality or political commitment. The consequence of more visible researcher/authors, through the use of, for example, the first person, begins to remove the mystique of the objective, disinterested researcher as well as giving a sense of responsibility, ownership and authorship of the research. Some researchers, such as the psychologist Wendy Hollway, have discussed the circumstances in formulating their topic. She ponders, 'at what point can I say that I started doing *research*?' (Hollway, 1989: 9). She explains that she was reading widely about her main interest in the relationship between the individual and the social, but she felt that she was also 'living the problem' (ibid.: 9) and keeping a notebook. This blurring of boundaries is a consequence of her own reasons for doing psychology at university which were a curiosity about herself and others, about what motivates us and how relationships involve power, dependence and change. Her own experience outside the academy informed her intellectual curiosity and dissatisfaction with the prescribed ways of doing research and the available theoretical frameworks. This point about an intellectual identity becoming indistinguishable from other identities is an important one and one that can help in thinking through who we are as researchers and how our research is actually being generated. It became, Hollway says, 'impossible to separate "me" from "theoretical ideas" from "field notes"'. In a similar vein, Wright Mills talks of 'the fusion of personal and intellectual life' and how 'you cannot split your work from your life – you must use both for enrichment of the other' (Wright Mills, 1959: 215), an observation with which many experienced researchers would concur.

Turning to your own project and bearing in mind the comments above about your particular research context, a good way to start formulating a topic is to get yourself in the mood to do a bit of free and creative thinking. However you do this is up to you, but it is important to be relaxed and not anxious. In this state you can begin to generate some initial ideas, producing a list of 'possible' themes or subjects or approaches. After the first session you will have a list which you can then talk about with your friends and colleagues. This 'talk work' is very important and productive, and you will most likely find that they make suggestions, or have ways of approaching the topic that had not occurred to you. Talking things through in this way will sharpen your ideas and enable you to move on to the next stage. At the risk of stating the obvious, you need to focus on an area that interests and engages you, given that you will be living with the project for some time. What motivates your choice and selection of the object of study will vary, but the scope is very wide. You can certainly investigate, examine and analyse some aspect of popular culture in which you have had a long investment, e.g. football or popular cinema, youth subcultures or popular music and no doubt you will be encouraged to do so. Wright Mills (1959) echoes our earlier discussion on the usefulness of our own experience when he suggests that we should be learning to use our life experience in our intellectual work and to continually examine and interpret it. You will, after all, be something of an 'insider' here with already accumulated knowledge that you will be able to draw on for your research. Similarly, you will most likely have an immediate network of 'devotees', fans or practitioners who can become part of your project.

Other motives for choice may be the exclusion or absence of your own interests or knowledge from the field, or from your specific curriculum. Thus you will be exploring the ignored or the absent - here you will be making an, albeit modest, intervention in the field.

Stuart Hall (1992) has recently described cultural studies as having to have 'something at stake'. I think this is a very useful way of thinking about your research. It avoids the 'so what?' question which you will certainly be asking yourself as you attempt to justify and make sense of what you are doing. Many of the best student dissertations I have read have come out of an urgent need to examine or explore some aspect of culture, sometimes as fans or critics, but very often anger or the feeling of being used or duped by powerful texts or forms is the stimulus. It is no coincidence, for example, that female students are often driven to research and write about eating disorders, or other topics involving the uses and abuses of the female body in contemporary culture. Put simply, it matters to them. Questions of identity are also pressing and take on a particular poignancy and urgency as students explore questions of their own and others' identities and the ways in which they are shaped by cultural forms. Less 'personal' motives lead students to investigate urban regeneration, cultural policy, schooling, etc. This potential of an interdisciplinary contemporary field such as cultural studies, requires that we develop research skills but it also requires that we find an appropriate 'place' for ourselves in our research. What are the implications of carrying out this work when we are so enmeshed in it, when we have experience of it, when the very things we are investigating have shaped us, influenced us, made us what we are and what we might become? In order to develop her project with working-class women, Beverley Skeggs (1994) drew on what Guba (1990) has argued are the three fundamental research questions that structure any research project:

1   What is there that can be known – what is knowable?

2   What is the relation of the knower to the known?

3   How do we find things out?

What is there that can be known - what is knowable?

This is an ontological question, it refers to the aspect of social reality to be studied, but it also deals with assumptions we are willing to make about the nature of reality. It requires you to take a position in relation to your project and to define your 'knowable space'. How you construct your knowable space and how you go about exploring and investigating that knowable space will depend upon your theoretical approach to the social world and the actors or texts involved. In *Learning to Labour*, Paul Willis sought to examine how young working-class men ended up moving in working-class jobs. He considered schooling, education and more broadly the state to be a key agent in shaping this process and the occupational choices open to working class youth. However, his theory of subjectivity saw the young men involved as agents within their own lives, not mere products of a repressive system, but active and creative human beings. He therefore chose to carry out participant observation and interviews with pupils over an extended period in a school. In this way he was able to examine and identify the ways in which the educational system positioned these lads and the often creative ways they resisted the attempts to 'educate' them. Willis could have examined his research question in different ways, but his methodological choices enabled him to mobilise his theories, his perspective on the aspect of the social world he wished to study.

What is the relation of the knower to the known?

This is an epistemological question and, put simply, asks how we know what we know. The assumptions that are made about this depend on how we perceive of the reality, and, although Guba does not suggest this, how we are located as subjects within our research. What we bring to our work, how our own knowledge and experience is brought to bear on the research itself will certainly shape it. This is not a question of being 'subjective', nor to suggest that we can only view aspects of the world from our own perspective. Rather, it is to acknowledge what we ourselves bring to our research in terms of our lived experience, certainly, but also our politics and our intellectual frameworks. It is important to make these explicit. The point about who we are and how we relate to the project itself is a key issue for researchers and, again, has informed many debates about research practice and the politics of knowledge generation. In Chapter 1, we noted how the figure of the objective, or neutral researcher has inhabited the social sciences and anthropology and while you are not expected to resolve these dilemmas, it does at least require that you think about this and reflect on your own position. One of the most interesting and illuminating accounts of grappling with these questions is given by Wendy Hollway when she states: 'It would be impossible to present these questions fully without talking about myself: the point that I was at in my life and aspects of its history, the cultural and political conditions that produced it, how these shaped my interest in certain areas of contemporary social theory' (1989: 4).

Note how Hollway speaks of her own life, but also the political and social context that influenced her and encouraged her interest in theory. This is of crucial importance. Theory is often considered to be an 'object' which the researcher or student must engage with and overcome. Hollway's approach renders theory more usable when she thinks of it in relation to the needs of the topic. Thus, looking for theory can be quite a liberating way of thinking, rather than theory looking for you!

While these questions of position and subjectivity must be asked of the researcher in all research work, they are, I would suggest, particularly acute when the study involves drawing on others' lives and accounts of their experience. We should certainly question and examine the politics and ethics of our research, and this will be discussed more fully below, but for the moment I want to explore how researchers might relate to their subjects of research. What aspects of life experience might you share with your respondents, e.g. age, gender, 'race', ethnicity, physical ability and class? How might these 'matches' or 'mismatches' influence and shape the study? How will they affect your relationship with your research subjects? If you are part of their milieu, to what extent must you step outside, in order to analyse, or interpret activities and processes? What are the implicit, or explicit, power relations of researcher and researched? How can you avoid abusing your privilege? Let us look at how some researchers have dealt with these dilemmas. I have chosen to look at Beverley Skeggs's study of working-class women *Formations of Class and Gender* (1997); Marie Gillespie's study of young South Asian people living in Southall, London *Television, Ethnicity and Cultural Change* (1995) and Claire Alexander's study of young Bengali men in London *The Asian Gang* (2000).

Beverley Skeggs, in a reflexive article about her study of the lives of working-class women, states that her work was motivated by her desire to 'do research which both filled the gap in existing knowledge about working-class women and which challenged many of the dominant ideas of the time. To do this I felt I had to speak to real working class women rather than relying on the representations available' (1995: 195). She also identifies herself as a working-class woman. 'I was learning to speak out from a limited and marginalised position as a working-class woman in academia' (ibid.: 195). She insists also that passion and involvement were an important dimension 'My research was and still is a highly emotive affair. Ideas are emotional: they can be inspiring, satisfying, rage and guilt inducing, terrifying, etc. They involve you' (ibid.: 194). In an earlier article she says that her key research question was 'why do young women, who are clearly not just passive victims of some ideological conspiracy, consent to a system of class and gender oppression, which appears to offer few rewards and little benefit?' (Skeggs, 1994: 72). Skeggs carried out ethnographic research that followed a group of young women's progress for three years. With some of the young women she had a social relationship and with others she chatted and carried out some interviews which elicited different kinds of information. She reflects: 'The time spent doing the ethnography was so intense that the boundary between my life inside and outside the research dissolved' (1984: 73). Skeggs was concerned to locate the 'view from below', that is the view, or perspective of young working-class women and was concerned to 'show how young women's experience of structure (their class and gender positioning) and institutions (education and the media) framed and informed their responses and how this process informed constructions of their own subjectivity' (ibid.: 74).

Marie Gillespie's study 'evolved over seven years of teaching in two Southall high schools where the popularity of 'Indian' films was evident' (Gillespie, 1989, in Gray and McGuigan, 1993: 147). Her aim was to explore with groups of young second-generation immigrants, questions of identity and ethnicity, with particular emphasis on the consumption and use of popular texts such as television programmes, films and advertisements. Gillespie speaks of how 'issues of power, detachment, gender and ethnicity' (1995: 72) influenced her fieldwork. During the research she was a part-time teacher in the school that her respondents attended. This dual role could have been problematic but Gillespie was aware of the need to maintain her professional role as teacher and not to let the imperatives of her research project take over. Her status as a part-time teacher gave her a more independent role in relation to the school authorities and the students themselves and in this way she was able to occupy a more negotiable position in relation to her power and authority. The familiarity she had with the young people presented some issues around her ability to detach herself from the way in which her relationship with them had developed in the years prior to the beginning of her research. She found it necessary to be vigilant and to make a real attempt to render the familiar strange once more. Her gender definitely influenced the shape of the project. Unsurprisingly, perhaps, she found it much easier to relate to young women and had some rather difficult encounters with groups of young men in her study. The result is that her female respondents outnumber the males, a fact to which she draws our attention (ibid.: 72).

Gillespie says: 'My status as a gori or "white woman" is of central importance to the fieldwork and to the ethnography' (ibid.: 72), both in terms of how she was perceived by and how she perceived her subjects. The fact that she had a basic knowledge of Punjabi was extremely important in that this was seen to be a mark of 'respect and recognition for "the culture" which, in turn, tends to make one more acceptable and accepted'(ibid.: 72). However, Gillespie is clear about the fact that 'one can never claim immunity to ethnocentrism or racism' (ibid.: 73) but she makes serious attempts to be constantly aware of her own perceptions, language and categorisations throughout her research. Clearly these aspects of the relationship between Gillespie and her respondents are crucial in shaping the study and it is to her credit that she has declared this in her discussion of methodology.

Claire Alexander, a young Asian woman, carried out research alongside a Bengali youth project, again based in London (Alexander, 2000). Ironically, she found the young women involved in the project the most difficult to relate to. She put this down to the 'culture' of the project where the young people were encouraged to regard the youth workers as 'older sisters'. As a result, young women regarded Alexander in the same way and treated her with polite distance. Thus she concluded that it was the combination of gender, ethnicity and age which created a barrier between her and the young women and not the fact that she was a researcher (ibid.: 31). The actual focus of her research was on Asian masculinities and she formed good and productive relationships with groups of young men involved in the project. Some anthropologists insist on the position of the innocent or the naïve researcher, assuming a lack of knowledge and taking up the role of 'student' to be 'educated' in the (mysterious) ways of the group or culture. For Alexander 'innocence' masks an enormous gulf between researcher and researched. This is a disingenuous strategy, cynical even, as what it denies above all is the relative power of the researcher, their institutional position and the value to them of doing the research (ibid.: 28).

These researchers bring to our attention the importance of acknowledging that, in cultural studies especially, we are part of the world which we study. We are not only participants in the cultural world, but are constructed by that world. This is what makes cultural studies both exciting and daunting, as we try to place ourselves as researchers in the often all too familiar world which we want to explore critically and analytically.

How do we find things out?

These are methodological questions. What kind of methods must I employ in order to know, or to put me in a position of being able to interpret and analyse this aspect of the social world? This, then, is where you can begin to think about the kinds of data you need and how to gather it in order to begin to explore your research questions, the subject of the following chapters.

Working in a group

This book, in common with other research methods texts, tends to assume that research is conducted by individuals. This is mainly the case in academic work and the kinds of assessed work you will be doing. However, you may well be involved in a group project as part of your degree course, and you will almost certainly find yourself working within a group when you enter the world of employment. It is worth discussing ways of approaching group work and here I am drawing on work developed during a Teaching and Learning project and which colleagues and I use for a group project on our course, *Modes of Cultural Analysis* (Hanson et al., 2000). This requires students to form small research groups and investigate a cultural site in the city of Birmingham. Students are asked to formulate their own topic, theoretical framework and methods appropriate to their chosen site and to produce: a visual display for exhibition in the department, prepare a presentation for the whole class at a day-school and produce an individual report on the group research process. Guidelines are provided for this work (see Figure 4.1).

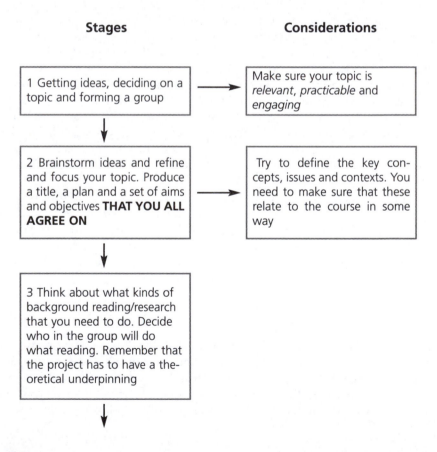

Stages	**Considerations**
1 Getting ideas, deciding on a topic and forming a group	Make sure your topic is *relevant, practicable* and *engaging*
2 Brainstorm ideas and refine and focus your topic. Produce a title, a plan and a set of aims and objectives **THAT YOU ALL AGREE ON**	Try to define the key concepts, issues and contexts. You need to make sure that these relate to the course in some way
3 Think about what kinds of background reading/research that you need to do. Decide who in the group will do what reading. Remember that the project has to have a theoretical underpinning	

4 Decide which information-gathering techniques you are going to use	Do you need to use interviews, questionnaires, participant observation and/or others? Think about the relevant strengths/weaknesses of each approach. Moreover, consider the time implications of different approaches (e.g. arranging to interview people)
5 Plan your project using timetable slots and organise group meetings. Decide on a division of labour and allocate tasks to each group member. **PRODUCE DEADLINES FOR ALL TASKS AND STICK TO THEM**	
6 Think about what resources you will need (e.g. cameras, tape recorders, photocopiers) and where you will obtain them	The department has equipment: cameras, tape recorders, which you can borrow. Take care of them and return them intact
7 Plan your Progress Presentation	Decide who will address which aspect of the project and make sure that you *all* attend. **DON'T LET YOUR COLLEAGUES DOWN**
8 Plan your display in the light of your research findings. Think about what materials are needed and how the display is to communicate the *focus of your project*	The display should be an **OUTCOME** of your project and the research you have generated. It *should not* determine the focus of your project
9 Plan your group presentation for the Day School. You can use OHP's, flipcharts, video and audio tapes. You should plan this carefully and do a rehearsal. *This is assessed*. Your display should be on the wall in the department on the day before the Day School	Decide who will address which aspect of the project and make sure that you *all* attend. **DON'T LET YOUR COLLEAGUES DOWN**

The case study

Returning to individual research, it is clear from the studies outlined in Chapter 3 and the studies examined in this chapter that the case study approach has been extremely valuable for cultural studies research and I will now indicate what a well-designed case study can offer. It is, by definition, focused on one case or instance as a 'bounded system' and for Robert Stake a 'case study is the study of the particularity and complexity of a single case, coming to understand its activity within important circumstances' (1995: xi). While case studies can be carried out in relation to quantitative research, either as the 'fleshing out' of a specific illustrative case, or as a preliminary, exploratory project which identifies key issues for further investigation, they can provide valuable, free-standing projects, producing useful knowledge and generating conceptual and theoretical work. The case study is a model frequently found in educational and other kinds of social and cultural research and, in addition to the above, its usefulness as an examination of 'issues' or problems has been highlighted by Stake. His work is primarily in the field of education where case study projects have been useful in examining issues and problems associated with schooling and other educational contexts. By focusing on an issue, the researcher has a clear focus and defined parameters for the study. Many students in cultural studies areas will find that formulating their projects as case studies or 'vantage points' focusing on an issue, for example, in relation to representation, in relation to cultural difference, to questions of access, within political struggles and community groups, a productive way of approaching their work.

Bell describes setting up a case study as the 'identification of an "instance" through which by questioning, observing, studying, you can explore the elements of the process – how it *works*' (1987: 8). For example, Nick Couldry, in his study of meetings between 'ordinary people' and the media in the UK (Couldry, 2000), selected a number of 'case studies' which demonstrated particular encounters between organisations of media, e.g. Greenham Common, the studio set of *Coronation Street* as a visitor attraction, and 'the public' and referred to these as 'specific vantage points on the social terrain'.

However, there is a further advantage to using the case study and this relates to a cultural studies interdisciplinary approach and its concern to examine different elements within social and cultural processes. Returning to Johnson's description of cultural studies as an attempt to 'tap into the structures', the identification of a specific and unique case study can enable the researcher to do just that, in revealing the multi-layered complexity of a given case. A well chosen case study can produce 'intensity' and an example of condensed layers of meaning which, through careful analysis, can produce insights into cultural processes. As we shall see below, work of this kind can be of value to further study and not simply confined to the seemingly 'individual case'.

A good example of an extended case study is the one carried out by Paul du Gay and Stuart Hall on the Sony Walkman (du Gay et al., 1997). In this study the process of analysis explores the complexity of the elements that are required to understand the particularities of a commodity such as the Walkman. Thus, they looked at the methods of design and production, the cultures of the industry and the workplace, the marketing and advertising images and the ways in which people actually used the product. Students read this study on a course I taught called 'Cultures of Consumption' and are then invited to carry out a small case study as part of the assessment. These are the guidelines I produced for students who took my course:

Consumpton, taste and identity in everyday life

'A case study is expected to catch the complexity of a single case.'

What is a case study?

We have already seen a very good example of a case study on this course, that of the Sony Walkman (du Gay et al., 1997). The process of analysis explores the complexity of elements that are required to understand the particularities of the case in point. For example, the study of the Walkman led researchers to look at methods of design and production; marketing and advertising images; the way in which people actually used the product. They looked at how the commodity interacted with its context(s).

Clearly you cannot be expected to carry out such an exhaustive case study. However, what I would like you to do is to take an 'instance' within what we now understand as our consumer society and culture, and subject it to analysis using the theoretical approaches, methods and ways of looking at commodities or consumer practices.

Deciding on a topic

You could think of approaching your topic under different categories, e.g.:

- commodities: e.g. trainers; instant cameras; cigarettes; asparagus from Peru; fitness gear; 'Designer' labels; Italian cars; food in different kinds of retail outlets. The magazines/media texts about these commodities.

- retailing: shopping malls; clothes shops; heritage shops; shop cultures; markets; car-boot sales; high street.

This is not an exhaustive list – you will be able to add to them. The important thing is to select a focus for your study. **Then ask some questions, such as:**

- who is this for: who uses it and how?

- what is it about this commodity or activity which characterises its user (design, taste, cost)?

- how is it advertised? What kinds of meanings are given to the commodity?

- where has it come from?

You might also want to look at a practice *rather than an* object e.g.

- shopping

- clubbing/eating/drinking (not too much fieldwork here in the interests of research!)

- walking around art galleries/going to the theatre/watching television and/or video

Deciding on an approach/method

Once you have decided on your object or practice – decide on your method. Say, for example, you choose trainers, then you need to have a list of the elements of this commodity which are of most significance, e.g. distinctions between different makes; who are they for?; how are they advertised?; how are they used?, and what do they mean to their users?

If you want to look at a site of consumption, such as a shopping centre or mall, then you will need to visit one – look at its design and layout; who is using it and how; how do the different stores 'address' you; where is it located.

Choosing a practice, such as going to art galleries or shopping or eating out would require some observational work, even – if you have time – some interviewing/discussions with users.

Evaluative criteria

While evaluative terms such as reliability, validity and representativeness were designed to interrogate the products and claims of social research utilising different kinds of methods, e.g. statistical surveys or quantifiable interview methods, the questions are often put to those studies based on qualitative research methods. Under such scrutiny these studies are considered to fall short of the requirements of social research. The responses can be hasty and defensive, rejecting the assumptions behind the questions, insisting that qualitative studies do not claim to be representative, or generalisable. However, it is important to be able to evaluate qualitative studies and it is therefore worth examining the assumptions behind the familiar criteria in order to see whether they can be useful in relation to the kinds of studies with which this book is concerned.

Reliability

This perhaps is the evaluative criteria most closely attached to quantitative studies. It is primarily concerned with the techniques of research design which produce reliable consistency. This is important in, for example, the use of questionnaires in large-scale survey research. The aim is to ensure that, through standardisation of the research techniques, different researchers conducting the same study would obtain consistent data, which could then be subjected to measurement, producing verifiable 'findings'. Most of the research projects we have looked at so far use a mixture of participant observation and conversational or life story interviews aimed at the free flow of discussion, of the development of topics throughout the interview and the potential of encountering something new and unexpected. Thus, any attempt to standardise 'questionnaires' or interview schedules would be inappropriate to the aims of the study.

Validity, representativeness and generalisability

Joke Hermes observes that qualitative research tends to be strong on 'validity', but weak on 'generalisability' (1995: 206). Here, validity is taken to refer to the accuracy of the picture presented of the subject and context of study. The ethnographer or qualitative researcher is close to and has first-hand accounts from actors involved. Furthermore, if what you are after is data of subjective accounts of what people are doing, how they account for their lives, their passions, their sense of self, then the most valid research method is that which will enable the researcher to listen to those accounts, those narratives, those stories of the everyday. Ken Plummer (2001) notes that a common critique of these kinds of methods is a number of biases which are potentially present in the research. These can be found in the conduct of the interviewee, the researcher her/himself and the ways in which the subject and researcher interact. All these elements, it is true, are open to unpredictability, to influence, to 'contamination'. But, as Plummer points, out, it is impossible to imagine any research project which could eliminate these biases. Far better to acknowledge that the researcher is part of the world which he/she is researching, that different factors will influence the interviewee, and to take account of these in the kinds of claims you might make on the basis of the data that is generated through this necessarily unpredictable and often shaky and perplexing process.

While a certain kind of 'validity' seems to be guaranteed by the immediacy of respondents, what is rendered problematic in small-scale, single researcher studies, is the question of the validation of the interpretations made of the data. There are recognised practices for dealing with this. The most obvious is to reflect on your methodological strategies and the claims you are making on the basis of your data. Another method is that of respondent validation where feedback is sought from respondents to the researcher's written account of, say, an interview. Undoubtedly this procedure has value within the politics of research in its open approach to the relationships with respondents. However, the purpose of the feedback is less obvious. Is the purpose to establish a more 'truthful' or 'accurate' account? If so, who has the prior claim to truth or accuracy? The data will be subjected to analysis and as such will not remain as a verbatim account in the research, rendering it difficult to read without a clear understanding of the analytical framework. A further strategy is referred to as 'triangulation', i.e. 'the checking of inferences drawn from one set of data sources by collecting data from others' (Hammersley and Atkinson, 1993: 231). In addition, 'technique triangulation' (ibid.: 231) can be used which is to contrast data gathered from different methods, for example, the interview with a written diary report. What people say to you and what they write in a diary may be very different. Comparing individual and group interviews may produce very different responses to the same research topic. The whole point of going through this kind of process is not to carry out triangulation for its own sake, but (a) to confront threats to the validity of the analysis and (b) to allow differences and contradictions to emerge. The second reason is important and a productive phase in the research process.

However, all of this may not be possible for reasons of scale and technique. You may be a lone researcher able to employ only one research method. Also, many of the assumptions behind questions of 'validity' and the guarantees of 'triangulation' assume a relatively stable research context and environment. Research into social and cultural practices and processes are subject to change. Indeed, that tenet of ethnography, reflexivity, presupposes the dynamic nature of the subject. Hermes' response to this in her discussion of 'validity' is that researchers should openly describe the changes, or disruptions in context and her responses to those changes. The reflexivity should be elaborated upon throughout the research process thus aiming for a kind of 'internal validity' which Wendy Hollway describes thus: 'Throughout the process of data collection and analysis, I was evolving the theoretical frame-work which fed back to inform both my analysis of data and the way I generated material in discussions with my participants' (1989: 4).

Generalisability presents a rather different set of problems for qualitative studies. Again, Hermes' reflections on the research process are useful. The requirements of generalisability, replicatability or, indeed, representativeness are that the 'results' or 'findings' of the study can be applied to similar phenomena in different contexts. Hermes' study of readers of women's magazines identified a number of cultural repertoires through which the different readers in her study made sense or meaning of different genres of magazines. The repertoires differed from respondent to respondent, although many were shared, and from genre to (sub-)genre of magazine. Thus, Hermes argues, it was not easy to transfer the range of repertoires that were connected to the different genres to other contexts, but it was possible to relate the different cultural repertoires accessed by respondents to their general ownership of cultural capital. This is an example of a theoretical generalisation based upon the perceived differences or distinctions within Hermes' sample of readers. Similarly, Wendy Hollway, in her study of gendered identities does not seek to generalise from her sample. If she is to generalise at all, it is on theoretical rather than statistical principles. Her sample was constructed on the basis of the comparative method, which as 'an important part of "grounded theory", is that through being faced with differences, concepts are generated which describe those differences which can then be applied to other phenomena' (Hollway, 1989: 17). Small-scale qualitative studies employing reflexive and innovative methods appropriate to the research questions, produce valuable insights which can be transferred to different contexts and certainly provide sources and often inspiration for new researchers. However, when researchers like Hermes and Hollway elaborate in such detail on the research process they can also provide transferable approaches, methods and strategies which, while not necessarily adopted lock, stock and barrel for a new project, can certainly function as a provisional 'blueprint' for future research design.

Richard Johnson has written on the subject of evaluation and argues that cultural studies research which is contextual and textual 'transgress the social science criteria of "representativeness"' (1997: 466). Rather, Johnson argues, these small-scale studies are 'intensive' and 'this enables the complex layered analysis of contradictory forms of consciousness and of the sayable and unsayable in situations of unequal power' (ibid.: 467). For Johnson, notions of cultural structure and formation are crucial and small-scale intensive studies, therefore, tap into these processes which are shared. These studies are not about 'individual' attitudes at all but about shared (or not shared) formations. Taken from this perspective, these small studies are 'likely to have a wider range of occurrence than the single example suggests' (ibid.: 467). Similarly, Ken Plummer thinks about what is involved in subjecting research based on the life story to the criteria of representativeness. His move is to detach the notion of representativeness from its usual statistical underpinnings and ask what it can tell us as cultural and social researchers. For Plummer, research has 'different goals and different kinds of data require different modes of evaluation' (2001: 153). He first of all suggests that in certain fields, oral history for example, it is the very uniqueness, not generalisability or replicability of the life story, which is important, where reflections can shed light on past events, or can produce different histories. Also, the life story can be told by a 'key informant' whose grasp of a particular cultural world can provide rich data that any amount of large scale surveys would simply not produce. Bob Connell, in his study of masculinities, uses the life-story method arguing, through analysis, that it is possible to bridge cultural, social, personal and the historical. In life stories, social structure, narrative and theory work together as he reflects on the way 'life history method always concerns the making of social life through time. It is literally history' (Connell, 1995: 89). Johnson, in his attempt to re-evaluate the idea of representativeness looks at it as a question of power. For him, the notion of representativeness implies presence and seeks to ask where and in what contexts can the same phenomenon be observed. He argues that if we start from 'the margins' or from 'culture from below', this often reveals more about the central categories than the focus on 'presence'. Representativeness should be judged in relation to exclusion of, for example, the points of view of subjugated minorities. Small-scale, modest studies, focusing as they do on cultures of subordination, practices of everyday life, etc. can 'reorder a taken for granted landscape' (Johnson, 1997: 470).

These questions of evaluative criteria are important, but, as Plummer says, he is not arguing for an 'anything goes' approach to research, rather, the reverse. Once we acknowledge the constructed nature of social knowledge, then this makes us much more aware of the range of determinates at play. The extent to which the researcher acknowledges this and reflects on the process and her or his role as researcher in the production of knowledge, should be an important 'validity' criteria – ironically one which would be ruled out by the 'reliability' criteria. Plummer summarises his thoughts on representativeness by seriously questioning the extent to which it is possible to arrive at a 'decontextualised' knowledge about any project upon which the external criteria of reliability, validity and representativeness depend.

Objectivity and subjectivity

Once again, these are important terms that occupy us when thinking about our research processes. The question of objectivity was discussed in Chapter 1, and, in particular, the impossibility of the kind of neutral objectivity assumed by the 'scientific' approach to research. It is pretty clear that the researcher plays a significant role in any study upon which he or she embarks and whilst neutral objectivity is an impossibility, it is possible to construct a project which accounts for its own framework, its methodology and reflects on changes and developments in the research process (Hermes, 1995).

However, what is meant by 'subjective' is also worth some elaboration. The issues raised by the subjective dimension to what we do are particularly highlighted in autobiographical writing (see Chapter 7) but also in those examples of research in which authors attempt to 'put themselves in the picture'. While often not fully-fledged autobiographies, examples of such work would use particular life experiences or knowledge through which specific aspects of cultural or social processes can be elaborated. Examples of this from Birmingham students have included explorations of the construction of masculinity and femininity; analysis of sub-cultures and identity, working-class identity using family albums, among others. Students grappling with this work often express anxieties which they articulate in terms of it being 'too subjective', or 'it is only subjective'. It is important to make a distinction between the meaning of the subjective: in my dictionary the definition is 'proceeding from, or relating to the mind of the thinking subject and not the nature of the object being considered' and a 'theory of the subject' which exposes the notion of the individual as an essentialist concept with which, as Stuart Hall describes it, 'it is no longer good to think with' (Hall and du Gay, 1996). Theories of the subject challenge the notion of the unified and centred 'individual' as author of social practice and suggest that the subject is made up of discursive practices which constitute that very subjectivity. Therefore, our own subjectivities are made up of our positions in and encounters with particular discourses and which we bring to our research. This, of course, is important when thinking about our research practice. Wendy Hollway refers to this in relation to the subjects of her study: 'A social theory of the subject implies that the information derived from any participant is valid because that account is a product (albeit complex) of the social domain' (1989: 15). If we reflect, therefore on our own subjectivities (and identities) in process and, at the very least, as the product of historical, social and cultural discourses, then it is possible to go beyond 'the subjective' when using our own (and others' experience) in our explorations of cultural processes.

Ethics and the politics of research

Ethical considerations must be taken seriously when we are proposing research that involves 'going out' or 'into the field' in order to construct some form of data for our analysis. Research language, like other forms of 'scientific' discourse, has a habit of sanitising and legitimising what should be seen as highly problematic actions and decisions. It is, I consider, my good fortune to have worked with many students, both undergraduate and postgraduate, who, when formulating their research projects and methods have asked the question 'What right have I/we to do this?' This question must stop us in our tracks and make us pause. 'We' are, after all, trying to convince people to participate in our research, to 'coax' information and stories from them, to do it for no recompense and, in the majority of cases, they will not even have the opportunity to read the resulting research report, article or book. Some have argued that there is a pleasure involved in the encounter with an interviewer. It is not often, after all, that there is someone who is interested in what you have to say and think, to the exclusion of all other distractions. There is certainly a pleasure in being invited to present yourself, or your life history to an interested listener. But it is enormously time-consuming and can unearth many unsettling elements of a life story, past and present. The researcher would rarely offer any kind of follow-up to allow the talk to continue.

Robert Coles reflects on these problems in *Doing Documentary Work* 'is it exploitative to do documentary work, to arrive on a given scene, ask for people's co-operation, time, energy and knowledge, do one's study or project, and soon enough, leave, thank yous presumably extended. How can we do such work honorably?' (1997: 76-7, quoted in Plummer, 2001).

Here is an extract from a student who was trying to get into a household to take some photos:

> I'll be sitting there in someone's home – I've interrupted their life, the nerve of me! – and I think to myself, this is wrong ... Why should that family let me hang around? ... I suppose I could try to bribe them, pay them. But that's not right – or is it? Why shouldn't they be paid? They're poor and they need the money, and I'll get something out of this, that's certain ... we get recognition, and we build our lives up, our careers – and they, there's nothing in it for them. They put up with us! (Coles, 1997: 82-3).

These are important issues and require consideration before assuming that you have the right to invade people's lives in the way Coles and his student felt they were doing. The point is that your current institutional location, its traditions, routines and assumptions, legitimise this practice in that it 'presumes' the right of students, researchers and academics to investigate people's lives. We need, therefore, at the very least, to be aware of this unspoken assumption, to approach our subjects of study as participants in our research, not as 'objects' to be investigated and to be respectful and open. It is important to answer their questions about your research, about how you plan to use the data and, above all, to respect requests for confidentiality. These notes of caution are even more important to bear in mind when people welcome you through their doors for an interview. This was my experience when I found that women were only too pleased to talk to me, to open up to me about their lives, with very little encouragement on my part. The pleasures gained from the interview are encapsulated in the phrase often used by my respondents: 'It's so good to have someone to talk to'. They said how good it was to be able to express their views and opinions about things from the routines and frustrations of their everyday lives to their plans and hopes for the future. As an interviewer I was asking people to talk about themselves, I was a keen listener who was interested in what they had to say and I encouraged them to speak on by uttering sympathetic noises. Leaving the homes of some of my respondents I caught myself thinking how well things were going – 'that was a good interview ... no problems with rapport there ... she seemed completely at ease'. But there were very disturbing interviews during the course of which some women spoke in detail of intimate aspects of their lives which must have been, and clearly was in some cases, quite traumatic for them. Some said that this was the first time they had articulated some of their concerns, dissatisfactions and feelings of oppression. Some expressed deep anxiety and loneliness in their lives. Like Coles' student, I was dashing off to transcribe the tape and to add it to my 'data' for analysis. Although I revisited some of the women, which served only as a salve to my conscience, I could not 'take back' what the research encounter had brought to life, nor could I feasibly do anything more useful than listening. Plummer puts it this way:

> The telling of a story of a life is a deeply problematic and ethical process in which researchers are fully implicated. In the hands of a novice researcher – and especially say a student rushing in to gather a life story for a dissertation – such awareness may be very thin and the damage that could be done, enormous. (2000: 224)

I fully endorse those calls for properly grounded empirical work which pay attention to actual human subjects and their lives but the actual consequences of this insistence can be overlooked. However, it is also very easy to feel completely incapacitated by consideration of these questions. But, by working through them carefully you will be encouraged to: think about your responsibilities to your respondents; approach them with respect and humility; be as open as you possibly can about the use of your material; offer to send transcripts, or the finished project to your respondents. You will also, by the way, be going a great deal further in dealing with these important issues than many established and successful researchers!

Part II

THE RESEARCH PROCESS

five	**Locating Instances and Generating Material**

Now you have a focus and a topic and, if you have read the previous chapter, you will be aware of the intellectual, political, ethical and personal issues at stake in embarking on your project. You next need to decide on the site or location for exploration and generation of your research material. I have deliberately avoided the term 'data' that is used in all sociological texts but also in Hammersley and Atkinson's (1993) book on Ethnography, for example their chapter on 'Recording and organizing data'. 'Data' has strong associations with 'evidence', 'information' and 'proof' as well as being associated with the products of more conventional sociological research methods. As such, I know it will be an immediate 'turn-off' for those of you who have come to cultural studies through more literary and textual routes. I don't want to lose you, so please read on.

My preference for the term 'research material' is not merely semantic, nor only a ploy to retain 'arts' students. The definition of 'material' encompasses the following dimensions all of which provide interesting keystones for cultural studies research.

1   In addition to more conventional notions of 'data', the term 'material' is inclusive of such things as, information, notes, work, as it were, the 'stuff' of research. This can therefore expand our understanding of empirical work to include: interview 'data', notes made on participant observation, personal research journals, autobiographies, dreams, etc. but also the products of literary and visual textual analysis.

2   It is also suggestive of substance and 'worldliness', if something is material, then it is grounded and embodied. This neatly encompasses both the kind of research material we produce, and also the way in which we do it. The connection, thus to the embodied researcher. Thus, neither the stuff of research, nor the researcher themselves are

free-floating or disembodied. Rather, both must be located and locatable.

3   By definition, something which is material is of consequence, meaningful and significant. A useful criteria to apply to research material.

4   A final dimension of the term that provides us with useful sets of questions is that it should be applicable, apposite and germane to the research topic and the task in hand.

Thus, the label 'research material' incorporates all the 'stuff' of our research, whether the product of participant observation, interviews, or the close analysis of texts, e.g. film, comics, television programmes, of documents e.g. historical papers, diaries, photographs, of government reports, print news coverage, etc. In addition, it offers useful suggestions about the way we approach our research. The research material that you generate will be the core of your research and is what makes it uniquely yours. It can perform different functions, but your particular method of research will define and shape the nature of the material and will limit or facilitate your interpretation and analysis. The important thing to bear in mind when setting up your project is that the material you gather fulfils the function you require of it.

The kinds of projects you might be interested in within a cultural studies perspective could be: interpretation and use of popular texts; membership of a fan or sub-culture; the construction of celebrity across different media; the work of identity in a national and global context; the performance of gender in different public and private spaces; the construction of markets; presentation of 'green' issues through the media; cultural and political activism. And finally, the cultural producers, institutions and organisations of culture, although it is true that this dimension of 'culture' has been neglected in cultural studies (Born, 2000; Meijer, 2001).

Let me try to detail some of the dimensions of the different relationships or formations which are implied by the above.

1   Interpretation and use of popular texts. Still one of the key areas in cultural studies, given its focus on the extent to which 'the cultural', as it is embodied in popular texts produced by large cultural industries, determine or shape a sense of self and the social more generally. If this is the primary area of concern, then a way must be found to explore how the connection between text or genres are interpreted and used by actual users and readers. Janice Radway, in her now classic study of romance readers (Radway, 1987), did exactly that in identifying a group of already defined readers of popular romantic fiction and, through questionnaires and interviews explored their interpretations and readings of romantic fiction. Her broader interest was in patriarchal positioning of women and the release which romance reading, and

the very act of reading itself, offered the women concerned. In other words, her broader research agenda looked at how romance as a powerful discourse within contemporary Western culture is commodified, circulated and consumed.

2   Membership of a fan or sub-culture. This requires a close and, indeed, participatory involvement with the group concerned. Henry Jenkins's work with the fans of *Star Trek* was an ethnographic account of this group written from an 'insider's' perspective. While the focus of the study is on the relationship between an enduring text of popular culture and its fans, Jenkins's study explores their interpretive strategies, the social organisation and cultural practices as well as its relationship to the mass media and consumer culture. Paul Hodkinson, himself a member of the Goth sub-culture, carried out research into his 'community' using participant observation and interviews in addition to textual analysis in his study. While interested in this specific cultural and social phenomenon, Hodkinson (2002) argues for a post-modern approach to the construction of identity and community, relating this to both material practice and the existence of virtual communities.

3   The work of identity in different global and national contexts. Marie Gillespie explored identity work of Punjabi Londoners through long ethnographic contact, interviews, discussions, as well as analysis of the discourses of specific films and other texts used by households (Gillespie, 1995). Although her study is based on a specific group, socially and geographically located, she explores through interpretation of her material the significance of popular forms, especially television and video, in the processes of identity formation.

Youth clubs and other 'public' groupings provide often highly condensed yet embodied examples of interactions and experimentations with identity, with belonging and not belonging, with finding your place and location (Back, 1996; Alexander, 2000).

4   The organisations and institutions of cultural producers. As we saw in Chapter 3, much less research energy has been put into this aspect of the cultural, but more recently, Georgina Born has carried out an ethnography of some of the BBC production contexts and Irene Costa Meijer interviewed the producers of three Dutch prime time soap operas in relation to their constructions of ethnicity (Bourne, 2000; Meijer, 2001).

Whatever your topic area, you will probably want to carry out some form of 'participant observation' and I now want to discuss this set of methods more generally before looking at some specific examples.

'Just looking' and participant observation

Paul Willis (1980) specified the following techniques which make up participant observation:

- Participation
- Observation
- Participation as observer
- Observation as participant
- Just 'being around'
- Group discussion
- Recorded group discussion
- Unfocused interview
- Recorded unfocused interview.

You may find that what you are investigating demands some or all of the techniques mentioned above. This is likely if, for example, you are interested in the ways in which people interact and relate to one another within given sites or spaces, for example, the classroom or a night club, a household or the shopfloor. This is usually referred to as 'participant observation' and is the central method of ethnography, indeed, Hammersley and Atkinson (1993) suggest that the terms, ethnography and participant observation, are synonymous. By employing this kind of method, you will be able to go beyond talking to the actors involved through, say, the interview or group discussion, but the material you gather in this process can also be used to complement your interviews or group discussions. In this way it would provide a kind of 'descriptive context' in setting the scene of the action for your readers. This often enriches or fills out the character of your interviewee and can say quite a lot about them which would not necessarily reveal itself in an interview alone. Examples here would be: appearance; clothing, style and demeanour; setting: at home or the workplace; a person's presence within their setting: are they easy or nervous?, do they move around their space with authority?, and so on. Some may be uncomfortable with what seems like a covert, or even voyeuristic practice. However, my point in bringing this to your attention is that you will be picking up these kinds of clues in your different research encounters anyway, and interpreting them, usually coming to some evaluations or judgements about your respondents. This is what Beverley Skeggs has referred to as the 'tacit knowledge' we have of a particular social process or context (1994: 70). By making this apparent within your analysis, not only are you using all your senses in data collection, but you are acting with integrity in regard to your respondents and your readers. Alasuutari, speaking of research into media cultures, goes further and suggests that 'we have the advantage of a very long personal field experience' in that we have inhabited the same culture which forms the background to our study (1999: 8). What I have just described is, if you like, a weaker use of participant observation than the more fully developed, long-term process which many researchers employ, in which extended observations are made of a particular setting or group. But what Willis describes as 'just being around' is an important part of research when you can 'feel the pulse' or take soundings of the people and places you want to explore further.

It is crucial to be clear about your purpose in embarking on this kind of field work and to understand your own role in this part of your research. It is very good to get into the practice of questioning yourself at different stages in the research. Here you might helpfully ask the following questions: to what extent must I be a participant in these activities: what role will I play during this research? How will I present myself to the subjects of my study? What is at stake in revelation and/or masquerade? How much do I declare of my purpose? What about trust, confidentiality, ethics?

These are not especially easy questions to answer but it is essential to clarify as much as you can about your intentions before you start. This will be necessary in order to give a clear signal when gaining access to your 'site' or group. You will obtain much more reliable and usable research material if you are able to operate on a sound footing.

Sarah Thornton, in her study of 'club cultures' which employed participant observation (Thornton, 1995), discusses the complication of her fieldwork by distinguishing between the two conflicting dimensions of ethnography: participation and observation. The former relies upon and legitimises what people *say*; the latter relies on what the researcher *sees*. We could go further than Thornton and suggest that the researcher as observer sees what people *do* rather than what they say. Junker (1960) further distinguishes between the 'complete participant', 'participant-as-observer', 'observer-as-participant', and 'complete observer'. This spectrum goes from the researcher's activities as wholly concealed where the researcher is incognito and is 'passing' as a member of the group, culture, community, to activities as observer where they are wholly detached and visible as observers. This is to indicate that each position requires particular kinds of research performance and will produce different kinds of research material.

In her research, in common with most examples used throughout this book, Thornton consciously performs a 'double move' in that she pursues a 'subjectivist' mode in her attempt to understand the world from the point of view of the clubbers but also pursues a more objectivist line of inquiry.

Thus, as participant/observers within a group, we can describe both how people account for their involvement in what they do, how they relate to each other, the way the atmosphere of the chosen site, etc. but in order to interpret and fully explore the answer to the question 'What is going on?', we need recourse to some analytical framework. This is to say, we begin to 'objectify' our data. Put simply, to analyse something is to take it apart. In order to do this we move into the abstract, we draw on concepts and theories, in order to offer some analysis of the action. Here we would be adopting the 'objectivist' mode. I want to complicate matters further, however, and suggest that, although they are useful epistemological distinctions, neither of these modes operates in a pure form. The 'real' world of research is always situated and able to be situated within a context and an important part of that context is the researcher her or himself. Our own subjectivity and social identities pre-date any specific research project and will determine, not only our choice of topic, but, quite literally, what we see.

Spatial metaphor/between familiarity and strangeness

As we have seen, the tension always exists in a project using participant obser-vation techniques between the 'external' view of the observer to the 'internal' view of the participant. It is the aim of the researcher to combine the two perspectives. This raises questions about your relationship to the group or culture of your study. Traditionally, anthropology aims to 'discover', through extended participant observation, the ways of life of particular cultures. Anthropologists use the distinctly problematic phrase 'going native' where the ethnographer becomes a part of the group and culture and is integrated into their daily lives, he/she becomes one of them. Doing cultural studies usually departs from this model in a number of ways. One of these is the researcher's knowledge of the chosen field of study and, often, of the partic-ipants themselves. Most obviously, this is because cultural studies seeks to analyse and understand cultural practices and processes which are much nearer to 'home'. Thus, at the very least, the researcher operates within the same overall cultural framework as his or her respondents. However, as undergrad-uate or postgraduate students, with limited time and funds, many of you will select aspects of culture and social groups for your research with which you are already familiar, if not a part. This is an almost inevitable part of doing cultural studies, and is often not only a question of pragmatics. It can also be, for example, a question of political commitment and desire for change, or a choice inspired by existing involvement and pleasures in, say, popular culture. There are distinct advantages to the knowledge which you can bring to your project based on your experience, but as discussed in Chapter 2, this is not without its problems and pitfalls. You will need to be aware of how this belonging and being part of the scene might also produce a partial account. That, while you 'know' the scene, you may be blind to different aspects of it. 'Over-identification' can also be an issue when the researcher identifies with a group and fails to critically analyse their activities, accounts or prac-tices. Mark Pursehouse in his study of *Sun* readers, speaks of his conflicting identity positions, the traces within his subjectivity which made him a subject for the *Sun*. He also had a group of friends who had not gone to university and who were readers of the *Sun*. He argues for the importance and advantage for him in his small-scale project of interviewing friends. 'I became increasingly grateful that I had some kind of prior knowledge to work with when I met the people I interviewed' (Pursehouse, 1989: 32). Here Pursehouse is acknowledging his experience and knowledge of the specific cultural community in which his readers are placed and the way in which he was able to mobilise that knowledge during his interviews. He goes further:

> I think there were significant advantages in me knowing them, or being known by them, in some way. Firstly, and obviously, it facilitated the actual process of getting to talk and feeling comfortable about speaking on a range of subjects. It also meant that there could be no pretending to the illusion that 'researcher' could somehow meet with 'researched' in some kind of empty social vacuum. I had ideas about the positions and cultures in which they were likely to live, and they could identify me both as the 'researcher' and as someone involved in other relations. Simply, they were never just going to be 'Sun readers', and I was never just going to be an 'academic researcher'. (ibid.: 33)

What Pursehouse did was to contextualise his small sample, in terms of their gender and ethnicity, but also in their geographical location, their regionality, the patterns of employment in the geographical region they all came from, thus providing that broader context, not of generalisation, but of theorisation. His textual analysis of the *Sun* and his conversational interviews revealed the complexity of both and the often contradictory nature of the *Sun* and its readers in the period of the late 1980s.

As Hammersley and Atkinson put it, 'the ethnographer needs to be intellectually poised between familiarity and strangeness; and, in overt participant observation, socially he or she will usually be poised between stranger and friend' (1993: 112). This is to emphasise the importance of reflexivity and to acknowledge that you, as researchers of the social, will inhabit different 'identities' throughout your project. The person who dresses formally to conduct an interview, or 'hangs around' with a group of musicians, is very different from the one who sits at her desk thinking about the material and writing an academic text.

There are, of course, sites or fields where your presence can go unnoticed, for example, 'public' spaces to which access is open. However, should you wish to study the workings of a news room of a television station, clearly questions of access become crucial and there will be a visibility of presence which will require some negotiation. But remember, however 'undercover' you might be, you are the agent with the gaze - you are doing the looking and seeing the world through your particular lens. You will always and already have your framework which will determine things you will notice which another researcher simply would not. Clearly, what we see is important but also what we do not see is equally revealing, for example, objects for which we have no available categories or behaviours, accounts of experience of which we have no knowledge and that we cannot interpret. To a great extent, therefore our research abilities and potential will depend on our competences and our available repertoires. There is therefore a necessity, to the extent that we are able, to reveal these to ourselves in order to be reflexive about our own position within our work. To do this is to begin to 'denaturalise' our own assumptions and prejudices as they are revealed within our research.

Being there

Most seminar discussions on the use of participant observer methods in research get rather bogged down in trying to answer the question 'What effect does the researcher have on the site of study?' This is clearly an issue but what underpins this question is the assumption that there is somehow, somewhere, an existing 'natural' site of interactive social beings which can, by implication, be 'captured' by the researcher. Certainly much conventional ethnographic writing constructs this version of the field. It tries to convince us of the 'truth' and 'reality' of the setting: 'this is what actually goes on'. You are, as a researcher, a participant in the field. The question is how you account for yourself in that position - both to the actors involved and within your research writing. Whatever you do, your presence will have an effect on what you are seeking to observe. You are part of the world you are studying, in a broader 'macro' sense of being part of the culture, but also in the 'micro' sense within the geography of your chosen setting or site. Returning to our definitions of 'material', you, literally, embody your research.

The kind of information you can gather through observing can be much richer and more revealing than simply asking the actors involved about their interest, their feelings and their attitudes towards the activity (whether a factory worker or shop worker or a shopper or night-clubber). However, we cannot treat this as 'raw material' or somehow imply that in carrying out this kind of research you are gaining access to the truth - the obviousness of being there is a dangerous fallacy. This material that you gather through your observations and the notes you will take afterwards, must be thought of as a set of data from a specific source and gathered in a particular way. And like all such data requires analysis and interpretation.

More practical things

In order to conduct your observation you will need to gain access to your chosen site. There are a number of well-known strategies here. For example, Les Back worked as a youth community helper during the period of his research into the changing ethnicities of young urban dwellers (1996). Others might be to persuade a group to allow you to sit in on their meetings or discussions. Whatever strategy you adopt it is important to become a familiar part of the scene, to establish rapport with your respondents and make the most of your time there. This involves active listening, engaging people in conversation and being responsive to what people are (or are not) telling you. Here are some more practical considerations when 'entering the field'.

Self-presentation

You are acting a role and need to think about the kind of person you should present. This will enable you to blend in to the surroundings, but also may conform to your respondents' expectations of you as a researcher. Interviewing or engaging in other kinds of participant observation can involve dressing up or dressing down. It is not meant to fool or trick people, but to make people feel comfortable and not to draw attention to yourself by wearing the wrong clothes. Most of the women in my study, for example, had clearly taken care over their appearance when I visited them at home. As a mark of respect I did the same (Gray, 1995).

Once at your location, here are the kinds of things you would be looking for as a participant observer:

- Setting and spatial elements: what is the place like?, what gives it its character?, and how do the spaces 'organise' people? (e.g. classroom – how the arrangement of furniture organises the actors), what does the place 'feel' like?, and how is it likely to make its inhabitants feel? (think of the differences between a library and a bookshop; an expensive restaurant and McDonald's; a museum and a shopping centre) and, crucially, what produces these environments?

- Social interaction: how do people 'behave' within the setting?, for example, how do people present themselves through body language? What are the codes of body space (think of differences between a playground and dance-floor)? How do people move within the environment, for example, groupings, clusterings, separations and who are the isolated ones?. How do people communicate with each other, for example, greetings; etiquette (who speaks to whom and when?); what are the 'rules of discourse'; who listens and who speaks?; are there conflicts and resolutions?, and what are the categories which matter: gender, ethnicity, age, ability, hierarchy (formal, e.g. teacher, informal, e.g. leader, head honcho of gang, etc.)?

- Patterns through and across time: movement through time; limits and constraints; rhythms in movement; narrators/actors/controllers/followers; timelessness; loss of self in time.

- Liminality: some spaces and sites are strongly time-structured – most obvious is the work-place where time is considered to be a commodity: it structures working practices and determines working days. But there are sites, mainly designated for leisure, where time is configured very differently: where subjects are encouraged to enter into a timeless world. For example, theme parks such as Disneyworld, require a kind of suspension of ourselves which includes our idea of self in time in order that we can engage in the 'total experience' on offer. Shopping malls also engender a timeless quality where wandering aimlessly through the building is encouraged. This is achieved through certain kinds of spatial organisation and a, paradoxically, controlled environment.

Dear diary: keeping a journal

We can see from the above that there is a lot to observe and attend to during fieldwork. It is therefore essential to keep a notebook or journal, specifically for your 'field notes'. If you are in the setting of your study, the only record of your experience there will be your notes. These are usually made after your visit. In your notebook should go your thoughts, observations, any quotes you want to make from what people said to you. Get this kind of detailed observation down as soon as you can. Don't attempt to organise it at this stage – you will already be selecting, shaping and editing in the act of writing. This again will be important data to add to your sources for analysis. Also it is important to pull out of your observations anything which you want to follow up. This could be requiring further information (e.g. about working practices) or suggestions for further research, such as conducting some interviews with 'key' actors. Equally your observations could connect to some of the theoretical work, or existing research: observations can be highly suggestive – nudging at theory, demonstrating concepts, confirming or questioning other research. As C. Wright Mills suggests, these ideas are your own – note them and develop them as the research proceeds. As researchers of social worlds and cultural processes you can be open to ideas, responsive to triggers.

The most important thing to grasp about this method is that, although it often parades itself as 'naturalistic' – you are observing some aspect of the social world as it happens in front of you – you as researcher should render it 'unnatural', open to question and as a constructed part of your research. It should be revealed, therefore, within your account as part of the research process. This will, of course, be obvious if participant observation is your main chosen method. However, there are many studies which often implicitly use aspects of participant observation in order to make sense of their topic, or 'flesh out' their study. The best examples of research will make this element explicit, will be rigorous in their accounts and analysis and clear about the basis for their interpretation. The worst will use this material implicitly, be less open about it – will 'fudge' it. This is often because researchers are not clear about the 'status' of this aspect of their engagement with the subject – is it legitimate, can I do this, isn't it being 'unscientific' and impressionistic? The answer to these questions is 'Yes', unless you are systematic about its use. To emphasise: this is an important feature of the kinds of research projects you are most likely to carry out and you will be doing your research a disservice unless you find some way of making use of this aspect of your research. It requires confidence and a certainty about the ground of your study – its ontology – and your relationship to it, which is an epistemological question. Furthermore, these are political and ethical questions. They involve you reflecting on your role as researcher and your attitude towards your respondents. How are you dealing with them? What validity are you awarding their statements? What are the issues between you in terms of your identity?: you, as initiator of the research, have certain kinds of power over the research, but, potentially, the researched. But what of other differences and similarities?: gender, ethnicity, age are all quite crucial markers in the kinds of relationships you might have with your interviewees or those you are seeking to describe. It is as well to acknowledge these differences and similarities from the start as they are bound to rise to the surface at some point in the progress of your research, and these will be discussed in more detail in the next section.

Working examples

I will now look briefly at some examples where this method has been employed and in particular the kinds of questions two researchers took into their participant observation and how they reflected upon the process.

Sarah Thornton: club cultures

Thornton's study is 'concerned with the attitudes and ideas of the youthful insiders whose social lives revolve around clubs and raves' (1995: 2). Thornton is particularly interested in notions of 'the mainstream'; how it operates as a trope within youth sub-cultures, how it is constructed by the media and how it has not been investigated by earlier youth sub-cultural theorists. In this work it is simply assumed as the 'other' of the underground, or specific sub-cultural groups. In this research these sub-cultures are described as being more authentic, vigorous and 'real' than the mainstream. Furthermore, as Thornton points out, the 'mainstream' is represented as commercial and feminine, as it were, the 'other' of masculinised authentic sub-cultural worlds. Also that there is a diversity of 'cultures' within the mainstream. She employed methods of media analysis in order to assess how the 'mainstream' and club culture were represented in the media. Her book also provides a brief history of the rise of the disco.

Thornton describes that part of her study which involved participant observation as follows: 'between 1988 and 1992, I acted as participant observer at over two hundred discos, clubs and raves and attended at least thirty live gigs for comparative purposes'. She insists that the purpose of the book is not to celebrate the creativity of dance culture. 'Despite having once been an avid clubber, I was an outsider to the cultures in which I conducted research for several reasons' (1995: 2). She identifies these as:

- Work v leisure: she was working as a researcher in the clubs whereas everyone else (bar the staff) was there for leisure. Difficult, she argues, to 'lose yourself' – one of the attractions of clubbing – if you are carrying out research.

- Age: she started her research when she was 23 and 'slowly aged out of the peer group I was studying' (ibid.: 3).

- National identity: as a North American investigating British clubs and raves 'I was, quite literally, a stranger in a strange land' (ibid.: 3).

In her study, Thornton follows the Chicago School's commitment to the idea that, in order to come to an understanding of certain kinds of social behaviour, then we must understand the 'symbolic world' in which our subjects live. Thus, her research strategy was to gain access to a number of clubs via a key informant in order to be a part of, but also to observe the clubs as cultural sites.

In Chapter 3 of her book, 'Exploring the Meaning of the Mainstream' Thornton gives an account of her field work in the 'subjective mode'. The chapter's full title is 'Exploring the Meaning of the Mainstream (or why Sharon and Tracy Dance around their Handbags), it is then subtitled 'a night of research'. On one occasion she is, not surprisingly, offered Ecstasy and describes the encounter:

> A white boy, wired and talking a mile a minute, stops me in my tracks: 'Want some "E"?' He's referring to 'Ecstasy' and he's eating his words ... He is a poor advertisement for the effects of his wares. From his aggressive and jumpy delivery, I assume that he is really on some speed concoction or perhaps this is his first night on the job. (ibid.: 88)

Thornton does not tell us at that point whether she accepts the Ecstasy or not. However, a little later she is offered some MDMA by her 'informant' clubber:

> We go to the toilets, cram into a cubicle where Kate opens the capsule and divides the contents. I put my share in my glass [of champagne] and drink. I'm not a personal fan of drugs – I worry about my brain cells. But they're a fact of this youth culture, so I submit myself to the experiment in the name of thorough research (thereby confirming every stereotype of the subcultural sociologist). (ibid.: 89)

Thornton does not describe the effects of the MDMA on her – but a couple of pages later describes a visit to a different nightclub – around 4 a.m. she meets a DJ:

He tells me he's been running clubs since 1979, then snorts some coke off the corner of a friend's Visa card. His blue eyes actually dart about like whirling disco spotlights and his conversation is a chaotic compilation of *non sequiturs*. Ecstasy turns banal thoughts into epiphanies. I see how club organizers, DJs and journalists – the professional clubbers – get lost within the excesses and irresponsibilities of youth. With no dividing line between work and leisure, those in the business of creating night-time fantasy world often become their own worst victims.

Thornton's study is a poignant analytical account of the youthful clubbing scene, she reflects on her observations both as a researcher and construct an apposite theoretical framework for an understanding of the operations of distinction and difference within the dance culture. In addition, she is critical of earlier studies of youth sub-cultures and the design and approach of her study seeks to provide a more appropriate way of addressing the phenomenon.

Beverley Skeggs: formations of class and gender

Beverley Skeggs, who, as we saw in Chapter 4, carried out a longitudinal ethnographic study of 83 white working-class women in the North of England, says that her research was motivated by the question 'why do women, who are clearly not just passive victims of some ideological conspiracy, consent to a system of class and gender oppression which appears to offer few rewards and little benefit?' She argues that responsibility and accountability were central to her conduct as a researcher and that her ethnography was 'politically motivated to provide a space for the articulations and experiences of the marginalised' (1997: 23). Her relationship with the women was ambivalent. She had a similar background to the women in her study, especially in relation to class and early education. However, she does not claim to be the 'same' as the women, especially as she had, by the time of the study, graduated from university and was pursuing a PhD. She describes her method thus:

> I had entry to different parts of the young women's lives in different ways. With some it was very social, with others it was a quiet chat; the different relationships elicited different types of information. The time spent doing the ethnography was so intense that the boundary between my life inside and outside of the research dissolved. (Skeggs, 1994)

Skeggs began her research with the belief that if she got to know these women, became part of their lives, she would be able to 'deliver their "real" (even "true") experiences'. Her approach was based on a 'naturalistic' belief in the powers of observation to reveal the truth. What she found was the opposite. The longer she spent with the women the more confused she became and the women's lives and particularly the formation of their identities were not revealed as she expected. This is an important insight into the process of participant observation and its usefulness as the kind of method which can tap into social and cultural processes and deeper structural formations of subjectivities. Thus, Skeggs constantly analysed what she was hearing from the young women throughout the research process and her theoretical reading continued throughout the process - each informing the other.

Les Back: new ethnicities and urban culture –
racisms and multi-culture in young lives

Les Back carried out an ethnographic account of multiculturalism and racism in young people's lives predominantly in two areas of London – post-war council estates. The research was conducted between 1985 and 1989 and entailed participant observation. One is a mainly white working-class area and the second is a multi-ethnic neighbourhood. During the research he lived in or at close proximity to the research area. He chose youth club settings and worked in the youth clubs.

In addition to participant observation he carried out semi-structured recorded interviews and group discussions. He states his rationale behind the methodology:

> To try to get an appreciation of the way young people articulated their notions of identity and ethnicity, but also the way identity was acted out within the context of adolescent interactions. This was particularly important in relation to the ways in which racism entered into the lives of these young people. Accounts given within the context of interviews would often be contradicted by actions and statements in other settings. Through using a flexible methodology I developed a close appreciation of both what young people *said* with regard to race, ethnicity and racism and also what they *did* in the context of interaction with peers. (ibid.: 22)

Back is insistent that he draws attention to his own position as researcher within the community:

> The point that I want to emphasise is that the following study should be read in the context of research relationships developed by a white male ethnographer. In this sense it is necessary for me to position myself within the field relations that facilitated the study. I am asking the reader to judge the 'truth claims' ... made in what follows in this context. Throughout the study I have tried to point to situations where my social identities may have been particularly important in interpreting the meaning of a particular event or interview extract. A position that I develop throughout the book is that the accounts quoted here constitute interactive samples and are the product of a particular social circumstance – be it an interviewer-interviewee relationship, a group discussion or a dramatic event involving numerous people. (ibid.: 22)

Back's study is an example of a full ethnography: it takes place over time, within specific settings, it employs a range of methods including participant observation. The researcher here literally gets to know, lives with, is part of the group he studies. It is structured thematically, but two major sections deal with the different neighbourhoods. There follows a chapter which looks at the musical cultures which are being created by young people in South London.

These three studies represent very different kinds of research. Their different use of participant observation is clearly a reflection of the aims. Thornton wished to explore the way in which a category of popular music culture 'the mainstream' operated within youth culture and specifically in club-culture. She therefore had to look at the ways in which 'mainstream' was identified and categorised by the relevant media as well as finding a way of understanding what it meant to people involved in going to clubs.

Skeggs, on the other hand, wanted to explore the formations of class and gender: how do we get to be who we are, could be the broadest question. She was also concerned about the powerless groups and how their subjectivities are formed into, she argues, disempowered subjectivities. Hers, then, involved a long-term study, taking some 80 women as 'case studies' in thinking through the complexities of subject and identity formation. Back's desire to examine the construction of urban identities meant he had to find a way of observing identity construction in action, in the public space of a youth community centre, but also on the streets of the different neighbourhoods. Thus, each of these researchers was able to employ participant observation in order to gain insights into the symbolic worlds of the people in their study. They each reflect on their position in relation to their chosen location and the issues arising for them in conducting the research.

Structured conversations (the interview)

I want to begin this section by re-thinking the notion of 'the interview' itself. This is partly because, as we saw in Chapter 1, the interview has a long history and Tolson and others should cause us to stop and think before we allow this mode to become a naturalised part of our research process. I do not, however, want to take the notion of the interview apart to render it unusable in our research. Indeed, I shall insist on its usefulness as a method and encourage ways of thinking about its diverse potential for doing cultural studies work. This potential remains unfulfilled which is in part due to the rather unimaginative and non-reflexive use of the interview. This chapter will explore some innovative approaches to the interview which are relevant to the kinds of questions we might want to ask in our research. It is the case that 'the interview' has entered the common-sense world and most of us have a notion of what constitutes 'an interview' and perhaps even what constitutes the 'correct' interview. Just think about it. You are probably imagining two people sitting opposite each other, one with clip-board or note-pad with a list of questions. This person would largely 'control' the event. The person to whom the questions are addressed is rendered passive, responding only to questions, waiting for the interviewer to set the agenda through their questions. The interviewer, on the other hand, while being in control, is not expected to release any information about themselves to their respondent, nor must they introduce 'leading questions' or agree or disagree with the respondent. The interviewer begins the interview and ends it. Now, depending on your exposure to discussions of research methods, you might recognise that description, but you will most likely see through it as an example of an 'ideal' type of interview. This kind of interview is carried out for such purposes as large surveys, market research, etc. The responses are coded and analysed through data-handling computer software. The method of this kind of research requires a reliable, measurable and quantifiable set of data which the controlled interview will reproduce across large numbers. There are 'gradations' of this tightly controlled model which social science methods have defined, but I think many of us carry this model, even subconsciously, when we plan our research and when we actually carry out interviews ourselves. We have the idea that there is a 'correct' way of interviewing, that we might be breaking the rules if we depart from the prescribed role of interviewer, thereby invalidating our research.

Let me begin to unearth some of the assumptions behind the notion of the ideal interview by suggesting that, rather than thinking about the ideal interview, we should ask ourselves what our research is trying to do. What kinds of disclosures are we hoping to elicit by interviewing people? Once we identify this, then, and only then can we begin to approach an interview design and strategy. It will be helpful here to return to Richard Johnson's distinction between sociological research and cultural studies research specifically in relation to what kind of material our research methods need to produce. He argues that sociological research is, in the main, still attached to the notion of 'population' and 'qualitative' interview methods are designed to examine 'attitudes, opinions, behaviours, etc.' Cultural studies, for Johnson, on the other hand, is interested through such methods as the interview, to 'tap into cultural structures and formations' with the researcher exploring this through a specific case study. Cultural studies projects have an intensity and depth and regard their subjects of study as individuals who are and have been socially and culturally shaped. These formations 'are precisely social or shared [and] are likely to have a larger range of occurrence than the simple samples suggest' (Johnson, 1997: 468). This observation has implications for questions of 'representativeness' which also tend to haunt researchers (see Chapter 4).

The interview: reflexivity and intensity

One useful tenet for the researcher is to think of this statement: 'If you want to know what I think or do, it would be as well to ask me.' However, the open interview is not just a chat. The aim is to establish a good rapport with the respondent, so that she or he gains confidence and feels comfortable in responding freely. It is better described as a structured conversation, but it is also a discursive event in which the two subjects involved are the key players.

Here we can see that the intentions of the cultural studies interview might have more in common with ethnographically oriented work than with sociology. However, this does not mean that we can abandon all structures, procedures, formalities and simply go off and chat to a few people. Indeed, there is no such thing as an unstructured interview, rather, all interviews are structured but each must be structured in relation to the aims of the specific interviews and the overall study. Hammersley and Atkinson suggest that what distinguishes the 'survey' interview and the ethnographic interview is that between 'standardised and reflexive interviewing'. Thus, 'Ethnographers do not usually decide beforehand the exact questions they want to ask, and do not ask each interviewee exactly the same questions, though they will usually enter the interviews with a list of issues to be covered' (Hammersley and Atkinson, 1993: 152). Using this technique, the interviewer must be an active listener. Thinking on your feet during the interview is important (see Holstein and Gubrium,1997, below).

Work developed by feminist researchers has challenged the strict codes and modes of interviewing for its masculinist bias with its belief in objectivity and denial of the emotionality of research. Feminists have developed a rich seam of work that addresses broader questions of epistemology as well as what a feminist research practice might be like. There are clearly issues around this and different feminists have claimed a feminist research method (Stanley and Wise) while others have argued for research which is conducted from a particular standpoint or position which can only be known by feminists. A feminist subject position, in other words. Here these epistemological positions are reflected in the approach to empirical work and the gathering of research material, be it a questioning of the politics of research, the power relations of the researcher and researched and the openness of the interview method.

Questions of reflexivity have now moved onto the agenda more generally, for example, Holstein and Gubrium pose the notion of the *active interview* which may be useful for your purposes. In this model the respondent is seen as an active producer of meaning, not, as in more traditional models, a wellspring of information, material or emotions. They argue that the interview as such is 'a concerted project for producing meaning' (1997: 121). Through the interview process itself the respondent constructs their subjectivity – builds their character, their stories, emotions, etc. 'The interview and its participants are constantly developing' (ibid.). 'The objective is not to dictate interpretation, but to provide an environment conducive to the production of the range and complexity of meanings that address relevant issues, and not be confined by predetermined agendas' (ibid.: 123).

This approach goes beyond the 'what' of the interview – the substantive topic of the research - but it goes into the 'how' of subjectivity too. The framework of a research project will inform the orientation of the interviews and the gathering of empirical material. What is interesting is how this framework can generate the kinds of exchanges within interviews that are productive. During my interviews with women, many remarked that they had either never talked about this before, or never thought about it before. Gender divisions and the inherent power relations in domestic life informed my study and my orientation. Thus, my conversations with women produced a framework and concepts through which they could discuss their lives and express their sense of themselves and experience within those particular frameworks. Some of this was clearly informed by a knowledge of the issues but in many cases it came through the structuring of the conversation.

This mode and way of approaching the interview relate it much more immediately to analysis, or make the framework much more visible throughout the interview with theoretical, empirical and analytical links being made through the process. There follows examples from research that has employed these kinds of interviewing strategies.

Many studies use interviewing as their main method of gathering material. Those within media and cultural studies which have sought to explore media consumption have been criticised for this. What the critics rarely discuss are the actual interview modes adopted by these studies and in particular the kinds of depth which can be plumbed and layers of meaning which can be produced through, say, adopting a life story method (see Chapter 6).

By way of example, I will now turn to Ruth Frankenberg's study of white women's relationship to racism for which she employed a dialogic approach to interviewing in which she encouraged women to tell their life stories but 'I positioned myself as explicitly involved in the questions, at time sharing with interviewees either information about my own life or elements of my own analysis of racism as it developed through the research process' (Frankenberg, 1993: 32).

Her topic was a sensitive one and called for careful approaches to potential interviewees and careful handling of the interviews themselves. Her open and dialogic approach, she argues, democratised the research process because she enabled women to explore their own feelings about race as well as the analysis and politics of race.

The 30 women she interviewed were all white, but came from different social backgrounds and had varying levels of awareness of the politics of race and feminism. Therefore, her interview approach had to take these differences into account. Although her aim was to collect 30 'life stories' no one interview was the same. Central to her dialogic method, she argues, were 'the ways in which I offered information both about myself as inscribed within racism and about my analysis of racism as systemic as well as personal'. By telling her own stories about whiteness, she effectively broke the silence of white discourses on colour and power – she gave the women 'permission' to speak of race and racism. In addition, she consciously employed different analyses of 'race' in her dialogues with the women, to enable them to express and articulate their experiences. Thus, she gave them a safe and secure discursive position from which to examine their own experiences and feelings. She uses the following example:

Evelyn, a self-styled Conservative in her fifties, but one who nonetheless views herself as 'not a prejudiced and biased person', talked toward the end of the interview about who her friends were:

RF: One final question, and then that's probably about it. And again, it sort of goes back to what I was saying about how I see, when I think about white women and race and contact with different ethnic groups, different racial groups. I know that for myself, I was raised in a very white, 99.9 per cent white environment ...

EVELYN: Mhm.

RF: ... and I also know that, the way that my life is set up, and probably the way most people's lives are set up, the people that you spend time with are usually people in the same income bracket, and the same ...

EVELYN: Mhm!!

RF: ... type of person. So I was wondering if that was the same for you? Is it the case that your friends are mainly in your same income bracket and mainly in your same racial group or ethnic group?

EVELYN: It's probably true. But I don't think it was done out of choosing, I think that it just ... well, you have to have a sense of having something in common in the first place ...

RF: Right.

EVELYN: ... and with women generally the first thing is, are you married ... then you have something in common. Do you have children ... then you have something in common. And then it's a question of the husbands ... can they talk to one another? And so it's true, most of our friends, they do have, certainly economically we're about the same level, most all of them are college graduates. A great many of them are engineers, businesspeople. It's true, but I don't think that we do it out of deliberately. I think it just happens to be the way our lives all fall together.

RF: No, that's why I phrased it the way I did.

EVELYN: Yeah.

RF: Because a lot of times, I think that if I asked somebody that question, they would feel challenged ...

EVELYN: Yes.

RF: ... criticised by the question. Which isn't my intention, because what I'm real interested in is just I think things shake down that way.

EVELYN: Mhm, mhm, I think they do too.

RF: And with me, it's been that way in the past, in terms of that my friends have been white people.

EVELYN: Mhm.

RF: And I don't know if that's been true of you, that your friends are ...

EVELYN: Uh, I have one friend that's an Argentinian. [Laughs] Where would I meet all these other people, you see? And so, as I say, it isn't anything that's done deliberately, I think it's our circumstances.

RF: Right.

EVELYN: And there again, when you have friends, friends are people that you can talk to, that can understand why you feel a certain way about a certain thing, you have something in common. And it wouldn't make any difference if they were black, green, yellow, or pink. It just happens ... that ... they ... [tails off and throw up her hands]. We have friends of different *religious* backgrounds ... atheist, staunch Catholic, and just as many that are Protestant. And also Republicans *and* Democrats. Now *there's* a difference. [Laughs]

(Frankenberg, 1993: 36-9)

What is striking about this interview is the way Frankenberg reveals her own experience in order to make her respondent feel comfortable. She refers to this as a 'battle of discourses' (ibid.: 39). And in this way: 'Interviewees were multi-positioned in relation to these life narratives. On the one hand, they were co-producers of the narratives. On the other hand, they were observers, both of their environments and of themselves as they retold and re-evaluated what had gone before' (ibid.: 42).

These interviews were central to Frankenberg's project, she did not spend time with the women other than during interviews, although these lasted between three and eight hours, usually over two sessions. What is important is her approach to the interviews. She insists that an interview is not simply a vehicle for the telling or expressing of experience, but is a socially constructed encounter. It is an 'incomplete story angled toward my questions and each woman's ever-changing sense of self and of how the world works' (ibid.: 41).

Listening for silences

Frankenberg's interviewing position is that of a 'knowing' interviewer. She consciously introduces discursive strategies which will enable her respondents to talk about a 'taboo' subject, that of race and racism. Another, rather different, dimension of the dialogic interview is discussed by Marjorie Devault (1990) employing feminist theories of language. She insists that many of the everyday practices that form the substance of women's experience and daily lives lack identifiable language and concepts through which to express this experience. She opens up a discussion about the problem of defining research 'topics' and to be able to open the boundaries of accepted or conventional 'topics' of social and other kinds of research in order to incorporate women's experience. Devault's research examines household routines for planning, cooking and serving meals. An everyday activity which all will acknowledge as a – quite literally – essential activity within households. The category available to her – that of housework - was too general to get at the very specific activities involved in 'the work of providing food' (Devault, 1990: 99). She started by telling her respondents about what she was interested in and told them she wanted to discuss 'all the housework that has to do with food – cooking, planning, shopping, cleaning up'. What she found was that the women, whether they liked cooking or hated it, spoke naturally about the various dimensions of the task easily because, as she argues, 'I identified, in a rough way, a category that made sense to my respondents because it was a category that organized their day-to-day activity' (ibid.: 99).

Drawing on this research experience, she argues that there are not always words available to 'fit' women's experiences, arguing for the importance of listening as interviewers. An obvious thing to say, perhaps, but as Devault insists, we might be listening for 'silences' too. Those moments when 'respondents got stuck' but were working hard at trying to find words for what they felt. By way of example she discusses a particular interview:

> One woman, talking about why she worked so hard at organising regular meals for her family, told me: 'My husband sees food as something you need to live. But – I don't quite know how to describe it – I really have an emphasis on the social aspects. I mean, the food is an important part, but it's kind of in that setting.

Another woman tried to define the difference between the regular 'drudgery' of cooking and the satisfaction you might get from providing a good meal – she referred to this as 'the good parts'. Also,

> several of my respondents referred to an immediate, improvisational kind of thinking they do while shopping. They did not know quite what to call this process. One told me: 'Most of the time, I kind of plan when I'm at the store, you know? Like OK, we have chicken Monday, pork chops Tuesday – I'll be kind of, you know, figuring out in my mind, as I shop, what's what. (ibid.: 103)

For Devault the most interesting points in the interviews are the 'inarticulate' moments, the fumbling for words, the 'you know's' for these are moments when people are trying to find words for what they do and what they feel about their lives. Those areas for which there are no 'ready made' descriptions or terms or concepts are thus being rendered 'speakable'. This is another example of the conversational or dialogic character of this kind of intensive interviewing. We can see here how the interviewer and her/his respondent come together in a collaborative project. What the interviewer wants to find are answers to questions, this drive and the respondent's willingness and desire to articulate their experience, produces a formidable 'search engine' of productive discourse which, if listened to carefully, can provide new ways of looking at the world. In this way, the standard topics of our research can be opened up, expanded and provide valuable knowledge for new research questions.

Strategic sampling

When I carried out my study into the uses of the VCR, as I knocked on the door of number 11, it could just as well have been someone at number 25. I was in the process of constructing an 'audience' or a community of users where attributes of subjectivity are used to identify and distinguish the women. Thus the respondents, or participants in the study come to stand for (usually) social categories. This is a way of shaping the research, of giving the data depth and meaning. Enabling the researcher, not to generalise, but to compare and contrast individuals located in different subjectivities and life-stages. Many of the small-scale empirical studies upon which cultural studies has been built have been done by graduate students carrying out research for doctoral degrees. This immediately places limitations upon what can be achieved. First, one of geographical location. It is likely that researchers will select respondents within easy access of their base, thereby cutting down travel costs and time. Second, questions of access are crucial. This selection of our 'sample' is a very difficult part of the research and one in which compromises must be made.

The spectre of representativeness is always present when we are thinking about constructing our 'sample', that is those people whom we hope to involve in our study. Perhaps the first problem is in the term 'sample'. Once again, this is a concept which refers to a diffrent research model and, as it implies, is designed to function as a representation of the whole. It certainly creates problems for the design of research projects. One of the commonest questions in discussing plans for research is 'how many people do I need to interview?' This is a question generated directly out of the notion of 'the sample'. The numbers, types, locations, identities and combinations of respondents will entirely depend upon what it is you are wanting to explore with them. What is the purpose of the research contact with them and what kind of data are you wishing to generate? In small-scale projects the core of respondents should be identified in relation to their capacity to provide as rich a set of data as can be managed. For example, in my study of women's use of the video cassette recorder, I interviewed 30 women, but, while they were culturally homogeneous, they differed in relation to age, class, education, occupation and number of children. It is important to stress once more, this was not intended as a representative sample of white women in the UK, rather, it provided a series of complex comparisons between the women in relation to a number of themes of the project. Bob Connell has helpfully discussed his approach to selecting respondents, a process which he calls 'strategic sampling'. He concentrated on 'a few situations where the theoretical yield should be high' (Connell, 1995: 90). We can think about our empirical work in this way by asking what potential exists for 'theoretical sampling' and how rich a very small number of interviews can be.

The interview itself

Setting up the interview

Procedures will vary depending on your relationship with your respondents, but it is always advisable to be formal in setting up the interview. An initial letter outlining your project and intentions for the interview, followed by a telephone call to agree a time and location places the relationship on a proper footing. It should go without saying that you must be punctual and not take any longer than you have agreed. While arranging interviews is usually considered to be a very practical and quite mundane part of research, this is not always the case.

In her study of women artists, Bette Kauffman (1992) was dismayed when she found how difficult it was to arrange interviews with them in New York. Many who had agreed to be interviewed broke appointments, re-arranged times, delayed the interview by days or weeks and, in some cases, refused to be interviewed in their studios, Kauffman's preferred location. In a very interesting piece which reflects on this, she explains how this difficulty, which was not experienced with a group of women artists in Philadelphia, was revealing of the very social identity that she wished to explore, that of the woman artist. She assumed that the New York women would feel more at ease on their own territory, thus shifting the power relations between researcher and researched. Most of their studios were in their homes and competed with domestic obligations and space and many of the women preferred to be interviewed in more public spaces, for example, in an art gallery or restaurant. She concluded that in this way the women confirmed their public personae as artists and that her methodology had not coincided with their experience and self-identity. The evasive strategies employed by the women artists were therefore a key element in Kauffman's eventual understanding of their self-identity. Kauffman's experience reminds us of the importance of getting the location right. What she did was to follow a methodological 'truism' as part of her training as a researcher which told her that interviewing people on their own patch will put them at ease and shift the power relations between researcher and researched.

Preparing for the interview

Taking into account the various kinds of interview available to you, think about what kinds of information or discussion you wish to facilitate. Whatever mode of interview you adopt you will need to draw up a list of 'topic areas' that you want to cover with your respondent. It is best to start off your discussion by asking a general question, for example, 'Could you start by telling me how you got interested in ...? Or 'Could you take me through your usual daily routine?' This category of question enables your respondent to start from a confident position of knowledge and gives them time to 'settle in' to the interview. If you are going to tape-record the interview, and this is highly desirable, you will have cleared this with your respondent and need to check that your technology is functioning efficiently. Make sure that you position the microphone nearer to your correspondent than yourself and, if you are at all uncertain, ask to do a 'sound check' before you start. When I tape-recorded interviews I noticed very often that the conversation changed and became much more relaxed when the recorder was switched off. Be prepared, therefore, to remember what is said during these more informal or 'off-stage' moments (Goffman, 1972).

During the interview

We have already discussed the dynamic nature of interviewing and there follows a discussion of the significance of gender, ethnicity, class and age differences during the encounter itself. Here I simply want to indicate some points for your consideration:

- A pilot interview is invaluable in determining whether your approach, your questions and your topics are effective. This can then be used to review your interview schedule and the ways in which you are asking the questions.

• Allow for diversification and be an active listener. This is obviously important for the dialogic interviews we have already discussed, but it is also important for more structured interviews too.

• Revealing something of yourself during the interviews often has surprising consequences as you will see from Song and Parker's discussion that follows. But it also opens up the discussion, enabling your respondent to have some knowledge of you, your research and your feelings towards the topic under consideration.

• Try to anticipate what your respondents expect of you. They will certainly have some expectations about you and what 'being interviewed' might entail. Depending on the interview type, you may have to begin by getting rid of the notion of the 'formal interview' model described at the beginning of this chapter. This will put your respondent at ease when you reassure them that it will be an informal discussion with no right or wrong answers!

• Most importantly, have respect for your respondents. They are being generous with their time and will be of great help to you. Turn up on time, thank them at the end of the interview, ask them if they have any questions and offer to let them see the transcript of the interview and/or the final product of your research.

Group 'interviews'

There are some research areas and approaches for which group interviews or discussions will provide useful material. However, as is the case for all decisions about method, you need to be clear about why the group interviews are useful, what kind of data are you expecting them to generate as well as an awareness of the specific problems group interviewing presents. One of the most obvious reasons for selecting groups to interview together is because you want to explore how people interact with each other in relation to your topic. How, for example, might people express their views on a popular television serial, or on growing up male, or their attitudes towards their work. This is to recognise and mobilise the importance of interaction in social identity and how people account for themselves in discussions with others. This might be very different from the ways in which we might account for ourselves in a one-to-one. Researchers who have used this method include David Morley (1980, 1986) and Liebes and Katz (1993), all of whom were interested in how groups generated discussions about popular television and how their understandings and interpretations could be seen to be ideologically formed. Marie Gillespie, in her study of young Punjabi people in South London, was interested in 'group talk' amongst her respondents rather than what they might say to her as a researcher. She therefore listened to 'friendship groups' as they talked about their likes and dislikes, the kinds of programmes they liked on television, etc. and in this way tapped into more 'naturalistic' talk. Her role in discussions 'involved surrendering the initiative and allowing talk to flow as far as possible without intervention on my part' (1995: 67). Another researcher interested in thinking about the dynamics of group talk is David Buckingham and we will look at his research in more detail in Chapter 7.

Group discussions can also be used at an early stage in a project. Talking to a group of interested and involved people about your topic in the early stages of your research can be an extremely useful way of generating ideas and concepts which can then be used to formulate your approach to further interviews. Of course employing group discussions presents problems associated with any group interaction. For example, some group members will dominate the discussion, will lead the discussion their way and focus on matters of interest to them, to the possible exclusion of other viewpoints. Groups may assume that you are looking for consensus and will aim their discussions towards agreement on issues, rather than allowing difference and contradictions to emerge. The discussion, therefore, will have to be managed and as facilitator you will need to develop strategies to get the maximum potential from a group discussion.

Class, gender, ethnicity, age: differences which make a difference

In discussions on method by feminists, the interview is recognised as a site of power relations (Roberts, 1981). This is to say that the researcher is in a more powerful position than her respondents both during the interview itself and often, although not always, in her acquisition of social and cultural capital. Feminists working on surveying, documenting, exploring women's lives and experience have argued for and practised a range of 'respondent-friendly' strategies. For example, open conversational interviews of the type discussed above, 'allowing' respondents to determine the agenda or direction of the interview and being open to questions from respondents. Les Back provides a rare example of a male researcher who has reflected on his role as a male researcher and ethnographer. He argues that the relationships which he developed with both male and female respondents during his fieldwork were 'ordered by [a] gendered form of participation' (Back, 1993: 230). Back begins his reflection on his fieldwork by acknowledging his reluctance to make contact with and interview women. This is a strategy that is underpinned by a feminist research politics which admits to the inappropriateness of a male researcher exploring women's lives. For Back this has two consequences. First, male researchers are allowed to disregard gender and, second, this strategy suggests that gender is not an issue in male-to-male, and we might add, female-to-female interviewing situations. Our identities as male/female, black/white, older/younger researchers crucially affects the research encounters and the openness, or otherwise, of our respondents and interviewees. We need to be able to acknowledge these complexities, the inequalities of gender and ethnic relations and the difference generation might make to power and authority.

Miri Song and David Parker take these reflections further by deploying theories of the fluidity of identity in their understanding of the shifting positions of the researcher during the interviewing process. They were both, in separate research projects, interviewing Chinese young people in Britain and found that their 'experiences of mixed descent Chinese-English and Korean-American researchers 'positioned [them] in terms of both commonality *and* difference *vis-à-vis* [their] interviewees' (Song and Parker, 1995: 241). Their cultural identities shifted, in the perceptions of their interviewees, in relation to, for example, their background, their mastery of language, their experience of racism, appearance, and so on, finding that their disclosures were helpful in developing the conversations. Parker summarises it thus:

> The contact that I had with other part-Chinese people in my research profoundly affected my conceptualisation of identity formation. These shared experiences encouraged me to venture more of my *own* experiences in a way that I did not with respondents who were not of dual heritage. The result was less stilted exchanges and telling remembrances of falling outside of the prevalent black/white, Chinese/non-Chinese categorisation systems. A number of the part-Chinese people I interviewed summarised their sense of identity in terms exactly corresponding to the sort of vocabulary for which I had been struggling. (ibid.: 246)

Song argues that notions of similarity of difference do not necessarily shape the way interviews proceed in any kind of predictable or systematic way. Rather, they were 'very much contingent upon each moment in each interview'. 'Interviewees' assumptions about my cultural identity were central in shaping what respondents chose to disclose to me, as well as the matter in which interviewees disclosed information about themselves' (ibid.: 248). However, for both Parker and Song, the key shared ground of experience between them and their interviewees was that of racial discrimination. Theirs is a usefully reflexive piece on the dynamics of interviewing and the highly contingent nature of the interview from moment and moment.

Ellen Seiter discusses the political problems of interviewing about such a popular form as television and in so doing raises the question of class difference. She usefully analyses in great detail a single and troubling interview that she and a colleague conducted as part of a study of soap opera viewing. She identifies class, gender and generational difference between researcher and researched as contributing to the 'failure' of the interview with two white men who had responded to their advertisement for a soap opera study:

> Throughout the interview, it was uppermost in these men's minds that we were academics. For them, it was an honour to talk to us and an opportunity to be heard by persons of authority and standing. They made a concerted

effort to appear cosmopolitan and sophisticated. For them, our visit offered a chance to reveal their own personal knowledge, and their opinions about society and the media. *They had no interest whatsoever in offering us interpretative, textual readings of television programs, as we wanted them to do. In fact, they exhibited a kind of 'incompetence' in this regard.* (Seiter 1990: 62, my emphasis)

Seiter suggests that what is at stake here is the difference in social identities between the academic researcher and their subjects. Her interviewees offended her feminist and socialist politics. They were recalcitrant and refused to 'behave like ordinary, everyday viewers'. Given that one of the men had responded to their newspaper advertisement asking to interview soap opera viewers, Seiter is understandably annoyed. While she is right to consider the class difference and the differently valued cultural capital of academic researchers and the ways in which this will influence and shape the interview, we could look at that interview text in a very different way. We could ask a number of questions which are highly significant with regard to the popular, distinction and class difference. An analysis of the interview could reveal the social formation of the two men - their working lives, their class and sexuality and explore questions of subjectivity and identity in relation to the popular as well as the academic understandings of 'ordinary' viewers. What is of interest here, I would argue, is the kind of interview method which sought to focus attention on specific readings and use of soap operas, running away from the researchers' control into more rich and revealing disclosures about class, gender and the popular. Thus, the interview and Seiter's welcome reflections on her experience of the encounter, provide an important example of the recalcitrant nature of respondents if they are determined to take control from the interviewee.

The interview is clearly a valuable research method but one that should be approached with caution, always being informed by the kinds of questions we have explored in this chapter. Also, we must be circumspect and beware of claiming too much on the basis of these constructed events, thus it is important to reveal those limitations and of the particularly contingent and provisional nature of the technique. In the following chapter I will look at other forms of 'interview' in examining the influence of autobiography in cultural studies.

six	I Want to Tell You a Story

The narratives of the world are numberless ... narrative is international, transhistorical, transcultural. It is simply there, like life itself. (Barthes, 1977: 79)

In our discussion of dialogic interviewing, we noted how respondents construct their stories. I now wish to consider the use of 'stories' in cultural studies and how they can become an intrinsic part of our research practice. Indeed, many, like Barthes, have suggested that narrative is the stuff of life. For example, Graham Dawson argues that the cultural importance of storytelling is not only to be found in the cultural products which circulate, but also in the stories we tell others and ourselves. 'It is a cultural practice deeply embedded in everyday life, a creative activity in which everyone engages' (1994: 22). We tell each other stories and we tell ourselves stories. Given the ubiquitous nature of stories we need to consider how we might deal with them in our research. It is often the case that the most pervasive forms of cultural practice are the most difficult to catch hold of but often, when we do they are the most fruitful for our understandings of the processes of culture and meaning in society.

I want to begin by telling you a story about my research into the video cassette recorder which will indicate how stories emerge through our research encounters. Mine was a qualitative study using the ethnographic interview as the main method of research. During my first phase of interviewing I discovered that the women I talked to wanted to tell me stories, or more specifically, 'their story'.

To begin with I felt that we were getting away from the topic, that it was nothing to do with their use of the VCR and worried that, as David Buckingham put it, 'this was not ... the stuff from which significant research is made' (1985: 159). When I began listening to the tapes, however, I realised that their life stories were a very significant part of each interview, for three main reasons.

First, the women were taking over control of the interview and telling me what they wanted to, rather than simply responding to my questions. Second, in constructing their autobiographies for me they revealed through self-commentary their articulation of their position within the social structure. This often involved their family history, from how their parents had lived out their relationship to each other, to domestic labour, to technology, to television and to reading. Some presented a teleological account of their history, with all events and experiences leading towards their present position with a certain inevitability, while others indicated fractures and breaks within their history which had changed their lives in some way. The cultures of different households, the relationships which exist within a structure of power and authority, across gender and age extend beyond the present generation, and many of the women reminded me of the importance of this cultural history in our understanding of the social use of television and video. And, third, there is a further potential in this mode of response. The problem of classifying women in terms of social class has been the subject of discussion and debate within feminist research. What the biographies reveal are the complexities of gender and class and ways in which they intersect manifestly in the options and 'choices' available to women within different social positions. Through these accounts emerged an impression of different class cultures.

As these, and other stories emerged through opening up questions about the uses of the VCR, it forced me to look at the whole and related area of women and their consumption of popular texts. Questions and answer formats tend to fragment 'experience' whereas story-telling allows the inter-relatedness of different areas of women's lives to emerge. It became necessary, for instance to think about domestic labour before considering how and when women watched television, to consider video recorders as technology before asking how they were used and so on.

This was a surprise to me and raised some important epistemological and ontological issues. First, the women were recounting their experience. They were telling me stories about their own lives, their pasts and, often, their aspirations and desires for the future. The stories tumbled out, spilling over the boundaries of my 'interview schedule' and my understanding of what qualified as 'good research practice'. The actual moment of the interview was a discursive event – it was an active and productive conversation in which together we were constructing a story. Here, we were moving into the epistemological mode, this became a way of knowing, not simply about the details of a person's life, but how and in what ways that life could be told. Carolyn Steedman (1997) suggests that to tell a life, or write a life is to produce 'a self'. This active production of self was often accompanied by a reflection on their story. Many of the women reflected on the way they were and how they felt at particular key moments in their lives that were often related to marriage and children. They held up the past 'self' for reflection and, often, fascination. Thus, the women were moving between their lived world, their material existence and the knowledge about that existence – where they were in the world and how they got there, and in one or two cases, their aspirations for the future.

Since carrying out my research in the mid-1980s I have since discovered very interesting work on the nature of stories and how they can be understood. If we consider the practice of storying more generally, the distinct elements are: a speaker; an enunciator of the story; the story itself; and a listener. These relationships are variable and complex. More specifically, there are different kinds of story-tellers, occupying a range of (speaking) positions and with differential access to experience and the means of telling the story. Stories themselves can take numerous forms, quite apart from the subjects or topics that they might cover. The stories are told through different media oral, print and electronic. Which reminds us of the proliferation of 'storying' in the broadcast media, for example, the confessional, the chat shows and the recording of 'ordinary' lives in documentary genres. Turning to the listener, questions such as their access, their social position and how they interpret the stories would open up another important dimension. This entire process is continuous and in flux, but the stories happen within specific contexts and at particular historical moments. However, as this is a book about research methods, we need to add another character to this process. That is the person who seeks, or 'coaxes' the story – the researcher. I have indicated a number of relationships between different elements which will play particular parts at each moment in the production of the research material, its interpretation and analysis. This can be expressed as follows:

- The researcher: can be the coaxer, but also can be the story-teller – either directly using autobiography, or as constructing the account of the research

- The story-teller: who is being coaxed to tell and what is the relationship between the teller and the story

- The story itself – the narrative, form, discourses and repertoires upon which it draws for expression. (adapted from Plummer 1995)

The social role of stories

Writing recently from a symbolic interactionist perspective, Ken Plummer (1995) has drawn attention to the importance of stories in understanding the social, for individuals and for those broader social stories which are in circulation. Similarly, Denzin (1992) uses the concept of story as a way of exploring the ways in which people use publicly available stories, for example from narrative cinema, in order to make sense of their lives. In this way, stories are seen as part of the flux and flow of identity, everyday life and the social. For Plummer society is made up of webs of storying, thus there is no abstract 'individual' and 'society' but rather a 'social order which heaves as a vast negotiated web of dialogue and conversation' (1995: 20). He insists, however, that the web is shot through with power. This is to say that some stories have more power than others and certain stories cannot be spoken at all. Of course, the human sciences and other discursive practices are not cut off or remote from this process, but are embedded within it, telling their own particular stories, some of which can be highly influential in the shaping and framing of possible narratives.

Plummer, in proposing a sociology of stories defines their different dimensions:

- *What is the nature and content of the story?* This is a textual question and will look at the structure of the narrative, what repertoires or codes are drawn upon. How the teller positions her or himself within the story, etc.

- *What is the social process of producing and consuming stories?* This is to ask how stories get produced and how people come to construct their particular stories at particular moments. Do the story-tellers own their own stories, or do they move into different authorship? What circumstances might prevent the story being told and what would encourage it? Why do people tell this particular kind of story rather than another and what social and cultural formations enable this story?

- *What social roles do stories play?* This is to question the significance of particular stories being enabled and how they relate to broader historical and social change. What are the power dimensions involved in the telling of particular stories? Who is able to speak and who is silenced? Why do some narratives become dominant and others always kept on the margins?

Plummer thus comes up with five questions in thinking about the social role of stories:

1   Which kinds of narratives work to empower people and which degrade, control and dominate (pathologisation, victimisation, cf. stories which sense human agency and survival ... stories told in different ways by different groups – talk from below may be marginalised and excluded – 'expert' talk given priority and credibility (powerful stories)?

2   The making of stories: what strategies enable stories to be told – what silences (role of the coaxer)?

3   Consuming: who has access to stories, cultural and economic resources?

4   Strategies: turn taking, style, mode, etc.

5   Stories in the wider world - powerful exercise over the agendas -
what can be told and how. (adapted from Plummer, 1995)

Plummer's insights, developed through his oral history and life story
research, will be valuable when we consider how to relate cultural texts to
lived cultures which is the topic of the next chapter, but for now I will continue to explore the notion of self in relation to storying.

Speaking the self

Another useful way of thinking about the 'characters' in this process is as a
collection of 'selves'. Theories of 'the self' and how we deal with questions
about who we are in the research process have produced some extremely
interesting work and emphasise the importance of exploring these questions
in our research. 'Who am I?' sounds like a deep philosophical question, but
it is one which often occurs to a researcher in the midst of their research. Not
only 'Who am I?' but 'Who am I in this research?' How do I find my place
or location within the research itself, as the theorist, the coaxer of stories, the
interpreter of texts and as author? As researchers and writers we cannot 'speak
from nowhere' but rather always speak and write from a particular 'speaking
position' which is always materially located. This, then, presents real dilemmas as to how and where we position our 'self' in relation to our work. In
order to explore these relationships and questions I will look at 'the researching self', specific kinds of stories and their relationship to the speaker,
auto/biography, life story and testament and, finally, provide some reflections
on narrativity in our work.

The central and most problematic concept here is the self and what we
understand it to be. Recent work, influenced largely by Foucault, has sought
to conceptualise the self, not as a unified individual with a central and stable
core, or essential being, but rather as a fragmented and decentred subject that
is constantly in the process of production. The extent to which the subject
and subjectivity is structured by and through the social is a matter for debate,
but, drawing on Giddens, we can at least speak of the self as a project insofar
as we are capable of reflecting on our past and the present and projecting ourselves into the future. But the potential for putting together our identity and
subjectivity is always shaped and constrained, or enabled, by our position
within the social structure, our access to education through our class position
would be an obvious example. Conceptualising the subject in this way recognises the complexities of individual experience within the social and suggests
that the social is spoken through the subject. The examples which follow will
serve to demonstrate these notions of the subject as they relate to the research
process.

Carolyn Steedman (1997) notes the explosion of autobiography which
now goes beyond its definition of a literary genre. She says that when a

'literary genre becomes more than itself – when it becomes, variously, a cognitive form, a mode of academic writing, a way of being in the world' (ibid.: 107), we must ask why. Steedman suggests that the self is now being foregrounded 'because it stands at the confluence of many post-Foucauldian understandings that have shaped and continue to shape postmodernist thought' (ibid.: 107). She goes on to examine how 'self-narration' became a 'taught and learned activity' (ibid.: 109) through particular pedagogic practices in creative writing, producing, at specific historical times, particular kinds of narratives. Writing the self, she suggests can bring the self into being, and as such, of course, can also be a disciplinary strategy via powerful institutions, for example, the state. For Plummer, discussing the importance of life stories, the very telling of the story confirms who and what we are. It is this process, this speaking and writing of the self that is so important to an understanding of culture and the social.

The researcher

As is clear from the example drawn from my own research and others in the previous chapter, the coaxer of the story, the researcher plays a constitutive part in the construction of research material. Bev Skeggs suggests that the researcher can usefully ask her or himself some autobiographical questions in order to locate their position within the research process:

- Why was the area of study chosen, what institutional, economic and socio-political factors underpinned the choice?

- Which frameworks of established knowledge were used, referred to, challenged, ignored, and why?

- Which methods were chosen for study and why? Why were other approaches not used?

- How did the initial questions and research relate to the final product?

- How did the process of writing influence the final product? (Skeggs, 1995: 4)

Putting these questions to ourselves in the process of our research demands a reflexive awareness of why we are making particular decisions at each stage of the process. Being answerable to ourselves is the first stage in ensuring an ethical and fair approach to our research. Of course, not all these questions are always relevant to the particular study in question, nor to they need to be written up in the 'final' text. An excess of self-absorption in a research text can be extremely tedious for the reader!

Valerie Walkerdine is a researcher who has constantly reflected upon her position within the research process, using a psychoanalytic framework to grasp what happens in the research encounter (Walkerdine, 1989). She points to the process of transference and counter-transference in fieldwork 'by examining precisely the issue of projection of the researcher on to the subjects and vice versa'. Walkerdine continues, 'I want to argue that the fantasies that come up on both sides are immensely important, and are not to be discounted even if they turn out not to be about the data in question.' She argues that this is going on, however we would like to deny it, and that it should not be ignored, but acknowledged as an important part of the research process itself. Walkerdine further insists that this indicates that the collection of data is not simple or superficial and that data, in itself, does not tell us anything. Using an example from her own research, Walkerdine discusses interviewing practice and the interpretation of data saying how three researchers involved in the same study could be seen to project their own fears and fantasies onto both the interviewee and the way in which they interpreted data. While Walkerdine's arguments are extremely important, the implications are questionable. The examples she gives suggest that the researcher herself is not at all in control of her own feelings, knowledge about herself and her desires and fears. Psychoanalysis tells us that the unconscious is in operation, but this does not take into account the process of intellectualising and theorising involved in this kind of research. As scholars we have 'shared' access to particular frameworks and concepts and it is possible to reflect upon our knowledge of ourselves. These important elements can give us some possibility of distance, not in the sense of objectivity, but of knowing ourselves in the process. Walkerdine's accounts of fieldwork suggest that we are almost totally vulnerable to our feelings and emotions. I consider this to be a potential mis-recognition of understanding human behaviour in this formal setting. I do not think we are prey to our selves in this extreme way. We can find ways of being aware of the process and our role within it. And we must not forget that the subjects of our research are also often acutely aware of their role in the activities of research. Walkerdine calls for the necessity of us placing ourselves more centre-stage in our research, in writing about our subjectivity. However, it is surely the case that there are many stories of our subjectivity which can be constructed and that not all of our experience is of relevance here.

Walkerdine and Hollway have written fascinating accounts of their research practice. However, their psychological frameworks and the topics of their research perhaps lend themselves to this particular kinds of psychoanalytic reflection on transference, projection, fantasy and fear. As Brunsdon (2000) points out, Walkerdine's portrait of the viewing of *Rocky* with the Coles family, discussed here in Chapter 3, is used to emphasise and explore methodological issues and to give full vent to the researcher's concerns and anxieties about her relationship to the subjects of her research. As Brunsdon also notes, the overwhelming point of identification and fantasy is Walkerdine and her identity as working class, her loss and her desire to be recognised by the Coles as working class. Walkerdine's choice of research topic and the kinds of questions she wants to raise in her studies focus specifically on the construction of working-class femininity. A choice already implicated in her own identity and desires. It is important to reflect on our own subjectivity and place within our research. The discussion above has drawn attention to the ways in which researchers have used different frameworks for self-reflection.

Different modes of storying

Bearing this in mind, I now want to move on in suggesting four different modes of storying which can be put into play in our research: autobiography, testimony, life story and memory.

(Auto)biography

As Steedman has noted, this is an increasingly influential genre within the humanities and social science. It has been especially important within feminist work and Elspeth Probyn examines the notion of the gendered self and the possibility, or otherwise, of 'speaking positions' for that self within cultural studies. (Probyn, 1993) She is concerned to find ways of using (our)selves and our experience in our intellectual work and critical analysis. Probyn notes how the self is 'legitimated and required' in some situations and locations and not in others. She wants to elaborate ways of tactically speaking in strategic loci where the sound of the self is unexpected and to 'reveal the self as both the possession of experience and emotion, and as a way of conceptualizing the effectivity of that possession' (ibid.: 87). She cites Carolyn Steedman's *Landscape for a Good Woman* (1986) as exemplary in this respect. Steedman draws on the memories of her past and, in particular, her relationship with her mother, and is able, through different theoretical perspectives, to reflect on both her (auto)biography and the adequacies of the theoretical accounts. Probyn describes this method as a kind of double move between an ontological register, a way of being in the world based on experience and an epistemological register through which that being/experience can become a way of knowing. Probyn's work is helpful in enabling cultural theorists and critics to find a speaking position within their own analyses, without necessarily slipping into a narrowly subjective mode. Clearly, autobiography is an important form for both cultural studies and feminism, concerned to draw on our own experience as a resource, but also in thinking more analytically about how that can find its place within our epistemological projects. Similarly, the category of experience can be tremendously effective in feminist or cultural studies pedagogic practice in encouraging students to reflect on their own knowledge of the world. Probyn's insight is useful as a strategy to think beyond experience and to encourage an understanding of the intersection of the public (social cultural) with the private (intimate/subjective).

In his important book *Documents of Life 2*, Ken Plummer (2001) distinguishes between different modes or functions of the life story: life story as *resource* and life story as *topic*. This is a helpful distinction in enabling us think about what we are expecting from the life story and how we might use it in our research.

If we regard the life story as *resource*, then we are most interested in how it increases our understanding of, say, an event or what it was like to live through particular events, or in specific conditions or at a particular period. It can enrich our knowledge about that world, that society, that culture and give us a sense of what it was like to be there. When we regard the life story as *topic*, then it becomes of interest in its own right as a discourse or a discursive event. We would ask of it how and in what ways this story was being told, what kinds of repertoires were being drawn on in the telling. We might also ask how did that person come to be telling this story in the first place, what were her formations of social and cultural life that enabled this story to be produced. Thus, the shaping and telling of the story become more significant than the content. It is, of course, possible to use the same story in different ways (see Summerfield 1998).

Testimony: resource

Something worth noting is that people live through particular events and witness incidents about which they have, often urgent, stories to tell. One very potent version of this mode of 'eye witness' account is that of 'testimony'. In one week in January 1982 Elisabeth Burgos-Debray listened to and recorded the story told to her by Rigoberta Menchu, a Quiche Indian woman, about her life and struggles in Guatemala. Although doubts have been cast on Menchu's motives (Stoll, 1999), it is still important for us to think about this form of storying. Introducing the narrative (Menchu, 1983), Burgos-Debray says of Menchu: 'Her life story is an account of contemporary history rather than of Guatemala itself. It is in this sense that it is exemplary: she speaks for all the Indians of the American subcontinent ... she is a privileged witness' (Burgos-Debray, 1984: xi).

This notion of privilege should be understood as that possessed by one who is consciously speaking for a subjugated people. Menchu does this through a detailed account of her own life as a Quiche Indian, a people whose lives have been shadowed by cultural discrimination throughout centuries of brutal regimes. Testimonies such as hers are a poignant example of the speaking of experience which is relatable to oral traditions and the role of storytellers within them. Walter Benjamin described the role of the story-teller as a person who had the ability 'to fashion the raw material of experience, his (*sic*) own and that of others, in a solid, useful and unique way' (Benjamin, 1973: 108). Burgos-Debray worked to 'faithfully reproduce' this account and not to subject it to interpretation or analysis in its published form. Clearly, this kind of account has a significance in the broader political and cultural context outside of the academy, but it should be a clear reminder that millions of people are painfully experiencing the consequences of brutal political and economic regimes and for whom the notion of 'fragmented subjectivity' is a painfully lived one. To quote Menchu's final words:

> [Therefore], my commitment to our struggle knows no boundaries nor limits. This is why I've travelled to many places where I've had the opportunity to talk about my people ... Nevertheless, I'm still keeping my Indian identity a secret. I'm still keeping secret what I think no-one should know. Not even anthropologists or intellectuals, no matter how many books they have, can find out all our secrets. (Menchu, 1983: 247)

A salutory reminder of the limits to knowledge indeed and that, in my view, there must be a place in our work for this experiential mode.

Life story: resource and topic

The life story technique is a well-established method in oral history where it has tended to be used in order to generate 'alternative' accounts of the world, in other words, as a resource. The gathering of life stories has been important in feminist work where women's experience was often hidden and unable to be spoken. First, it is important to insist that the life story is not a direct expression of one's life – this is an impossibility. It will always be a tale told, that is, it will be constructed, it will have a narrative form and pattern. It will not necessarily stay the same. It will speak of the present in the past. It will, in other words, use conventions and be inherently unstable and unfixed.

The post-structuralist insistence on the problematic nature of experience as giving direct access to the 'truth' or the 'real lives' which people live prompted much debate between feminist historians (see the discussion in Chapter 2). Many believed that women's experience and their accounts of life stories were authentic accounts and should be treated as such. While experience should not be lost, Kathleen Canning suggest that the task in listening to accounts is 'to untangle the relationships between discourses and experiences by exploring the ways in which subjects mediated or transformed discourses in specific historical settings' (Canning 1994, quoted in Summerfield, 1998: 17).

A very good example of the employment of a version of this method is Ruth Frankenberg's study already referred to in Chapter 5, who draws on women's accounts of their lives as a resource for analysing racialised society. Frankenberg argues that these life stories need to be explained and understood by 'mapping' them onto broader social processes. Hers is a clear statement of the complexity of the life story and the intensity and richness of data which it can achieve. Frankenberg captures the shifting dynamics and positionalities adopted during the interviews, but also the self-reflexivity of the interviewees as they told their stories. It is in this self-reflexive space which the work of the production of the self is going on and it is the self-awareness of the subjects of her study which is simply not acknowledged in more conventional uses of life story and the conversational interview. Frankenberg goes on to discuss the interview narratives: 'They are self-reflexive, and they confirm as well as contradict other accounts of the social world outside of the project. In a wider sense, they intersect with other local and global histories' (1993: 42). Frankenberg's study, among other things, is able to '[make] explicit and tangible some of the ways in which white women's life experience is racially structured' (ibid.: 22).

While I would argue that cultural studies and feminism needs to continue working towards more sophisticated methods which engage with 'lived cultures', those subjects must be allowed to be the knowledgeable and knowing subjects. Working with the life story and ideas of narrative in our analysis will enable us to conceptualise experience as, in de Lauretis' words:

> The process by which, for all social beings, subjectivity is constructed. Through that process one places oneself or is placed in social reality and so perceives and comprehends as subjective (referring to, originating in oneself) those relations – material, economic and inter-personal – which are in fact social, and, in a larger perspective, historical. (1984: 27)

Accounts of experience, as they might be given, remain a rich and necessary source for our work. Both feminism and cultural studies have, in different and similar ways, recognised this fact. It is my view that a post-structuralist feminist-informed methodology insisting as it does on the problematising of all categories, of a clarity and openness in method and approach and a genuine reflexivity, can continue to enlighten and enrich the processes of research into cultures.

Bob Connell's study of masculinities, following Plummer, employs the life history method and argues that such histories 'give rich documentation of personal experience, ideology and subjectivity ... [B]ut life histories also, paradoxically, document social structures, social movements and institutions. That is to say, they give rich evidence about impersonal and collective processes as well as about subjectivity' (Connell, 1995: 89). He further argues that life history is an important method for understanding social change: 'life history method always concerns the making of social life through time. It is literally history.' Connell acknowledges, however, that it is a hugely time-consuming and labour-intensive method, but what the method loses in scope it gains in depth. The trick is to focus on a number of situations which he hoped would provide a rich 'theoretical yield'. This is to say that he identified what he calls 'crisis tendencies in the gender order', identifying groups of men for whom, for different reasons, 'the construction or integration of masculinity was under pressure' (ibid.: 90). These were men working with feminists where 'gender hierarchy had lost all legitimacy'; men in gay and bisexual networks; young working-class men without regular employment and middle-class professionals in 'new' occupations which lack 'the social authority of capital and the old professions'. Connell's strategy is of great interest and a valuable way of intensifying the life history method and, while the researchers asked the men for 'the story of your life', they focused on what actually happened to men in the various settings of their lives, thus:

> We used transitions between institutions (e.g. entry to high school) as pegs for memory; but we also asked for accounts of relationships within institutions such as families and workplaces. We sought evidence about each of the structures of gender (power, labour and cathexis) from different periods of life. In a field interview it was not possible to explore unconscious motives. Nevertheless we sought clues to emotional dynamics by asking about early memories, family constellations, relationship crises and wishes for the future. (ibid.: 91)

From this we can see that Connell's interviews were far from the coaxing of a free-flowing general life history and for Connell produced 'rich and fascinating narratives'. We will look at his strategy for analysis in Chapter 8, but he emphasises that, although language, narrative turns, figures of speech and silences were obviously an important feature of the stories, '[the] autobiographical story is evidence for a great deal beyond its own language. The evidence is not necessarily easy to use; it takes time and effort to examine the story from different angles and compare it with other evidence' (ibid.: 91). In other words, it takes a leap of the imagination, the sociological imagination, to see what the stories can reveal.

Penny Summerfield (1998) has written about the process of life story interviews raising slightly different issues and emphasises the instability experienced during the life story interview for researcher and respondent. She cites Graham Dawson's concept of composure as usefully describing the activity of speaking or telling ones life story (Dawson, 1994). Composure implies both a putting together of the story, literally, composing the self for the listener or reader, and a more psychic process of orientation or self-possession in telling the story, a kind of equilibrium is achieved through the careful telling of the story. Dawson and his fellow researchers in the Popular Memory Group at the CCCS referred to this kind of story as a 'safe story' and contrasted it to a 'risky story'. Of course, the role of the interviewer, or coaxer of the story is key to the potential shifts in the telling of the life story. Summerfield identifies the characteristics of the interview which can lead to (dis)composure. First, there will most likely be some disjunctures or lack of fit between the interviewer's research frame and the interviewee's memory frame. The researcher will have a clear notion of the kinds of areas she wishes to probe during the interview and these may not have found a place in the memory frame which shapes the story as it is to be told/remembered. The researcher can, therefore, intervene in the memory frame, inserting a new topic or encouraging the interviewee to take a different approach to her story. The second feature of life story interviewing which can unearth previously hidden feelings or events in memory is the process of 'interviewing for interiority'. This is to encourage the telling of more personal and intimate feelings and clearly can lead to (dis)composure. Finally, Summerfield draws our attention to the interpersonal dynamics of the interview itself - the interviewer's dress, demeanour and body language can encourage (or discourage) confessions around different topics. This can lead to unpredicted revelations and shifts from 'safe' to 'risky' stories.

An interesting example can be drawn from one of my interviews to demonstrate the shifts. My first interview with 'Janet' lasted over two hours. She defined herself as a 'housewife' and at the time of the interview her three children were aged 12, 10 and 7. Her husband was an electrical engineer and his work took him abroad for weeks at a time. Janet left school at 15 and worked as a counter assistant at Boots before she had her first child at the age of 22. Janet's story emerged through the interview, although, looking back on the transcripts now, I was doing my best to return her to my 'research framework' of questions about the video recorder, television viewing and leisure time in the home. What is interesting, and in the light of Dawson's concept of 'composure', is how her story began with one of the 'composed' and fulfilled full-time mother and housewife, but, as the interview progressed, she began to (dis)compose this version of herself and opened up a much more contradictory identity. I began all my interviews by asking about their daily routines, starting with the previous day and getting a sense of a routine week. Janet described a week made up of childcare, taking children to and from school, cleaning and cooking, plus two days when she went shopping, one of which took her near her parents whom she called to see. Getting to Friday, and in response to my third question of the interview, she said:

> and then it's the weekend and, you know, really, I honestly don't think I'd have time to work. It might sound silly, but you know, when people say 'oo don't you get bored at home?', I don't. Because there's always something to do, you know, I mean, I don't dislike being, you know, a housewife and all that ... you know, I've always liked that.

The interview then proceeded with questions about radio, television and video – what she liked to listen to and watch and how the VCR was used. After a short time she began to express feelings of guilt about sitting down and watching television, but especially video recordings, during the day: 'I'm not one for having the television on through the day, unless there's something I really want to watch because I think you can get addicted to it and everything else goes to pot then, so I don't watch it a lot through the day.'

There was an exception, an American daytime drama serial called *Falcon Crest* which she did watch and if she was out shopping, she would record it. I started to ask her about *Falcon Crest*, but she interrupted:

Going back now to having a video, watching television through the day, I think I would feel guilty ... I mean it isn't that my husband's coming home saying ... I don't mean for that, I'd just myself feel that I was cheating. I sort of look upon it as a job, you know, it is my work really ... like you go out to work, but this is my job and I think if I'm sat I'm not doing my job, that is just in my own mind, ... I think it's a bit of guilt really.

Here Janet re-claims her notion of 'her job' as housewife, comparing it to my job and, implicitly, my sense of commitments and obligation. I then picked up again on what she recorded and when she found the time to watch the tapes. This was met again by her saying that she found it difficult to find the time to watch because of her domestic obligations. We then moved to talk about reading for a little while. I then brought the conversation back to television and asked if she put the television on when the children came home from school.

J: They put it on for the children's programmes, yes, they do.

AG: Does it then tend to stay on, even if nobody's particularly watching?

J: Well ... if the children are in, yes ... but if they're out I'll many a time turn it off, and I'd put a record on or the radio, you know, if there's nothing I really want to watch ... I tend to ... I'm not one that can iron and watch television, I can't concentrate ... I get that involved in my ironing ... I can't, some people like television on, now I can't iron and watch the television.

Once again, Janet is returning to her sense of professionalism in how she approaches her work, insisting that for her, it takes priority over television. The discussion then moved on to the programmes and films she liked. She was a *Dallas* and *Dynasty* fan and enjoyed talking about the characters, the current story lines and so on. She then said she enjoyed some quiz programmes and another revelation was made:

J: I like some quiz programmes, I used to like that kid's one that was on, *Blockbusters* ... now I thought that was great ... probably because I could answer some of the questions ... and I love *Mastermind* ...

AG: What do you like about it?

J: I think you feel really great if you can answer one ... you can probably answer a lot [laughs].. ... but I love *Mastermind*. I get so, oo, you know, and like when that lad won last week, I really wanted him to win, and you know he was just - I'm not saying *just* an ambulance driver – but you know when you're up against people ... you know, school teachers and things like that, I thought it was really great ... like when that taxi driver won it ... but yet obviously he must have read a lot and studied a lot to get to that level ... and you're against very clever people, and to get that ... I think it's great. I think ... oo he's achieved something, you know I really think that they have achieved something.

Again Janet refers to me – 'you can probably answer a lot', but she then starts talking about people without formal educational qualifications achieving something and, most importantly, beating school teachers and very clever people. This thrilled her and the sense of achievement that people, with whom she clearly identified, must feel, was to come up again as she began to speak of herself in rather a different way. Janet proceeded to set herself and her present situation against a desired self, one who had 'achieved something'. Our conversation turned to her husband's personal computer. She said she had picked up some of the computer magazines to which her husband subscribed but 'I just can't honestly understand them', then she said:

J: ... well, like I keep saying to my husband, I'm always telling him I'm going to write a book, so he laughs, they all laugh, and I say, I'm telling you I'm going to write a book ... so buy me a typewriter ... he goes, you don't need a typewriter, just get a word processor, and goodness knows what, and a printer ... you know, but whether or not I will do ... I might do. I get these ideas you see.

AG: What kind of book would it be?

She told me that it would be a book for children because she thought she could do better than some of the books at the library where she takes her little girl. She had told her sister-in-law, who has a day centre for children who said she should write the book and that she would test it out on the children. Janet, again:

J: I says I'll show you all one day and I'd love to ... I'd love to do that and be a success and think, well ... because when you tend to be at home looking after children there's not much ... like, I go to my sister in law ... she works full-time, you know, looking after children and goodness knows what – they have been ill treated and all that type of thing ... and I go ... you've really got something in life, you can say ... you know you've got something, I have nothing. She says I admire you for being content to stop at home and look after your children. I'd love to do something just to say, well, I've done that ... do you know what I mean? ... or is that daft?

Janet then continued to talk about the fact that she feels undervalued, drawing attention to the repetitive nature of housework and the fact that she feel she has nothing to offer socially, 'I'm alright with my own friends ... er ... yes I'm fine with them, but I don't like, you know, like, I'd have a heart attack if my husband expected me to go out with somebody from work or something like that ... because, well what do you talk about ... you know, really, what on earth do you talk about?'

Janet was clearly becoming upset and anxious. I knew we were into 'risky story' territory and I asked if she would think of taking on some work outside the home:

> **J**:   No, because I can't really, because, I mean, he's not here and they are my responsibility. I've had them and they're mine to ... that's the way I look at it, you know ... I don't think they appreciate it ... I don't know, I don't know ... I keep threatening to leave, but I don't know where I'd go [laughs] ... you know, when I get mad and I just think ... they just think I'm here like some days I'll have a tantrum, and ... washing, I'm sick of washing ... I think that's all I'm here for, tied to the washer, and I really feel like, Oh ... I don't know, running off and getting a job ... I'll show them, type of thing ... [laughs]

This was upsetting and this confession of her frustrations and feelings of being taken for granted created, I then said, 'Perhaps the story writing's a good idea.'

J: Yes, yes, ... because I think ... what can you do in your own home? And that is something you can do in your own home ... without going out ... I mean I couldn't go out to work because of the school holidays ... but when I see some of them books in the library ... there's some real rubbish ... that's where I got the idea from.

AG: Mmm ... a lot of the famous women novelists who wrote the classics all wrote because they were confined to the home.

J: Yes, but then a lot that find that do writing, they're going out, like if they're writing about anywhere, they're going out and finding out ... I couldn't do anything about that, research ...

AG: But a lot of women write about their own experiences ...

J: Like that Barbara Taylor Bradford ... actually, she used to live in the same street as my mum and she always reads hers because, they, you know, I mean because she knew her ...

AG: Do you read them?

J: Yes, and I've seen them on TV, I enjoyed them.

AG: Would you tape those?

Thus, the dedicated researcher returns the interview to the 'safe' territory of her research framework. These lengthy extracts from my interview with Janet demonstrate her initial composure within the discourse of 'fulfilled mother and housewife' through to feelings of guilt, frustration, anger and aspiration. On a 'realist' reading of the interview this would be seen as someone contradicting herself, and certainly there is evidence of her comparing herself to others and to me in what she revealed. However, Janet demonstrates her movement in, and out of, different versions of herself. There was a point in the interview where she got into risk territory where I felt she could not re-compose herself. Hence my returning to writing and attempting to be positive about what was possible. This gave her the opportunity to re-iterate the constraints on her domestic life, but enabled her to positively consider a different future, one in which she was able to 'show them' what she could do.

Memory

As we have seen, life stories, autobiographies and testimonies involve, to a greater or lesser extent, what Ken Plummer calls 'digging about in the past' this activity is carried out in what Studs Terkel (1978) calls 'memory sites'. This metaphor is suggestive of the problematics of memory. That memory is not simply there to be re-presented in ones reflections on life, but something which must be selected, constructed and told to the listener. Understandings and conceptualisation of what memory is have undergone a number of shifts. Largely this can be seen as a move from the personal and individual memory in which the individual has a stock of memories about the past and tells them, to a sense of a collective, social or cultural dimension to memory. Here the narratives of memory are understood to be expressed within and through a framework in which certain narratives become possible. In this view certain conditions must prevail before the personal story can be told. A good example of this would be the stories of child abuse which have emerged within a social and cultural framework of recognition of the remembering or forgetting of the past and traumatic events which one undergoes. Here narratives or stories become public and can circulate, can, quite literally, be spoken. Terkel calls these frameworks, or cultural knowledges, technologies of memory that facilitate the digging around and enable particular stories to be told. All this then presents problems for questions of 'truth' or even, more modestly, what kind of 'truth' is being told. Plummer summarises the different approaches to questions of truth in life stories thus: there is a general acceptance now that life stories cannot simply be 'told', but are 'composed': 'the stories of our lives are indeed constructed, fabricated, invented, made up' (Plummer, 2001: 238). The question for the researcher is how that story is being composed, what is being 'made up' and how? This is not to say that life stories are fiction, but they are always 'artificial, variable and partial' (Alessandro Portelli, quoted in Plummer, 2001: 238).

A final quote from Myerhoff succinctly summarises what is involved in the life-history technique:

> When one takes a very long, careful life history of another person, complex changes occur between subject and object. Inventions and distortions emerge; neither party remains the same. A new creation is constituted when two points of view are engaged in examining one life. The new creation has its own integrity but should not be mistaken for the spontaneous, unframed life as lived person who existed before the interview began. This could be called an 'ethnoperson', the third person who is born by virtue of the collusion between interlocutor and subject. (1988: 281)

Textuality

In listening to personal narratives, including our own, it is clear that processes of interpretation are occurring and are necessary in analysis of the material composed. The next chapter will address questions of 'the text' as more conventionally understood, i.e. as, to paraphrase Williams, 'the documents of a culture' for example, literary work, the photograph, film, television or radio programme, advertisements, etc. but it is clear from our discussions here that personal narratives possess a 'textuality' as the enunciator of the narrative goes about the process of selection, exclusion, combination, narrative shaping which can be used to describe the production of more formal texts.

However, Ken Plummer, whose work has been an inspiration for this chapter, insists that life stories and personal narratives cannot and should not be thought of as 'texts' like any other cultural product. In his book, *Telling Sexual Stories* which, as the title suggests takes as its focus the telling of intimate personal experience, Plummer says:

> Such stories are not simply 'languages' or 'texts' or even 'discourses'. I want to move right away from the current, almost obsessive, concern of much analysis which reduces dense, empirical human life to texts. Social reality may be approached metaphorically as a text, but it is not in actuality a text. ... *the sexual stories I will be discussing must be seen to be socially produced in social contexts by embodied concrete people experiencing the thoughts and feelings of everyday life.* (1995: 16, original emphasis)

'If they are "texts", then they are texts embodied by breathing passionate people in the full stream of social life' (ibid. 16). This is an impassioned plea for a humanism and a position shared by Paul Willis. However, this entirely honourable and highly ethical stance can tend towards an over-identification with one's subject and in some instances a lack of critical distance between the researcher and their subjects. There is a fine line to be negotiated between the desire to honour and acknowledge the eloquent life stories and personal accounts given by individuals who are often disempowered and whose stories

are neither heard nor listened to and the desire to analyse and critically interpret those stories. In other words, and to return to Probyn, the far from
simple or direct relationship between the ontological and epistemological which
is the researcher's lonely problem. We could, however, take a rather different
perspective from Plummer whose concept of the text is one taken from literary
theory. A cultural studies analysis of a text would seek to contextualise, to
place the text within its process of production, distribution and consumption
and insist on understanding its worldliness, or the conditions which gave rise
to its production and shaped its consumption. Jackie Stacey, whose research
into memories of Hollywood and cinema going in the 1930s and 1940s
relied on written accounts from cinema-goers and film fans, suggests that
'These memories of Hollywood stars do need to be treated as texts *in so far
as they are forms of representation produced within certain cultural conventions'*
(1994: 76, my emphasis). She goes on to discuss the status of these accounts:

> However, to take such an approach is not to argue that what my respondents
> wrote to me is fictional, and thus of only relative significance to other fictions.
> Taking account of the narrative formations of audiences' memories is not to
> rob them of their specificity, or to treat them as fictional narratives like the
> films they were watching. This would be to confuse the categories of narrative
> and of fiction. (ibid.: 76)

And to quote Connell once more:

> There is a tendency, in recent discussions of method, to treat any story as a 'fic-
> tion' ... Any serious researcher using life-histories must be aware of these fea-
> tures of stories. But if the language is all we can see, then we are missing the
> point of a life-history - and spurning the effort that the respondents make to
> speak the truth. (1995: 91)

For Plummer, Stacey and Connell the narrative accounts of life histories and
experiences should be treated as texts which are produced through conventions of representation, and within a specific set of conditions, but always in
a way which respects the story-tellers' 'effort to truth telling'.

Issues of textuality are now turned to in the next chapter.

seven

Tying in the Texts

The main purpose of this book is to look at appropriate methodologies and methods that enable the exploration of those everyday practices which together make up lived cultures. Accounts of what people do in their daily lives and how they express the activities and the meanings those activities hold for them are an important part of many cultural studies projects. However, cultural studies is also interested in the production, circulation and consumption of 'texts' written, verbal, broadcast, visual, musical, etc. and as an interdisciplinary project, cultural studies is able to incorporate an understanding of lived practices with some exploration of the consumption and use of texts. Cultural studies has insisted upon the constitutive role of 'texts' in everyday lives and in the production of experiential accounts.

As we shall see, the research examples I draw on for this chapter seek to relate texts to their users and, in some cases, situate them within their sites of production. However, this is not to say that there is nothing to be gained from close textual analysis. For example, there has been important work which carried out 'new' readings of 'old' texts. This has been most poignantly developed within postcolonial studies (referred to in Chapter 1) in which the discourses of the text are related to their wider social and cultural context. There is much value, for instance, in indicating how the Western 'canons' of literature and art produced in the nineteenth century relate to and repeat the tropes of colonialism (the 'oriental' the 'other', etc.). This is to investigate the text in its wider socio-political historic context. Similarly, examination of visual texts, for example, early photography, can reveal important patterns of exclusion and domination rendered 'natural' in their time (Tagg, 1988). Feminist critics have brought new insights into the representations of gender and sexuality in popular forms such as film, television, advertising and the press. In the previous section we looked at life story and autobiography as important technologies providing articulated access to the past, but in many cases individuals have not survived to tell the story. What remains for the cultural historian are texts and an approach which analyses texts within a culture/power matrix can be extremely revealing (e.g. readings of government documents, press and other official reports, educational policy documents, as well as diaries, letters, and domestic photography).

So, how do we approach the text in cultural studies? If I were to single out one key factor in textual analysis for cultural studies I would once again refer to Stuart Hall's insistence that there must be 'something at stake' in carrying out the analysis, or, to use Ien Ang's term, the analysis should involve a 'cultural politics'. Thus, there must be a reason for exploring the text to be determined by asking the following questions: What is the question being put to the text and what is its point? How does the text relate to its production and its consumption and what methods have been adopted to examine those relationships? In Chapter 1, we noted the pervasiveness of texts within late modern societies and the increasing permeability of texts which demand new ways of understanding text and textuality, but also new ways of understanding the relationship between 'texts' and their 'consumers'. These challenges are the subject of this chapter. It will begin by looking at how cultural studies has approached the text and textual analysis and follow by looking at research which has attempted to 'tie in the text' to lived cultures and everyday life.

Texts and their analysis are at the heart of the humanities but from the early stages of its development cultural studies diverged from the ways in which texts were dealt with in the academy. Raymond Williams, for example, identified the construction of a canon of 'English' Literature which was selective and exclusive. He argued that literary texts, often valued as timeless and universal and of unquestioned 'quality', were a product of social and political formations, as were their election and acceptance into the 'canon'. This both deconstructed the canon as selective and exclusive, but methodologically, questioned the status of 'the text' as the central and unquestioned focus of attention. Richard Hoggart insisted that literature departments should address forms of communication other than literature, e.g. the popular press, women's magazines, and popular literature and should find appropriate ways of analysing them. Two factors underpin the early development of cultural studies' approaches to text: the visual and the popular. Ways had to be found of critically analysing the visual and the popular which held on to the specificity of such texts and did not carry the value judgements of 'the canon'

Semiotics

Structuralism and semiotics offered 'scientific' modes of textual analysis which avoided impressionistic forms of analysis. The aim here was to identify underlying, and repeated, narrative structures of the text. Cultural studies drew on the work done by Vladimir Propp on the analysis of fairy tales identifying underlying structures which could then be detected in a wide range of texts both 'literary' and 'popular', e.g. drama, the novel, films, folk-tales, etc. (Propp, 1968). Also, Roland Barthes' (1977) semiotic analysis of visual and other forms of representation employing the concepts of myth and ideology enabled scholars to analyse pervasive forms such as advertising. Through these theoretical developments the texts could be seen as significant in themselves, rather than, for example, reflections of an outer reality. The questions raised by semiotics are how texts produce meaning, rather than the search for meaning itself which had informed earlier analysis. It is true, however, that Barthes and his followers sought to detect the ideological operations of such texts in, for example, naturalising social hierarchies and other aspects of social and cultural life. Thus, 'the family' was portrayed as the 'natural' unit of living, along with heterosexual romance, femininity and masculinity. However, the quest for underlying 'universal' narrative structures ran the risk of evacuating any kind of context for the text. This context would include a sense of the historical, the social and the political as well as the mode of production and reception of the text. While cultural studies drew on more formalistic modes of textual analysis, there have been a number of moves which have attempted to explore the historical, social and political dimensions of the symbolic and the cultural embedded within the texts or documents of a culture. What follows is an account of the travails of the text within cultural studies with particular emphasis on methods of analysis.

The all-determining text

The ideological paradigm suggested that texts were shaped by strong ideologies which operated in the main to mask the workings of an exploitative system, whether that was understood as capitalism and the exploitation of labour, or patriarchy and exploitation of women. Textual analyses were then undertaken to identify the ideological messages or assumptions of the texts and in some studies audiences and readers were simply assumed to inhabit the ideological framework of the text and in others questions were asked of audiences/readers as to how they interpreted or made sense of the text. This strong version of the determination of the text informed a number of projects within cultural studies, especially those which sought to analyse the output of 'mass' media and other popular forms. Early experiments with textual analysis via cultural studies insisted that popular texts be taken seriously and that appropriate modes of analysis be established. Frameworks were developed which, drawing on structuralism, sought to locate the organising principles of meaning within texts which were largely identified as ideological, for example, as demonstrating and celebrating capitalist values, patriarchy, white dominance and rendering these as natural. Texts worked ideologically, argued these analyses, and their 'popularity' or 'mass appeal' was seen as evidence of the maintenance and reproduction of capitalist and patriarchal society. Marxist and feminist politics informed these analyses and tended to make certain assumptions about the ways in which readers or users of these texts would be positioned by them and, in turn, influenced by them (Williamson, 1978; Winship, 1987). Initially very little attention was paid to actual readers. In these, and other analyses, connections were made between social structure and ideology i.e. traditional femininity and masculinity and the representations within the texts, asserting the ways in which certain kinds of values and belief systems were rendered natural through popular culture. A relationship between popular texts and the broader society was often simply assumed rather than demonstrated through an understanding of actual readers and viewers.

Clearly, an understanding of the significance of popular texts within society, the ways in which they are consumed and the meanings which people might take from them are an appropriate field for cultural studies but there are some tricky ontological and epistemological problems to be faced in setting up a piece of research through which to examine this relationship.

Encoding/decoding model: the 'semiotic' and the 'social'

In what is now acknowledged as a 'first attempt' at formulating a model of 'meaning making' in the communication process, Stuart Hall proposed that the process of textual readings must be considered as consisting of at least two related instances. First, the process of meaning production, which involves all those practices and procedures involved in the putting together of a cultural text. Hall was particularly interested in understanding the production of television texts in this way. The second instance was that of 'reading' when the viewer engaged with the text. The first instance involves encoding particular meaning(s) through the use of codes and conventions available and appropriate to the particular type of programming and the second proposed an active role for a socially constructed audience. His reasons for developing this model were strategic in that it was a challenge to the then dominant communication model and to existing positivistic notions of content analysis and audience understanding. Hall's model insists that meaning is multi-layered/multi-referential and, as such, imported the then new fields of semiotics and structuralism into the study of mass communication. Also, for Hall, the model was part of a wider debate within Marxism itself and signals the move from the over-determination of the dominant ideology thesis to the more complex notion suggested by Gramsci's hegemony model. However, the encoding/decoding model was concerned with power, specifically with the idea of the encoding of 'preferred meanings' into media products. These are the product of institutional processes, working within the broader cultural and ideological world and, Hall suggests, working within the dominant ideology.

Hall's suggestive model provided the theoretical framework for the groundbreaking *Nationwide* study (Morley, 1980) which brought together the constructed text (Brunsdon and Morley, 1978) with its perceived preferred reading and the interpreting groups of readers with their determinations. The

Nationwide study sought to combine textual construction and interpretation, it granted viewers interpretative status (but always within shaping structural determinations) and developed ways of conceiving of the audience as socially structured suggesting that decoding is not homogeneous. Using this conception of a socially structured audience, Morley and Brunsdon had previously carried out a specific textual analysis of the early evening magazine programme, which identified its ideological terrain and the dominant or preferred meanings generated. The text was shown to 29 already established occupational groups whose members occupied different positions within the social structure, followed by interviews designed to reveal the extent to which the groups accepted, negotiated or opposed the preferred meaning in the decoding process. The project challenged both the predominant conceptions of the audience, reformulating this into an active, socially constituted one, and those theories which privileged the text as the site of meaning, leaving no space for the active reading subject.

While this study significantly attempted a 'double move' into the notion of the socially constructed audience and ideologically constructed text, it also shifted from 'straight' news and current affairs to an understanding of the encoding of the more popular 'entertainment' magazine format of *Nationwide*. It thus challenged the 'hard news' focus of existing work, it placed textuality clearly in the communication dynamic and it was suggestive of different reader positions.

The limitations of the *Nationwide* study were acknowledged by Morley in a postscript to the study. These are: the 'contrived', non-domestic, setting of the viewing groups – which took place in their work-place; the possibility of contradictory decodings which subjects may make across different types of texts and within different contexts; the specific genres preferred by particular sub-groups of the audience.

Here the relationship of the text to reader was heavily determined and rather static, with an assumed reader whose interpretations and reading positions 'matched' the textual analysis. The model also implied a distinction between text, as an isolatable and analysable object, and the reader or audience as the other dimension of the model. These problems are interesting and are a salutory reminder of the value of empirical work in allowing us to interrogate such theoretical or conceptual models. The shortcomings of the decoding model were:

1   The notion of the preferred meaning of the text applied to 'factual' products: how could it be understood in relation to other genres, such as, say, the soap opera?

2   The model was too linear, and therefore similar to previous communication models which implied sender, text, receiver. Also, the tendency was towards a conveyor belt of content, upon which the 'preferred meaning' travelled to the decoder.

3   The decoding process suggests a 'single act of reading' the text
(Morley, 1992: 121) rather than allowing for a mixture of processes of
recognition, attention, relevance, choice and competence.

Hall insists that if the model has '*any* purchase, now and later, it's a model
because of what it suggests. It suggests an approach; it opens up new questions. It maps the terrain. But it's a model which has to be worked with and
developed and changed' (Cruz and Lewis, 1994: 255). Hall locates the
encoding/decoding paper at a conjuncture, or paradigm shift. He characterises it as the one which Barthes made 'from the interpretation of the codes
into the notion of textuality, and then later into the notion of desire and the
pleasure of the text'. He sees this as a key development which 'took cultural
studies from communication studies to literary theory, to the cinematic text,
to psychoanalysis, to feminism, and to the beginnings of post structuralism'
(ibid.: 271).

Just as the notion of the encoding part of the process was problematic, so
the way of understanding readers, viewers or decoders was found wanting.
This was seen to be sociologically limited, with the emphasis on ideology constructing the audience in relation to class distinction. This ignored other
dimensions of difference, such as gender, ethnicity and age. The three reading positions which Hall proposed did not allow for sufficient variation, or
sub-variations within reading positions, not did they allow for difference of
context or initial reasons for wanting to watch the programme/text.

Morley's response to these shortcomings was to try to find ways of exploring choice and genre competence in relation to texts and different contexts
and the way in which they shaped or pressured different interpretations and
readings. This research trajectory took him from the notion of de-coding
upon which he focused in the *Nationwide* audience study to the viewing context in his project *Family Television* (see Chapter 3) in which he quotes
Richard Dyer who insightfully suggests in his attempt at interpreting *Victim*:

> One cannot conclude from a person's class, race, gender, sexual orientation
> and so on, how she or he will read a given text (though these factors do indi-
> cate what cultural code she or he has access to). It is also a question of how
> she or he thinks and feels about living her/his social situation. (Dyer, R.
> '*Victim*: Hermeneutic Project' in *Film Form*, vol. 1, no. 2. Autumn 1977,
> quoted in Morley, 1986: 43)

Morley goes further and paraphrases Sartre 'it is a question of what we make
of what history has made of us' (Morley, 1985: 43). The problem had then
become a search for a method which would enable the exploration of the
complex social subject in history and the ways in which she/he inhabits the
cultural dimension of her/his life without, on the one hand, implying a
mechanistic and deterministic relationship to the deep structures, and on the
other sliding into methodological individualism. In other words, the project

became one of finding a way of understanding the dialectic between the social determinants and the active human subject as they map into the cultural sphere. The studies which began to look at the context and social practice associated with popular forms, especially television, moved the focus away from 'the text' altogether and research became much more 'audience led'. This led to concern about the loss of the text and Charlotte Brunsdon (1981) insisted that studies should explore 'the interplay of social reader and social text'.

The suggestive text

This tension is at the heart of the cultural studies approach to texts. It expresses the way in which cultural studies straddles the humanities (text-based) and the social sciences (empirical world) and this tension can still be felt in current debates about cultural studies. I now want to return to developments in forms of textual analysis before looking at examples of further research.

Hall notes the important contribution made to the development of the *Nationwide* study by Charlotte Brunsdon who was beginning to work on the analysis of popular television genres from a feminist perspective (Cruz and Lewis, 1994: 272). The encoding/decoding model gestured towards the influences of structuralism and semiotics, and at the same time textual analyses of popular entertainment genres which were identifying reader/subject positions offered by the text were also coming from literary and film theory, especially from a feminist perspective. Feminist film theory has for the past three decades produced challenging and important work largely based on he textual analysis of film. As an important cultural artefact and one with which cultural studies has also been concerned, it is useful to take a brief look at the different approaches and theories employed.

Psychoanalytic theory has informed much critical feminist work on film and this has in the main been based in textual analysis. Important here is the way in which these critical analyses have insisted on the specificity of the visual (see Rose, 2001, as a useful practical text in visual methodologies) That is to say, the conventions and characteristics of the visual text have received their close attention. The approaches have explored the psychic structuring of film, and in particular, the Hollywood film. They have emphasised the role of such popular texts in producing sexual differentiation. While these analyses have been extremely useful in revealing the 'unconscious' of cinematic forms, their exponents in the main were not interested in 'actual audiences'. There was, therefore, little attempt to examine empirically the way in which the films worked for different audiences. In her discussion of feminist film analysis, Jackie Stacey draws attention to two writers who are brutally frank about this lack of interest. Mary Ann Doane says, 'I have never thought of the female spectator as synonymous with the woman sitting in front of the screen, munching her popcorn ... The female spectator is a concept, not a person'

(Doane, 1989: 142, quoted in Stacey, 1994: 23) In a similar vein, Guiliana Bruno says 'I am not interested in an empirical analysis of the phenomenon of female spectatorship ... I cannot get over an old semiotic diffidence for any notion of empirical "truth"' (Bruno, 1989: 106,quoted in Stacey, 1994: 23).

This staggering disregard for the social dimensions of cinema and the meanings and interpretations which different cinema goings might produce is probably what led cultural studies researchers to react so much against film theory. However, the important question which these textual analyses raise is that this approach to texts identified the spectator in the text – the spectator is, as Doane suggests, a concept and not a real person. Other feminist scholars turned their attention to popular forms such as television, but we can see that although she gestures outwards to the reader, she remains firmly within the text.

Tania Modleski, for example, provided a textual analysis of US daytime television which assumed an ideal reader, distracted, rendered incapable of concentrated and focused viewing (Modleski, 1983). Her more detailed analysis of the structure of the soap opera, such as its multiple storylines and the possibility of multiple character identifications inscribes, according to Modleski (1982), the 'ideal viewer/reader as an "ideal" mother'. In the UK scholars were also looking closely at the soap opera in terms of their strong female characters (Dyer et al., 1981), but a more complex formulation of text and reader pleasures came from Brunsdon's suggestion that pleasures offered by soaps required particular 'feminine' skills and competencies, e.g. 'reading' emotional turmoil, understanding the complexities of familial relationships, which were, in turn, validated within the text, e.g. a foregrounding of the domestic and the everyday (Brunsdon, 1981).

In her more recent study of the feminist analysis of soap opera Brunsdon notes how psychoanalytic theories of fantasy, pleasure and desire have been routinely applied to investigations of 'non-realist' texts, such as fantasy genres, melodrama, etc. while analysis of British 'realist' products have been limited to a realist mode (Brunsdon, 2000: 66). This can also be applied to the ways in which viewers or users of these forms have been conceptualised. Thus, cinema viewers are afforded fantasy, desire and pleasure while television viewers are assumed to have a much more rational relationship with the form, and especially relate to the form in a much more social way – whether in terms of their role as women or how they use the texts, storylines, characters to make sense of their world, to converse with others, etc. Brunsdon insists that if 'ideas of fantasy allow us to conceptualize one of the ways in which readers/viewers invest in fictional narrative ... there is an impoverishing literalism in making this investment genre/mode specific' (ibid.: 67). Brunsdon goes on to discuss the significance of fantasies of achieved or successful femininity which the British soap opera can offer. However, we can use Brunsdon's arguments to extend our understanding of the relationship between viewer/reader/users of popular forms.

In the early forms of textual analyses adopted by cultural studies scholars, the reader/viewer stepped into and out of the text and as such they can be seen as significant inter-disciplinary 'moments' within the development of cultural studies. Thus, while the text was understood to offer 'preferred' reading viewer/interpretative positions, the questions begged were about how and in what ways were actual readers taking up those positions. A number of studies mobilised these questions in relation to popular genres; Hobson on the then popular British soap opera *Crossroads*, Ang, and Katz and Liebes on *Dallas* and Buckingham on *EastEnders* (Hobson, 1982; Ang, 1995; Liebes and Katz, 1993; Buckingham, 1987). In the second half of this chapter I look in some detail at more recent studies which have used different methods for 'tying in the text'. The studies represent developments in 'audience' research in terms of its method and practice. As we will see from these examples, the studies represent different questions and problematics, different ways of conceptualising 'the audience' and especially in relation to everyday life. The studies also reflect major changes in national and transnational media landscapes.

Janice Radway: *Reading the Romance*

In her introduction to the British edition of *Reading the Romance* (1987) Janice Radway speaks of her ignorance of British cultural studies before embarking on her study of female romance readers in the United States. Her study was inspired by a desire to investigate the consumption of the widest selling popular genre - the romance (published by Harlequin in the USA and Mills and Boon in the UK). She was also responding to the refusal of her discipline American Studies to take these texts seriously and to find appropriate ways of analysing the text and to investigate the interpretations which 'real' readers make of these texts.

> To know ... why people do what they do, read romances, for example, it becomes necessary to discover the constructions they place on their behaviour, the interpretations they make of their actions. A good cultural analysis of the romance ought to specify not only how the women understand the novels themselves but also how they comprehend the very act of picking up a book in the first place. (Radway, 1984: 8)

In addition to this aim, Radway insists on the importance of understanding the processes and strategies of romance publication and marketing. Within the context of her study of the cultural industries of publishing and production of popular romance fiction, she analyses the romance genre, but also explores how these novels are used by a group of identified romance 'fans', in their everyday lives.

As we noted above, Brunsdon and Morley, working within the encoding/decoding model, carried out a semiotic analysis of a number of *Nationwide* programmes, identifying the preferred meaning against which audience readings could be measured. The bridge between text and audience/reader was established by an academic or 'expert' reading of the text and the differential interpretations made by the readers. Radway's strategy differed dramatically from this in that she first of all established, through questionnaires, group discussions and individual interviews, which romance titles the women in her study held up as 'good' romances and, conversely, which they considered to be 'bad' romances. Working with these two clusters of texts she then carried out a structural analysis of texts within each group in an attempt to identify the sequences of narrative functions contained in the texts. In addition, acknowledging the weakness of a purely structural analysis, she identified the kinds of characters appearing in the texts as the women themselves had perceived them. Radway's purpose in doing this analysis was to go into more depth about the pleasures gained from reading romance literature. Radway listened to what the women had to say about their likes and dislikes, allowing this to inform her analytical framework. But she wanted more explanatory power than the women's expressions could afford. 'Consequently, I have used this set to probe into the psychological significance of the genre for its readers and to infer further unconscious needs that underpin and reinforce the more conscious motives investigated earlier that prompt them to seek out the romantic fantasy' (Radway, 1984: 120).

The important point here is that her analysis was led by her interview data, not imposed upon it from an intellectual or theoretical perspective. Here we can see Radway's attempt at creating a dialogue between her respondent's readings and a theoretical framework developed within structuralist literary theory. Radway allowed her respondents to determine which texts should be included in the study and she also drew on their own analysis and interpretation of the texts themselves. Her emphasis on the importance of the 'actual act of reading' enabled Radway to suggest that the consumption of such popular genres performed a function over and above the texts themselves. For the women in her study this was a form of resistance to the obligations and constraints imposed upon them within the confines of traditional heterosexual family life. Her study used a mixture of methods: textual analysis, research into the publishing industry, questionnaires, group discussions and interviews, as well as forming friendship with one of her key informants in the group. The next example I want to discuss draws on much more intense group discussions to produce a discursive analysis of 'television talk'.

David Buckingham: children talking television

David Buckingham's consistently thoughtful and painstaking work on children and television stems from his primary interest in media education and media literacy and especially how critics and educators alike tend to devalue children's media literacy. This, he argues, leads to patronising approaches to education and to over-protective strategies of parenting. His research strategy, therefore, across a number of years, has been to find ways of demonstrating how young people actively make sense of television and the ways in which they use sophisticated categories and criteria in their readings. Buckingham's strategy has been to create situations whereby children are encouraged to talk about television. Buckingham treats the social act and process of 'television talk' not as 'product'-focused, but as a site where identities and subject positions are constituted. Television use and interpretation are not simply about how children occupy different subject positions.

> Social positions and biological categories are obviously determined by material factors; yet their meanings are actively constructed and negotiated, defined and redefined, in the process of talk. What it means to be male or female, working-class or middle-class, black or white, an adult or a child, is not given or pre-determined. (Buckingham, 1993: 268)

For Buckingham, then, different ways of 'talking about television are thus not simply a reflection of children's given social relationships and identities. On the contrary, it is at least partly through talking about television that those identities and relationships themselves are constructed and defined' (ibid.: 269). Buckingham wants to investigate how televisual discourses both frame and enable active engagement with the meanings generated through texts. In a study published in 1993, Buckingham and his colleagues carried out interviews with groups of 5 children aged between 7 and 12 as well as more focused activities. The interviews and activities were undertaken in the children's schools and Buckingham is appropriately reflexive about the significance of the context and the roles of the researchers in relation to the children. However, in the early stages of the project the researchers simply said to the children 'We want to find out about what you think about television', going on to ask 'What do you like about television?' This relatively unfocused approach enabled the researchers to identify both the kinds of television the children watched and also to follow up with discussions around the ways in which the children 'inhabited' these programmes. As noted above, Buckingham was centrally interested in the importance of television talk to the children's development of identity and subject positions. This kind of data gave Buckingham clues as to the textual universe which the children inhabit and a sense of their textual tactics from which significant categories emerged, such as genre, modality, audience, narrative, character. Buckingham and his colleagues explored these tactics and categorisations in order to reveal the ways in which children actively engage with television.

Radway and Buckingham provide examples of attempts to conceptualise the relationships between popular texts and the users or readers. They employ a range of empirical methods which provide rich data to be subjected to different analytical frameworks. For Radway drawing on structuralist literary theories and psychoanalytic object relations and for Buckingham, discourse analysis and theories of identity. The following three examples are what might described as 'media ethnographies' in that the researchers carried out extended periods of study with their respondents and draw on more anthropologically and sociologically informed strategies.

Marie Gillespie: television, ethnicity and cultural change

Marie Gillespie's ethnography of 'young Punjabi Londoners' explores in great detail the ways in which television is central to the formation and trans-formation of identity within this group. Her aims are to mobilise broader questions of the 'transnationalisation' of culture(s) by examining them from the local and domestic point of view (Gillespie, 1995). Gillespie began by drawing on a broader survey of young people in the Southall area of London which identified particular uses of television within her target group, but in the main she allows specific favoured genres to emerge from listening to the young people's 'talk'. These genres were introduced by members of the group in the 'Did you see ...?' mode of general social conversation. Neale's very useful definition of 'genre' is apposite: 'genres are not to be seen as forms of textual codifications, but as systems of orientations, expectations and conventions that circulate between industry, text and subject' (Neale, 1981: 19). The three genres identified for special consideration and interest were TV news, soap opera and advertising. Gillespie is interested in the ways in which these genres address young people differently 'News addresses young people as citizens, soaps address them as social actors, ads address them as consumers' (Gillespie, 1995: 26). This broad attention to generic categories of texts enables her to explore how the young people inhabit the different reading positions offered within their discussions about television and how the themes, topics and issues which arise within the texts are negotiated in terms of their individual and collective identities. In common with Buckingham, Gillespie believes that attention to 'TV talk' is to be understood as the site of 'recreative reception' (a term taken from Cheesman, 1994).

> TV talk is not only a form of social interaction integral to the peer group's sense of common identity. It furnishes and refines shared cultural resources which young people collectively harness, for purposes of comparison and cri-tique, as they negotiate relations within the peer group, with parents and other elders, and with the 'significant others' of the wider world, in Britain, in the Punjabi diaspora, and beyond. TV talk is a major forum for contest and debate over 'old' and 'new' identities, and for the formulation of cosmopolitan aspi-rations. (Gillespie, 1995: 24)

Gillespie listens to the way in which television reception is constitutive in everyday talk in opening up spaces for shifting subject positions for a group of young people who are part of a broad Indian diaspora located in London. Her study also has a chapter on the viewing of 'sacred texts' and explores how these are consumed within families and households as important vehicles for the translation of tradition between generations. Gillespie insists that her approach requires a full and extended ethnography.

Purnima Mankekar: screening culture, viewing politics

Purnima Mankekar was also interested in interpretations of a popular form, in her case popular entertainment television, and specifically within the context of family life. She carried out ethnographic research in New Delhi, India, analysing how the popular entertainment forms of the Indian state broadcasting organisation, Doordarshan, are attempting to construct a 'new' national identity around tropes of 'development' and 'consumption'. Her thesis suggests that the Indian woman is central to this construct and her ethnographic study of viewing families looks at how these representations are negotiated within the formation of class and gender identities: 'I became increasingly interested in understanding the relationship between the narratives of Doordarshan programmes and those that viewers wove of their own lives, between popular culture and viewers' perceptions of themselves and Indian men and women' (Mankekar, 1999: 8).

Her approach sought to place the subjects of her study within their social and cultural context and her analysis 'highlights the fact that meaning is unstable: it is frequently contested by viewers who are historical subjects living in particular discursive formations rather than positioned by a single text' (ibid.: 8).

The use of notions of 'discursive formation' and reference to the instability of meaning indicate Mankekar's approach to textuality and the interpretations made. She wished to explore the ways in which a state broadcasting organisation mobilised versions of Indian womanhood in their attempt to (re)construct ideas of the nation and national identity. Following the liberalisation of India's economy, the encouragement of a consumer culture and 'middle class life style' became important for the success of these new policies. Thus the state broadcasting channel began transmitting aspirational fictional series, especially focusing on women's lives. Although Mankekar was interested in the texts themselves, she saw them as products emerging from and circulating within a specific formation of discursive strategies. And, of course, the audience for these very popular series also inhabited these discourses. We can see, then, that Mankekar's 'text' is not only linked to the reader/viewer, but also connected to the wider social and cultural discourses of gender, class and nationhood. Her research asked: 'What subject positions were created for women at the center, so to speak, of nationalist discourses?' (ibid.: 16). Mankekar used the Gramscian concept of hegemony as she focused on viewers' negotiation of televisual narratives in her attempt to 'emphasize the inherently unstable nature of hegemonic discourses' (ibid.: 19).

A popular text, such as a long-running serial has the capacity, she suggests of 're-ordering collective memory through acts of remembering and forget-ting'. Her intention within her project is 'to show how realms of our identi-ties that we might mistakenly relegate to the "innermost recesses" of subjectivity might, in fact, be constituted through mass media, such as televi-sion' (ibid.: 18).

Mankekar's study affords emphatic intent to the texts – not simply that they play a didactic role (cf. Brazilian *telenovela*'s role in health care, edu-cation, etc.) but in suggesting new formations of identity, new senses of subjectivity and nationhood, in (re)constructing narratives of nation. Mankekar insists that the text is inextricably linked to the context of its con-sumption. Therefore, her choice of method should enable her to explore this context. Her choice of ethnography led her to view television with the dif-ferent household members in her study as well as to conduct individual inter-views. She insists that 'the analysis of television cannot be reduced to the text on the screen, but instead must extend to the spaces occupied by television in the daily lives and practices of viewers' (ibid.: 20).

Looking at the constitution of women viewers as national and gendered subjects she aimed, through her ethnography, to 'represent women's narra-tives and practices as *enactments* of their interpellation by television's dis-courses' (ibid.: 23, original emphasis). Thus, her aim is to go beyond understanding meanings and interpretations made by viewers and to look at the ways in which texts weave in and out of everyday life with material con-sequences. But how does she integrate the text into daily life? She argues that, although viewer interpretation and analysis are the core of her study, she pres-ents specific television narratives as nodes of discourses and sees these as rep-resentative of *discontinuities* in what is an attempt, as she sees it, of the television narratives to present unified subject positions around gender, class and nationhood and especially for women viewers. The text itself, then, is much less fixed and stable, but can be understood as overlapping with and seeping into these broader discourses. Mankekar analysed several pro-grammes produced by Doordashan with special emphasis on what she called 'woman-oriented' programmes, looking for common themes within the nar-ratives across the different texts. Thus, all these narratives were set within 'the family', and themes such as gender and class, unmarried women as daughters, married women as daughters-in-law, education and the 'uplift' of women were identified by Mankekar and her viewers. The themes dealt with the fig-uration of Indian womanhood as *both* modern and traditional, thus attempt-ing to unify within the narrative the often highly contradictory subject positions inhabited by Indian women from a working class background (ibid.: 104-62). What is especially interesting about Mankekar's approach is that her textual analysis is interspersed with 'scenes' or 'moments' of observation or conversations from her ethnography which resonate with the discourses iden-tified in the analysis. Thus she avoids the common pattern of separation of text and viewer by insisting that the two must be thought of together in the ways in which the (especially female) viewers are positioned. In addition to the address to the texts, Mankekar also interviewed the writer and director of one of the popular series. She insists that this is not to give authorial agency to the producers, but it serves to give her study another level of material. She identified the discourses informing their accounts of their approach to and involvement in the production of the television series as a significant element of the 'nodes of discourse' from which the textual and the viewing practices emerge. Thus the text and ethnography are interwoven throughout *Screening Culture, Viewing Politics* and this impressive study goes a long way towards satisfying Brunsdon's call to produce studies of socially produced texts and audiences.

Thomas Tufte: *living with the Rubbish Queen*

In a similarly complex and multi-layered study, Thomas Tufte (2000) argues the case for the media ethnography as a set of methods which can capture the ubiquitous nature of the media. His study of the history, production and reception of the Brazilian *telenovela* in three different regions of Brazil, is impressive in that he uses a range of methods which include quantitative survey, qualitative interviews and participant observation, including photography to examine that remarkable and distinctive popular cultural form, the *telenovela*. Tufte provides the reader with information on the particular Latin American/Brazilian context and, drawing on Martin-Barbero, suggests that:

> Whether it takes the form of a tango, a soap opera, a Mexican film or a cheap crime story, the melodrama taps into and stirs up a deep vein of collecting cultural imagination. And there is no access to historical memory or projection of dreams into the future which does not pass through this cultural imagination. (Martin-Barbero 1993)

In insisting on the importance of locally grounded cultural research, Tufte's work recognises what scholars such as Canclini mean when they talk of 'another modernity existing in Latin America'. Tufte concludes that as a Danish researcher it was important that he interrogated the assumptions made by and within 'western' audience and reception studies. For example, like Irene Penacchioni, he draws attention to the public nature of television in Brazil. Penacchioni suggests that television exists in a 'sound space in which there is no split between inside and outside, between the private sphere of intimacy and silence on the one hand, and the collective public sphere of togetherness and communication on the other (1984: 340)

Penacchioni was speaking of her observations in Fortaleza, North-east Brazil, but Ondina Fachel Leal, working in Porto Alegre in the South East also notes some distinctions in the place of television in society (Leal, 1990). She notes the importance, in working class households, of the public display of the television set. Thus the television set is always visible from the street and embellished by artefacts such as embroidered cloths, vases of flowers which she describes as the TV entourage, the display of which signifies modernity, urban rationality and aspiration to the passer-by.

Tufte, whose studies took place in different regions of Brazil, also notes the blurring of the public and private in the neighbourhoods and how television is articulated within what he describes as a 'hybrid sphere' of signification. Along with the very different organisation of time and space in routine daily life, these distinctions reveal much of what is assumed in western studies and alert us to the specificities of theoretical and methodological frameworks.

Tufte's 'micro-sociological' study in three different neighbourhoods looks at the social relations of viewing, organisation of time and space and the gossip networks within which *telenovelas* are central. He suggests that *telenovelas* have potential for the construction and articulation of what he calls 'cultural citizenship'. Within the often harsh socio-economic conditions his respondents demonstrated, in their social and cultural practices, for example, religious beliefs, aspirations, dreams and hopes for the future and Tufte's analysis suggests that the *telenovela* is central to these intimate and public negotiations.

These examples of media ethnography have responded to the deeply embedded nature of popular cultural forms, such as television and film, finding ways of exploring them in their dynamic processes and practice. Mankekar, Gillespie and Tufte have refused to separate the text from its fullest context, even analytically, insisting that this false move evacuates much of the actual complexity of media use. In addition, Radway, Mankekar and Tufte have provided a critical account of the production of the popular forms which are central to the readers/viewers in their study and in this way they are presenting a multi-layered and complex analysis of the cultural process.

In different ways these studies are concerned to place media readings and use within complex webs of determinations, not only of the texts and the contexts of their consumption, but also those deeper structural determinants, such as class, gender and, still, to a lesser extent, race and ethnicity. These studies have also shed light on the ways in which public and private discourses intersect and are lived out within the intimate and routine practices of daily life. In addition, all reflect on their research methods, and especially the location of the researcher in her or his study and Mankekar and Tufte, from different vantage points, raise critical questions about the dominance of the West in the definitions of 'knowledge sites' and the assumptions made by western frameworks. Thus, in spite of their small scale, each, in different ways, poses broader questions of structure and agency within the socially structured world of practices and subjectivity, and many reflect on the institutional context of research itself. What underpins the questions and problematics of the studies are those of agency and structure. Studies show how the public and the private are absorbed into the everyday, the mundane, the ordinary. Such studies recognise the false distinctions between micro and macro, between text and the contexts of its production and consumption, and demonstrate how discourses flow in and out of constructions of identity, self, private and public, national, local and global. Boundaries, thus, are permeable, unstable and uneasy, demanding a new way of thinking and looking at the 'audience', the user, the text and the complexity of relations and discourses that surround and are part of it.

Turkle, Jenkins and *Big Brother*

It is perhaps the case that the above examples are near to the 'peoples and culture' model of anthropology. Although all three ethnographers are aware of the constitutive role of culture which is not bounded by space and place, nevertheless, their studies focus on a bounded community, or, in Tufte's case, communities for their empirical research. I want to conclude this chapter by looking briefly at other kinds of community, already referred to in Chapter 3: the fan community. Along with new communications and entertainment technologies which are being made increasingly available, come new textual (and intertextual) forms and new kinds of 'audiences', if that term can be used to describe users of the Internet or active members of fan sub-cultures. The term audience does not now seem to grasp the complex range of activities which are involved in the engagement with certain forms of popular culture.

Sherry Turkle has studied computer use over the last decade. Her most recent study looks at users of the Internet. Here users interact with both the 'virtual text' and with other previously unknown individuals. As a psychologist she is interested in questions of identity and how the metaphor of 'machine' is increasingly being used to describe human activity, especially, she argues, in relation to the computer. She explores the ways in which humans relate to the machine and the potential that Internet sites, such as chat lines and multi-user domains offer for performance of multiple identities. Clearly, the development of such practices and potential crosses a number of boundaries – space and time, geographical boundaries – but also the boundaries we have assumed between the 'text' and the 'reader' Furthermore, for Turkle, 'the new practice of entering virtual worlds raises fundamental questions about our communities and ourselves' (1995: 232). She notes that her respondents' pleasures in their uses of the Internet are neither 'escape' nor 'resistance' but rather involve building an 'alternative reality'. Fiske describes the activities of fans of popular forms thus:

- Semiotic productivity: making meanings (essentially interior).

- Enunciative productivity: fan talk within a local community.

- Textual productivity: zines, web-sites and more ambitious artefacts. (Fiske, 1992: 35)

Henry Jenkins in his study of Trekkies describes fan reading as: a social process through which individual interpretations are shaped and reinforced through ongoing discussions with other readers (1992: 45). In support of this argument, he quotes fan writer Jean Lorrah:

> Trekfandom ... is friends and letters and crafts and fanzines and trivia and costumes and artwork and folksongs and buttons and film clips and conventions - something for everybody who has in common the inspiration of a television show which grew far beyond its TV and film incarnations to become a living part of world culture (ibid.: 45)

As Jenkins suggests, many of the traditionally assumed boundaries, such as that between producer and consumer and between commercial and creative products are broken down. 'Fandom here becomes a participatory culture which transforms the experience of media consumption into the production of new texts, indeed of a new culture and a new community' (ibid.: 46).

Turkle's and Jenkins' work indicates the ways in which the audience/text/everyday life problematic is shifting along with technological and other media imperatives. While earlier audience studies sought to examine the understandings which readers brought to texts, researchers must now look at how audiences are intervening in texts. Although texts themselves have long been intertextual, the active and participatory 'audience' is now providing yet another text in the production of popular forms. A particular, and contemporary example, is the latest television 'reality' show *Big Brother* which originated in The Netherlands, but has been screened in different versions in the UK, Europe and the USA. *Big Brother* is a 'multi-platform' product. It is a complex TV genre combining game-show and 'fly-on-the-wall' documentary in which a number of people are confined within one house, but with connected web-sites enabling viewers to vote for which member should leave. The remaining individual, i.e. the most popular, gets a large cash prize. In the UK, the show, while taking some time to build up an audience, became, through tabloid and other media exposure, a big talking point. Even if you had not seen *Big Brother*, you knew about it in the summer of 2000. Ticknell and Raghuram point to the 'sheer availability of access to *Big Brother* across multiple sites such as the on-line diaries, the web-cam, the official web-sites, the chat-sites, together with the take-up of the show by other more traditional media' (Ticknell and Raghuram, 2001). This confounds any attempt to identify, or locate, or say who is the audience for this product. The activities and the engagement with the 'text' are multiple, can happen 24 hours a day. At the very least, these developments require us to re-think the relationship between audience and media.

What this work within cultural studies suggests is the impossibility of dealing with texts as isolated and separable from their context. The false division between the 'textual' and the 'social' is certainly a consequence of disciplinarity, but one advantage of an interdisciplinary approach such as cultural studies to the social and cultural processes of making meaning, is that this boundary can be usurped. As Richard Johnson has argued, at its best cultural studies has worked across this division. However, just how this can be achieved is certainly an issue.

Looking at some examples enables us to identify the shift from what we might call the 'ideological' paradigm across to the 'discursive' paradigm. This suggests that a cultural studies approach to 'texts' is always as part of their broader context. And importantly the analysis and understanding of those texts begin from and through the reader/subjects in the case of reader/audience/use studies; in relation to broader social and historical discourses and in relation to the institutions and organisations which produce those texts. The discourse approach indicates an understanding of narratives or cultural repertoires upon which the texts are constructed and to which the readers/users have access in constructing their own interpretations and readings of the texts. The studies we have looked at in this chapter have all produced rich and interesting data/material. The following chapter turns to questions of analysis.

eight	Strategies and Tactics in Analysis

Many researchers are now writing about their role and position within the research process, and especially, as we have seen, in relation to 'field work' of different kinds. However, the ways in which researchers go about organising and analysing their data and research material are rarely discussed. This is strange because, arguably, this is one of the most creative parts of the process where the researcher puts their own unique stamp on the project through their interpretation and analysis. There are some notable, and welcome, exceptions to this rule, for example, Joke Hermes and Bob Connell, whose research publications, *Reading Women's Magazines* and *Masculinities* include discussions of their methods of analysis and Wendy Hollway whose monograph, *Subjectivity and Method in Psychology*, reflects on her own research methods. These authors will be discussed later in this chapter.

We are concerned here with the analysis and interpretation of research material. Quite simply, to analyse something, be it interview data, document or visual text, is to take it apart and interpretation is the process whereby theoretical reflection is brought to bear on the data for the explanatory insights it can offer. However, this does not happen in one 'move' but is a process of journey and arrival at different points. Carrying out ethnographic or qualitative research is a process of continuous interpretation. Here we are concerned with that phase of research which is more usually described as the analytical stage. The data can be interpreted and shaped in a number of ways (if it is good qualitative data, of course) and it is important to be experimental with your data. My own experience, and one which is often expressed by students, is not knowing where to begin when you are faced with your data.

What am I asking of the material?

Ken Plummer's categorisation of life histories as either 'resource' or 'topic' (see Chapter 6), is a good starting point. For the moment, this distinction can best be thought of as that between 'content' and 'form'. That is, the content, or substance of what the respondents are telling me, compared with the way in which they are formulating their accounts. This suggests different ways of dealing with your research material.

In the first instance, your respondents have provided, for example, a particular perspective on some events, new information about everyday life or ways of thinking which challenge dominant versions of events. The account of a familiar event from a particular perspective or, as we saw in the Rigoberta Menchu example, the testimony of one person which aims to speak for many. This kind of material can be crucial in opening up new avenues of research, of formulating different, usually suppressed, versions of events and requires 'documentation'.

In the second instance you are not only interested in what people say, but in how they say it. You want to ask questions about the subjectivity and subject position of your respondents, about the language they use, and the interpretive frames or cultural repertoires which they can call on in order to articulate their experience. However, although I have kept these analytically separate, it is possible to deal with both dimensions in our research material and in this way making the most of the type of intense interviewing which forms our research practice.

In my experience, open conversational interviews often encourage stories of life, if not more fully-fledged life stories. In addition, we have seen that many argue for the active interview approach, treating the interview encounter as a creative and productive part of research. Life stories, according to Thomas and Znaniecki (1958), are not only useful for sociology but they are 'the perfect type of sociological material'. By employing these kinds of interviewing strategies, the respondent is invited to engage in the presentation of self and, again to quote Thomas and Znaniecki, reveal some of the conditions of the processes of 'social becoming'. This is precisely what cultural studies is interested in understanding, so let us look at some ways of analysis material which makes the most of this multi-layered approach.

Hammersley and Atkinson (1993) identify key phases in data handling: generating concepts and developing typologies. This is a useful starting point for more practical advice in which the aim is, according to Atkinson, to disaggregate the text (transcript) into fragments, then to regroup them into themes. This is a rather conventional approach to 'qualitative data' and one which I adopted in my study of the use of the video recorder, from which I shall draw my first examples.

How I organised my transcripts

I carried out two pilot tape-recorded interviews and transcribed these verbatim. I also listened to these tapes with my supervisor during which we identified problems and discussed revisions to my interview approach. When I began my 'sample' interviews, at first I tried selecting sections for transcription, but soon discovered that this was far too limiting. I was editing as I transcribed and at this early stage I was unclear as to what might be relevant and what not. I therefore decided to transcribe my interviews verbatim, putting them straight into my computer, using a foot-operated transcription machine with headphones. I am fortunate in that I learnt to touch type when very young and I would recommend it highly as a relatively easily attained but very useful skill. Overall, I had some 60 hours of tapes, but I made it a golden rule to transcribe as I went along. This was important in the development of the project and future interviews. Transcription may seem onerous but the advantages are as follows: in transcribing the tapes I was listening very carefully to the recorded interview in a profound engagement with the material. This was often productive and revealing in that I noticed new things about my respondent and myself. For example, as we have seen from Devault's work, pauses and awkwardness in answering were often significant.

The process also lodged the material firmly in my mind. I found that each interview remained 'in my head'. The voice quality, the setting of the interview, how each respondent presented herself to me, the interruptions, for telephones or children and how these were dealt with, were all vividly recalled through listening. Thus, I gathered an overall sense of the interviews which took shape in my mind where I envisaged them as a whole with their different and distinct dimensions.

During the transcribing process I began to make links and connections which provided insights for the development of prescriptive concepts, but also those which were more suggestive of emergent theoretical themes. In this way analysis and interpretation became part of the process of research. This is when I was able to use my imagination, being sensitive to the material and experimental in my analysis. It provided an important interlude for 'trying things out' and for developing my analytical framework. If my ideas did not work out, then I tried something else!

I have talked about the importance of organising research material elsewhere but it is at this stage that a filing system comes into its own. As the project develops and before the material-gathering period, key concepts, themes, topics begin to shape the work. It is important that this shaping is given 'material' existence. The best, and most reassuring, way of doing this is to start a good filing and retrieval system. This provides the project with a structure which will then help in planning further reading and research. As reading progresses, photocopies accumulated and notes made, these should be filed and cross-referenced where necessary.

I describe the presence of files as reassuring. They are, because it is very easy to lose direction, or a sense of the overall project. Many researchers try to keep all this in their heads, afraid to write and afraid to impose shape on their project. They are making themselves extremely vulnerable to loss of confidence and lack of gumption. This is to be avoided at all costs. Organising and building up a filing system are very important grounding practices. Furthermore, files and filing provide you with the basis for reflexive activity which is at one and the same time productive, but not 'challenging'. Sorting files, re-visiting them and adding to them, is a time for reflection which can often provide the reassurance needed about the state of a project (Plummer, 2001: 151).

Lest you think that this sounds too mundane a task to take seriously, here is what C. Wright Mills has to say about re-organising a filing system:

> As you rearrange a filing system, you often find that you are, as it were, loosening your imagination. Apparently this occurs by means of your attempt to combine various ideas and notes on different topics. It is a sort of logic of combination, and 'chance' sometimes plays a curiously large part in it. In a relaxed way, you try to engage your intellectual resources, as exemplified in the file, with the new themes. (1959: 221)

These two activities, transcribing and filing, are intensely practical and the former is infinitely time-consuming, but they are also intensely creative and intellectual and can make important contributions to the development of the research. My point here is to encourage you to think of all aspects of your research as making specific contributions to its development, rather than as 'chores' which must be got through before getting onto the exciting or challenging work. What follows is an account of the analytical and interpretive strategies I adopted in my study of the VCR.

My strategy

First, I organised my 30 respondents into 'class' groupings, giving them each a code, identified through A/B/C/D. This immediately gave the sample some shape – but I was to find that they had to be grouped differently depending on the topic in hand as each group shared different attributes in different ways.

I then opened files (this can be done on the computer, although at the time I found it as easy to do it manually) for each of the main themes, i.e. the kinds of substantive material I was looking at: mine broadly became the chapters of my thesis, thus:

- Organisation of time and domestic work
- Leisure: going out and staying in
- Decisions to buy the VCR
- Questions about technology
- Watching television – with whom and when
- Hiring videos – the video shop
- Watching videos – with whom and when

• Cultural taste and preferences

I then worked through each interview, pulling out what each woman had said within the different categories – literally cutting out the sections – making sure the code was on the cutting.

Following this, I looked at the patterns which were beginning to emerge – then re-grouped the cuttings into the class differences, and so on. By working with the material in this way I was able to shift my categories and move the women in out of the gender/class distinctions depending on the topic. Thus, class was a highly significant variable in relation to 'viewing preferences' – questions of cultural taste in choice of programming and film hire – but much less so when discussing domestic labour and the uses of technology in the household. It was important to allow my categories to be flexible enough to acknowledge these differences within my sample.

A number of times I went back to the complete interviews constantly trying to retain a sense of the individual responses in their entirety, so that the particular formations were not lost or flattened out in the process. We noted Devault's strategies for allowing interview dialogue to produce concepts and categories (see Chapter 5), and when analysing data it is also crucial to respect your respondent's speech by allowing this data to challenge your sociological and cultural categories. Devault reminds us of the dangers of 'smoothing out' our data so that it fits into our pre-defined categories. Thus, just as she described the importance of listening to new ways of describing experiences during the interview, the analytical approach must be sufficiently flexible to enable the richness of the data: 'as I transcribed I developed the rudiments of a system for preserving some of the 'messiness' of everyday talk' (Devault, 1990: 109). Thus, she included the para-linguistic elements, such as pauses, repetition, contradiction, laughter, etc. Paget warns of the dangers in editing out pauses, hesitations, false starts when these could indeed be extremely significant. Pauses, repetition, hesitation and emphasis can all give us a clue to emotion and meaning, and these should in turn be building blocks for analysis. Thus, a sensitive analysis should pay attention to 'the dynamic construction of what was said' (Paget, 1983: 87).

Out of the key themes I developed some concepts which gave some explanatory power to the accounts of daily life which my respondents provided. The women themselves introduced the necessity for a range of concepts, or new ways of thinking about technology in the household. The ways in which the women described their own attitudes towards different kinds of technology and the ways in which they negotiated their position in relation to both the technology and members of their family required some organising concepts. These, such as 'calculated ignorance' whereby certain of the women feigned ignorance of technology in order to avoid becoming responsible for yet one more task; the formulation of 'blue' and 'pink' technologies was an enabling method during interviews, but also became a useful conceptual organising strategy in reproducing the minute differences and distinctions between and within particular kinds of household technologies. Second, the women spoke a lot about 'time' and how they felt about time spent in the household. This required fine-grained concepts which distinguished between 'guilty time', 'stolen time' 'my own time', etc. When I came to the analysis of viewing preferences I turned to concepts of popular aesthetic, critical distance, drawn from Bourdieu, as well as insights from the textual construction of different genres.

The purpose in developing these concepts was to be able to think across the different respondents and to organise their accounts in such a way as to identify similarities and difference in the substance of their accounts.

It was important, however, to constantly reflect and relate the concepts and themes to the data, so that I was not forcing the data to fit into my concepts. Here an awareness of the contradictions within and across the data was crucial.

Having gone through this process, I was then faced with the decision about how to present the material. I considered, first of all, producing 'portraits' in order to give a sense of the different 'household cultures'. Clearly, I did not have the space to treat each of my respondents in this way so I experimented with the idea of 'composite' portraits which would reflect, say, different households defined by class. I felt, however, that this strategy would lose the very specific details and dimensions of the household use of media and new entertainment technologies, the very details which had not previously been taken into account when considering 'audiences' for television and video. It was important for me to illuminate these areas and especially as they were dealing with women's everyday lives. It would have been too easy for these dull, routine and common-place activities which, nevertheless, had a powerful shaping force on women's lives and their uses of media, to simply be overlooked or lost within the life-story or portrait format. I was also struck by the significance of class in my small sample and again, I wanted to be able to indicate the complexity of the intersections between gender and class in the women's accounts. I further decided that I would quote extensively from my interview material in order to keep the distinctive voices of the women in my text, to enable readers to have greater access to the interview material and in order to make the book readable, potentially for a wider than merely academic audience.

By way of example, I want to introduce you to one of the women I interviewed and work through the material in different ways.

The case of 'Hilary'

As I have indicated, my mode of analysis followed the fragments/themes pattern. I organised my interview data across a number of grids: categories were related to age, class, occupation, numbers and ages of children and other significant variables. While this gave me the opportunity of discussing what I thought were important aspects of women's lives, such as the crucial importance of domestic labour and the organisation of time, to their sense of their own leisure time and therefore viewing habits, it did not enable the kind of analysis of the formation of subjectivity and identity which could equally well have emerged from my interview material.

Thus, the voices and expressions of the women in my study were fragmented and they appeared as characters under a number of category headings. What was lost was the sense of the whole person, or household they were describing.

Here is an extract from the index to *Video Playtime* showing the page numbers where 'Hilary' appears. Thus, extracts from our long interview are included in all the chapters and in many of the sub-headings of chapters: 'Hilary' 38, 44-5, 46-7, 55, 69, 85, 89-90, 151-2, 154-5, 167, 175, 180-1, 192, 205, 208-9, 228, 229, 231.

What follows is a brief extract from the chapter entitled 'Organisation of Spare Time':

... Hilary reflected on her personal history and family background, but also set it within a socio-historic context:

> I mean, I'm not telling you I do lots of Women's Institute and knitting, you know. I'm not a sort of standard housewife. I think you are fairly subscribed, except I suspect people are a little ... you see I'm a little bit old ... you see I went to university in 1960, really the beginning of the explosion, and I suspect people that are ten years younger than me or those who were rather more avant-garde than I was ... I mean I was the complete antithesis of avant-garde because I was very narrowly brought up, a very subscribed Northern background which I found it difficult to break away from ... I suspect that people ten years younger who also had the pill when they were younger, this is the thing ... actually have more equal relationships with their partners whereas mind is really quite traditional. (Hilary)

She then went on to say that this was in spite of the fact of her being a graduate and both her and her husband being 'university people' and continued,

> I think that now I've got to my age I've become quite, as it were, limited in this way, and looking back it is rather difficult to see how it happened. I think it pre-eminently happened when I had children, but I also think it was because I had a very deeply rooted into me very, very old-fashioned, rigid ideas about male and female roles which you never really break away from ... I mean, you just don't expect the man you're married to make the tea, that's just not an expectation you have ... I often think about this because I wonder quite how one did arrive as limited as I am ... I mean, I'm really making a blow for freedom taking Sarah [daughter] away with me and that's only because I earn my own money, there's no way I could do that if I didn't. (Hilary)

This woman, aged 44, whose education and material circumstances placed her in a position of apparent privilege, reveals in her autobiographical account the complexity of her experience. The strong ideological pull of her family background with its assumptions about women and men could not be resisted through her university education. But there are also significant material factors influencing her life. Not having adequate contraception, lack of state provision for maternity leave and child care led almost inevitably to her adopting the role of full-time mother and housewife, thereby establishing a pattern of living which now seems impossible to change. Her domestic servicing undoubtedly enabled her husband's career to develop ('he never changed a nappy or thought of washing the children's hair') as he was always free of childcare and domestic responsibilities. Her attempt to return to full-time teaching also demonstrates the vulnerability of women in her position and their dependence on the vagaries of the labour market. Financial autonomy, as she pointed out, is the key to her 'blows for freedom', to be able to do things on her own. Women in her position, married to successful and well-paid husbands, live within constraints which would not be immediately obvious. (Gray, 1992: 44-5)

Fragments of my interview with Hilary appear across all chapters dealing with the key themes of the research. Here, by way of comparison, is the interview presented in 'portrait' form in which I have attempted to include all the key themes. There now follows my writing of Hilary as 'portrait' which I did during the process of reworking my thesis for *Video Playtime*.

'Hilary's portrait'

I'm not a standard sort of housewife.

On my arrival at Hilary's house, a large Edwardian terrace, at 3 p.m. on an afternoon in November, I was shown into the dining room at the rear and offered tea. Several of the women I had interviewed offered me drinks of various kinds. I had usually declined, mainly because I loathe instant coffee and like very weak tea without milk, but sometimes, sensing a refusal would cause offence, I had accepted. However, there was no refusing Hilary; a tea tray had been prepared, with scones and jam, and set on the dining table. Apart from the fact that I wasn't very hungry (I learned quite soon to eat well before interviews, thus avoiding embarrassing gurgles from an empty stomach, tiredness and loss of concentration) I found the handling of plate, scone, butter, jam, napkin, tea, etc. and tape recorder, clip board, etc. rather intimidating. On the one hand, this was a very kind and hospitable gesture on Hilary's part and, I would imagine, her usual practice when visitors arrive at teatime. On the other, the tea tray in effect made Hilary's mark on the occasion, establishing a particular kind of relationship between us in which I was put firmly in my place as a guest in her house and as a (socially inferior?) student.

Hilary is married to a university professor, she was 44 at the time of our conversation, had graduated in the early 1960s with an English degree and, after obtaining a Post-Graduate Certificate in Education, went into secondary school teaching until her first child was born. She met her husband at university and they embarked on their marriage with certain kinds of expectations:

> I mean, I think the other thing that influenced us was that my husband became much more successful than we expected ... we never really expected ... because he's only got a white tile degree [laughs] he never expected to end up as a university professor.

According to her, this meant that his career had taken precedence over both her career and their family. During our conversation she was trying to find ways of explaining how 'one did arrive as limited as I am' occupying an apparently very traditional role of wife and mother. Her two children had been born in 1970 and 1973 respectively and she had left her job as a schoolteacher when her first child arrived. Her expectation was to be able to return to teaching when her children reached school age. She observed that the job market had changed completely in that period and she was currently supply school-teaching part time, a job which she found unrewarding and unstimulating. Although she had domestic help 'I have a cleaning lady who comes twice a week – it's quite a big house', she obviously carried out many domestic duties. Her husband worked long hours and also required her to 'entertain' visitors in connection with his work. The pink and blue coding was quite clear-cut in this household in relation to domestic technology *and* the performance of domestic tasks. When we were talking about the operation of the VCR Hilary told me that she tended not to operate the timer, pointing out that someone else was usually around to do it. She did not consider herself to be technologically minded, but felt that the reason she did not use the timer on the VCR was 'laziness'. Her husband, who she described as 'a scientist' could not operate the washing machine or the timer on the oven but she put that down to his lack of time and also, as she pointed out, 'he doesn't know where a lot of things are in the kitchen'. This man never cooked, or discussed 'planning food and menus' but, 'He doesn't like things not tidy and he doesn't like things not clean, so, if there are a lot of bits on the floor he Hoovers, er ... he tends to always tidy up the sink, I mean, if it's messy ... that sort of thing.'

When it came to leisure activities her husband was equally reluctant. She considered family outings to be important but, more often than not, found herself organising these alone with her children; 'my husband hates days out, we're home by three o'clock'. While Hilary laughed as she told me this she was obviously disappointed that family outings weren't more pleasurable and also said that she was 'making a real blow for freedom' having decided to take her daughter to Spain for a holiday. This she was able to do because she earned money and 'it means I can buy the children clothes and things like that, and do a lot of things that I wouldn't do otherwise'.

She told me about her job, teaching English as a second language in schools, and explained that for the first time in nine years she was teaching in one school. The normal pattern was that she had a number of children in different schools; teaching one session and then moving onto the next school: 'it's rather lonely, it's rewarding in some ways, but it's not really a social job'. I asked her if she had considered trying a different kind of job:

> Well, I've tried, I tried a few times going back into schools but it's hell [laughs] it's terrible, it makes me very difficult to live with and I think I've too many commitments here to do either very satisfactorily and I'm also a bit old ... [her daughter arrives home from school and walks into the room] ... this is Sarah ... there is some soup you can heat up, there's some ham and cottage cheese in the fridge. Was it a nice day and do you have any homework? There's some nice soup I made if you heat it up, have as much as you like, there's some French bread into which you may put one slice of ham and some cottage cheese and then I'll come and sort you out. [Sarah leaves, having mumbled a brief reply, and Hilary turns to me] She's going ice skating at five o'clock.

This is a very interesting interlude in our conversation. While Hilary had earlier rationalised her position in terms of employment as being contingent on the job market and therefore out of her control, what she is now saying is that she did try going back into school teaching, but found it impossible to manage given her domestic commitments. With her daughter's arrival, as if on cue, Hilary switched into the role of 'good' mother; the provision of nourishing food (homemade soup and French bread) questions about school and homework, to which Sarah mumbled a brief reply, and being available to transport her to the skating rink which, incidentally, was some thirty miles away. Far from her position being completely determined, therefore, Hilary has obviously made certain choices around her responsibilities and to her home and family versus her career, but doesn't seem to see it in those terms. While we could characterise this as the typical dilemma for well-educated middle-class women with children, I think the kernel in this account is the fact that full-time teaching made her 'very difficult to live with' for her family, presumably, but also very undermining in terms of her notions of being a mother.

In their re-interpretation of a study of mothers and daughters, Valerie Walkerdine and Helen Lucey suggest that one of the characteristics of middle-class mothers and their households is an observable lack of conflict; power relations, conflicts, struggles and difficulties are, by a variety of strategies, performed by women, rendered invisible. 'There is no way that, for instance, power conflicts will not arise, that they will be Absent. The secret of their apparent disappearance, however, lies in how that conflict is dealt with; how particular strategies for dealing with power and conflict make it seem as if they had simply gone away' (Walkerdine and Lucey, 1989: 104).

While my study is not about mothering this is, for many of the women I talked to, the central focus of their identity: a fundamental aspect of their lives and as such has an important bearing on their use and consumption of cultural products such as novels, television and film and particularly in the way they account for this use. Before focusing on this I want to explore one of the key strategies identified by Walkerdine and Lucey in relation to Hilary, that of 'intellectualisation'.

We have seen that Hilary rationalises her position with reference to the 'external' vagaries of the job market, but she also has another story to tell through which she accounts for the very traditional relationship which she has with her husband. To put it simply, she produces an exposition of their socialisation into stereotypical gender roles, but, more complexly, we can see from the following extract, she is also aware of the contradictions which exist in her autobiography:

> I was very sort of narrowly brought up, very subscribed Northern background which I found it difficult to break away from ... I suspect that people ten years younger who also had the pill ... this is the thing, actually have more equal relationships with their partners whereas mine is really quite a traditional ... in spite of the fact that we're university people and ... in many ways, in the sense of having advanced ideas - the top 10 per cent or 3 per cent whatever - but still we have quite a traditional thing ... it pre-eminently happened when I had children, but I also think it was because I had very deeply rooted into me very very rigid old fashioned ideas about male/female roles which you never really break away from so your pattern of behaviour is that you do make the tea and you never expect that the man you're married to will make it ... And in my husband's family there were just the two boys and I think it makes a great difference when a man is brought up in a family where there are no girls, because I think it has conditioned his response to women. His father died when he was very young and he was brought up only by women, so his expectations of what a woman does, her role, as his hostess ... and all these sorts of things are very deeply ingrained. I mean, my husband's modified his attitude and so have I but it is very difficult to break away from that early sort of patterning. I mean, he does a tremendously complicated job. It requires a ... I mean, it's not much good me expecting him to run the house ... he hasn't got the time ... he's working most evenings until 10 o'clock. I mean it does cause resentment, I'm not good about it all the time, I do get fed up and bitchy on occasions.

Walkerdine and Lucey identify 'intellectualisation' as a strategy which middle class mothers encourage their daughters to deal with conflict, often around gender/power relations and I think we can see in Hilary's account a similar kind of strategy being employed in order to understand what she sees as her own narrow and rather limited life. She is constantly trying to rationalise and explain the reasons for her husband's lack of involvement in the household and family: his upbringing, his demanding job, producing a person with certain expectations and assumptions about his role and those of his wife. Her phrase 'I'm not good about it all the time' is a telling one which clearly indicates *her* own expectations about herself in relation to him. She feels she should accept the situation, but her anger and frustration is displaced onto 'bitchiness' which she obviously tries to contain, smoothing over the potential problems. She constantly tries to distance her own difficulties through a process of intellectualisation and rationalisation.

> How then to achieve harmony where discord previously ruled, to replace tem-per with reason, bad power with equality? For this is exactly what many of the middle-class women especially strive to achieve but never can, precisely because the search for harmony is the search for a pot of gold – it does not, cannot exist in this way except as a fantasy. (Walkerdine and Lucey 1989: 104)

Apart from the brief encounter during the interview, I have no means of knowing the nature of her relationship with her daughter, but her account of her daughter's television viewing and her general attitude to television and video confirms a certain intellectual/rational ethos which she constantly invokes. Her daughter watched *Dallas* and *Dynasty*:

> I think they're a group ethos. I think they do get involved with the characters although they know it's ridiculous, but most children you ask say, 'because they look attractive, they like the clothes, the easy life-style and the glam-ourousness [*sic*] of it' ... they do get involved with the characters but it is so ridiculous that they can't always take it seriously, I think they watch it for the glamour of it. They do get involved with the characters but they know ration-ally it's ridiculous.

Her daughter's viewing behaviour is seen as part of a group ethos so, although my question was specifically about her daughter, she immediately began to talk in more general terms, but constructed them as 'rational' view-ers. Her son and husband watched 'grotty trash' to relax after their intense work in the evening and in describing their television watching she did not refer to their rationality, rather their need to relax after their work. Her own viewing, she reported, was very light, often leaving the room if the television was on, preferring 'quality' programmes, mainly plays. But they had all watched *Paradise Postponed*, *First Among Equals* and *Blott on the Landscape* all of which were series adapted from novels which she had previously read, by John Mortimer, Jeffrey Archer and Tom Sharpe respectively and on a number of occasions they had used the VCR to record missed episodes. She insisted that she had always read the book before watching a series (quickly explaining that the Jeffrey Archer novel was 'one of the only readable books in the Scottish hotel in which we found ourselves'). The VCR had been a 'spontaneous' purchase at Christmas four years earlier and when we moved on to talk about her film hiring, she said:

H: Well, I want to hire *The Spiderwoman* [*sic*] because I haven't seen it, but it depends at that moment in time, a lot of the ones you want to see aren't available on video of course. And it depends what's come out of the ... what I would call quality films that I would like to see. I've missed, for example, and I think it is on video now, *Letter to Brezhnev* and I would quite like to see that so when Philip's [husband] away I'll see if I can hire that.

AG: So you tend to hire films that you've read or heard about?

H: Oh yes, I would never hire a film I didn't really know.

I would suggest that this is another version of intellectualisation in her approach to her viewing and, as we shall see, her reading. This knowledge gives her the intellectual distance required for what Bourdieu referred to as the 'bourgeoise aesthetic', which gives the viewer/reader power and control over the text and distinctively differs from the 'popular aesthetic'. Hilary attempts to maintain a strong sense of 'self' by ensuring her prior knowledge of the texts she consumes.

Hilary claimed that reading was her main leisure activity, getting through about two books a week. She rarely read on her own during the day, unless she was ill, but always read in the late evening. She selected her books by reading book reviews in the newspaper, following the Booker Prize and had an informal exchange network with wives of her husband's colleagues whom she met in the evenings 'on the dinner party circuit'. Hilary referred to her 'social circle' more than once during our conversation, not always positively, and it is clear that her reading of particular books provided important cultural 'currency' within this network. She cited Anita Brookner and Margaret Drabble 'that sort of thing' and said she often re-read the 'classics'. I asked her why she read so much and what sort of pleasure she got out of it:

It is relaxing because it takes you outside – I'm not going to use the word escapist ... it takes you outside of the environment in which you live and my environment as a child, and even now as an adult running a family is very restricting ... it's like the armchair traveller; it's the next best thing to doing it yourself and it stops you getting ... I mean, you know ... God forbid that you're the sort of person that all you can think about is what are the best sort of dishwashers to buy, or what sort of clothes you wear and the best way to ... anyway I can't stand that sort of thing ... I have very limited contact with people that I can talk to on an intellectual basis. I can't read absolute trash, so there's this middle market which does make you think ... it pushes you forward, it's well written, because, after all, I was trained ... I cannot be a person who can live entirely through my children's achievements, entirely for my husband, or my home ... But of necessity one's life is very subscribed, perhaps everyone's life is, of course ... and the way out of that is to read. I think that's why I read.

Hilary's comments obviously have relevance to Janice Radway's study of women readers of romantic fiction. Radway identifies particular resistances in the reading of romance by women in 'traditional' marriages and patriarchal structures and while Hilary intellectualises her reading practice it nevertheless is seen by her as compensatory, allowing her to experience, vicariously, a dimension of her life which she feels to be missing. While Radway equates the structure of romance with the actual position of the women in her study, arguing that romance at one and the same time validates women's lives in patriarchal marriage and provides the sense of nurture and care missing from their primary relationship, Hilary's case is more complex. She does not read romantic fiction, as such, therefore the 'fit' is not so neat but undoubtedly it is the strictures of patriarchal marriage which she finds so 'intellectually' limiting and constraining and from which she feels a sense of release when she reads her 'middle-brow' books. For all her busy life, Hilary seemed to be an intensely lonely person (a term which I would use to describe many of the women I talked to) and her reading practice seemed to compensate in some ways for that loneliness.

The interview with Hilary began with her giving fairly brief responses to questions about her leisure activities and reading and viewing habits. The trigger which marked a shift in her presentation of self was the question about who operated the timer in the VCR. Here she said that she was not technologically minded, 'I think it's almost inevitable, if I'm married to a scientist and I've got a son who's a scientist, and I'm an arts graduate.' She then started talking about her past and her responses to my prompt questions became longer and more revealing of her feelings of isolation and loneliness. However, towards the end of the interview Hilary turned the tables on me and asked about my research. She said she would like to see what I did with the research data, and especially with these kinds of interviews. She was particularly interested in the working-class women in my sample and their reading, whom she assumed would not read so much. I said that many in my sample did read and cited Mills and Boon and other kinds of popular fiction. She asked 'Do they know why they read?' I gave her some examples of explanations for reading practice and she said 'They don't read it thinking it's going to be real?' I said, 'No.'

Themes of class and gender, mothering, of generation specific experience, taste and power relations emerge through this portrait of an individual woman in my study. The reason for presenting the material in this way is to give readers a sense of the whole culture of one middle-class household with something of the complexity of the Mother/Wife's position within it. Furthermore, as Hilary reflected on her own biography, it is possible to locate it to broader historical changes within society. To use Connell's terms, this kind of data can have a high theoretical yield.

However, this form of presentation is not without its problems. On reading this portrait I want to consider two short-comings, to relate them back to the format I actually adopted for the book, and to questions of power and respect. First of all, we actually seem to lose sight of 'Hilary' in the way I have written this account and, second, the use of conceptual frameworks in my analysis and the way this positions me as author of the text tends to place Hilary like a butterfly on the dissecting table of my analysis. In other words, I am suggesting that I know better than Hilary about what motivates her choices and her behaviour. I have become, in this mode, the all-knowing narrator. Paradoxically, on reading through *Video Playtime*, I have a much stronger sense of Hilary than this portrait presents but, more importantly, I was able to reflect theoretically on her accounts in a more distanced way. The adoption of the portrait mode, where the respondent is produced as a 'whole person' is not necessarily the most respectful nor analytically productive mode of analysis and presentation.

Thus, by employing different analytical strategies, frameworks, the same interview, provided it is open enough, can be used in different ways. The most important questions to ask yourself are:

- What purpose is the interview going to serve in my overall research?

- How do alternative strategies position the respondents? Do they maintain their dignity and integrity or is my voice rendered more powerful in the text?

I eventually made the decision to fragment and categorise. In this way it enabled me to identify some patterns of use across the households, but also indicate differences and distinctions in areas as diverse as doing the housework, using technology and reading and viewing pleasures.

Thoughts on analytical strategies:

Rigidity in your analysis will not do justice to your method and you will have spent a lot of time interviewing which will be wasted. Your data should be allowed to fulfil its potential for your study. It is worth stepping back again and again and looking at what you are doing through your analysis and asking:

- Is the framework too rigid? You can sense this if you are having to condense or deny aspects of your material.

- Are the categories sufficiently flexible or is the material forcing you to question your categorical assumptions?

- What happens if you move things around, multiply your topics and categories to make them more complex?

• Can you group and re-group your sample? Your original group-ings may not work for every topic.

• Are there differences in the kinds of responses you are getting in the interviews that might require a different form of analysis?

• By what means can you reveal contradiction and difference, as well as similarities, within your sample?

Other strategies

Wendy Hollway declares that: 'Making sense of the transcript in terms of the research questions is the most harrowing part of all. The more unstructured it is, the greater the anxiety that it is going to be impossible to analyse rigor-ously' (1989: 21). She, like me, tried to code her manuscripts identifying dif-ferent themes: she had six major theoretical categories and then sub-headings, then sub-subheadings. But, unlike me, she concluded:

> The result was unsatisfactory in several respects. Most importantly, it made me realize that what I was trying to understand was a complex whole, and the cat-egories were only of explanatory status. By separating them, I was doing vio-lence to the relations between categories, which were internal relations in a whole. I lost the integrity of a case study of a person or couple which could illustrate the relations between these aspects. (ibid.: 21)

She decided that what was important were the relations between categories in the specific instances rather than coding the transcripts according to one of several categories. She needed to demonstrate the relations in her analysis. She concluded that her transcripts should not be 'chopped up' in the inter-ests of some methodological 'rigour'.

Hermes (1995) noted a similar problem when analysing her interviews through repertoire analysis, in that she lost a sense of the overall structure of daily routines and the complexity of shifting uses of women's magazines over time. For this she conducted two much longer 'life history' type interviews in order to discover how women's magazine reading are predicated on everyday routines. Her conclusion was that in order to explain how women's maga-zines are used it is necessary to have knowledge of readers daily lives, histo-ries and routines which would be indicative of the complexity of the meanings and consumption of popular genres.

Hermes' account is helpful especially as she combined qualitative inter-views, of which she did a large number, with two longer life history type inter-views in order to grasp the place that magazine reading has in people's lives, their memories and their achievement of feminine identity. The need to pro-duce these 'portraits' of magazine use as an attempt to present the 'whole story' and, arguably, a more ethnographically informed account came from the interviews themselves. Time and again the people she interviewed indicated that their use of magazines was intricately woven into their everyday lives and that this shaped their readings and their pleasures of the magazines. This is an interesting example of the respondents pushing the researcher into adopting a different methodological strategy in order to 'capture' the phenomenon under study. Of course, this was brought about by her reflexive research practice and the desire (and necessary energy) to do justice to her topic. I want to dwell a little on this phenomenon – that of the demands which listening to our respondents can make on the research process and the ways in that the boundaries can be broken down. I have already discussed this in relation to storying, I now want to take it up in relation to the analysis of research material.

Connell's procedure for analysis of life histories

Connell, in his book *Masculinities*, describes the process in detail:

> In the first phase of analysis I listened to tapes, read transcripts, indexed, and wrote up each interview as a case study. In each case study the interview as a whole was examined from three points of view:
>
> • the narrative sequence of events
>
> • a structural analysis using a grid provided by the three structures of gender relations
>
> • a dynamic analysis, tracing the making and unmaking of masculinity, trying to grasp the gender project involved.

Writing up each case study was both an attempt at a portrait of a person, and a reflection on the portrait's meaning as evidence about social change.

In the second phase I reanalysed the case studies in groups. Here the goal was to explore the similarities and differences in the trajectories of men in a certain social location, and to understand their collective location in large-scale change. Again I used a grid derived from gender theory to make these comparisons systematic. I abstracted and reindexed the cases so that, as each topic came to be analysed, the whole group was in view, while the narrative shape of each life was preserved. I wrote this analysis for each group separately, making each report an attempt at a collective portrait of men caught up in a certain process of change. (Connell, 1995: 92)

From Connell's account we can see that his analysis went through a number of stages during which the interview material was subjected to different frameworks which posed different questions of the material. The reanalysis phase in which he regrouped the individual interviews enabled both differences and similarities to emerge in the stories and he emphasises again his use of a theoretical frame to shed light on the life stories and their 'yield'.

He insists that 'these four studies are not intended in themselves as a map of large-scale change', in other words, Connell is not claiming that the accounts are representative of more general social change, 'Their purpose is to illuminate particular situations which might be strategic. On this basis I use their findings when discussing broader issues ... The studies have of course also fed back into the theoretical arguments' (ibid.: 92).

In a wry comment Connell acknowledges that not all are convinced by the usefulness of this approach. His fieldwork was financed by the national funding body, the Australian Research Grants Committee and 'Before any findings were published, this project was attacked by the federal parliamentary "Wastewatch Committee" of the Liberal and National Parties ... as a conspicuous waste of public funds' (ibid.: 92).

Discourse analysis

The above discussion focuses our attention on breaking up the texts in different ways and we should always bear in mind that how we approach our analysis totally depends on what we want to texts to reveal. As we have suggested, this sometimes cannot be predicted and good reflexive practice will enable the full potential of such qualitative data to be revealed through analysis and interpretation. An imaginative and flexible approach, therefore, to analysis is important.

More recently, a number of researchers in cultural and media studies have employed discourse analysis in their interpretation of data. Ros Gill (2000) indicates four main themes of discourse analysis, thus:

1   Discourse is the topic – all forms of talk and texts. Discourse analysis is interested in texts in their own right and not as access to some underlying 'truth'.

2   Language is constructive. Discourse is manufactured out of pre-existing linguistic resources. Accounts are assembled from a range of choices, although these are not infinite. Texts of various kinds construct our world.

3   Discourse is occasioned. It is contingent and context dependent.

4   Texts are organised rhetorically and can give a sense of competing versions of the world.

The advantages of discourse analysis for cultural studies projects are that it can be employed in a mixture of different kinds of research material, that the 'discursive regimes' can be observed both at 'micro' and wider social levels and, at the 'macro' level, these regimes of discourse can be identified as discourses of power.

Thus, discourse and communication have both micro and macro dimensions and their analysis thus offers new ways of analysing complex social and political problem areas. This is not merely providing the 'backdrop' for a smaller scale or 'micro' study, but can demonstrate how those wider discourses of power can be enacted within social relations. Also, by examining the discursive relations within specific, or local contexts, we can explore how relations can reproduce more global levels of societal structure and culture.

The advantages of a discourse approach for cultural studies work is that it is possible to use the same framework of analysis for a whole range of texts that might make up one research project. Thus, cultural products, popular texts, gestures, interview dialogue and conversation, written documents, etc. can all be subjected to discourse analysis. We saw the usefulness of this approach when we looked at Mankekar's study and the ways in which discursive clusters were seen to underpin both the production of popular texts, but also the lived experience of the viewing families.

Penny Summerfield's (1998) study of women's wartime lives employed a discourse approach in that it sought to understand how 'official' discourses, assumed to be produced from a male point of view or perspective, provided certain ways of accounting for experience. These discourses tended to marginalise, or discount how and in what ways women experienced the war. In other words, discourse, for Summerfield, is gendered. In contrast, women's accounts of their experience were told by accessing different kinds of repertoires. Her life story interviews were designed to examine the links between gender, subjectivity, inter-subjectivity and discourse, thus establishing a relationship between the sense of who we are, how we experience particular events, or ways of life, and what available repertoires we have to construct our version of events. Summerfield's approach thus avoids the trap of the notion of the 'authentic voice of experience', but also shifts attention away from discourse alone. She is concerned with the interviews as resource and topic.

Cultural repertoires

This has been a particularly useful concept drawn from discourse analytic work and one which was employed by Joke Hermes in her study of magazine reading. Hermes uses Potter and Wetherell's definition of repertoires as 'currently used systems of terms used for characterising and evaluating actions, events and other phenomena' (Potter and Wetherell, 1987: 149). The social subject is conceptualised as the user of the repertoires seen as an active and creative language user and not the subject of pre-determined language systems. Furthermore, the advantages in thinking of interpretive repertoires, according to Jonathan Potter, as 'systematically related sets of terms' (Potter, 2000: 131) is that they can be considered to make up an important part of the 'common sense' of a culture. Often this 'common sense' is assumed by both interviewer and respondent and the analysis must first of all make this strange, in order to reveal these often deeply embedded discursive clusters. This notion, according to Potter, accommodates two important factors. First, they can be thought of as 'off the shelf' resources or discourses which can be used in a range of settings, but by different individuals. Second, they can be selectively drawn upon and reworked depending on the different contexts or settings. This, obviously, would include the context of the interview itself. Potter suggests that interviews are very useful vehicles for getting at these commonly used repertoires. He asks of the data: 'How is a particular version of the world made to seem solid and unproblematic? [common sense, natural, obvious] and 'How are social categories constructed and managed in practice?' (ibid: 131).

We can look in a very detailed and contextualised manner at how particular versions of the world are embedded and legitimated in speech and practice. (ibid: 131) Hermes was keen to identify the ways in which her respondents used and understood women's magazines. Her reading across her interview data began to establish specific interpretative repertoires, or positions, which her readers adopted in their articulation of their use of the magazines. These were the repertoires of 'practical knowledge' and 'emotional learning and connected knowing'. While these boundaries were not always clear, and indeed, had sub-repertoires, they provided a structure of shared meaning positions across Hermes' research respondents. As in Summerfield's study, this enabled her to both address the specific and the particular, and to relate it to a wider setting of meaning making, or common-sense assumptions. Both researchers adopt the constructivist approach to language and discourse and the social world more generally in their study, but neither become intricately involved in the specifics of language which some versions of discourse analysis, for example, conversation analysis, employ. What is crucial for both Hermes and Summerfield are the social and cultural contexts within and through which their respondents are inhabiting their subject positions and availing themselves of occasioned repertoires.

Hermes suggests drawing on Knorr-Cetina's suggestion of the presence of the macro in the micro:

> The macro structure is seen to reside within ... micro episodes where it results from the structuring practices of agents. The outcome of these practices are representations which thrive upon an alleged correspondence to that which they represent, but which at the same time can be seen as highly situated constructions which involve several layers of interpretation and selection ... Agents routinely transform situated micro-events into summary representations by relying on practices through which they convince themselves of having achieved appropriate representation. (Knorr-Cetina, 1981: 34, quoted in Hermes, 1995: 26)

This is to suggest that the repertoires selected, re-worked and mobilised at the micro-level are indicative of the wider culture. Again this resonates with Mankekar's approach and enables a theoretical generalisation to be made from specific examples. Hermes describes her use of repertoire analysis as not prescriptive nor particularly rigorous, but rather consisting of:

Going back and forth through the text, summarizing interview transcripts according to different criteria, for as long as it takes to organize the bits and pieces in meaningful structures. One looks for statements or manners of speech that recur in different interviews. Once such key elements have been found, it is a matter of trying to fit them together. (Hermes, 1995: 27)

The uses and abuses of technology

There now exist a number of software packages to enable the analysis of qualitative data. As these are constantly being refined and new versions introduced, it would be unwise to present detailed information on any existing packages. However, what I can say is that it is important to use computing towards your own ends, not as an end in itself. This is especially important in handling qualitative data in not allowing the software to restrict and impoverish the richness of analysis.

Hammersley and Atkinson warn that 'No system of filing or coding and retrieval can ever remove the necessity to remain sensitive to the social context of speech and action' (1993: 194) and Lofland (1971) argues that 'in the case of analytic categories it pays to be "wild", to include anything, however long a shot'.

One of the early packages was Ethnograph which is a 'Code-and-retrieve system' based on identifying and retrieving chunks of data. Tesch (1990) refers to this process as 'decontextualising' data segments, and 'recontextualising' them into thematic files and that 'in essence the coding strategy is a "flat" one'. Thus, the software cannot recognise some codes as being general categories that include more specific ones. Such software emulates manual searching quite efficiently and comprehensively. But its version of coding recapitulates what has been called 'the culture of fragmentation' (Atkinson, 1992) as a general approach to qualitative data. That is, it reflects a general assumption that data reduction and aggregation lie at the heart of data management. This is not necessarily faithful to all versions of ethnographic and other qualitative enquiry, particularly those concerned with detailed sequential analysis of social interaction' (Hammersley and Atkinson, 1993: 200) Those software packages which go beyond the more conventional approach, for example, NUDIST enable system relations to be established between codes themselves. Thus large numbers of codings can be organised and arranged as desired. With KWALITAN it is possible for the researcher to work with 'grounded theory' so segments of analytic and methodological text can be included in specific segments of data. Thus the packages now are attempting to go beyond the code and retrieval process into that of analysis. Hypertext, however, breaks with the basic approach of 'coding and segmentation'. Hypertext software allows the analyst to find complex routes and pathways within the database, rather than the fragmentation method (Fischer, 1994). Hyperqual suggests that it is possible to treat all materials from a research project for interrogation: this is much closer to an ethnographic enterprise than the coding and fragmenting method of qualitative studies. Here, journal notes, interviews, observations, theoretical commentary, or other writers could be recognised as research material. This, of course, is what the imaginative ethnographer or sociologist or cultural analyst is doing in their research. A computing facility which held all this in its head, as it were, is probably going to be more reliable than any individual. However, even this 'multi-layered' software process cannot replace those moments of wild thinking and imagination – they can just help us to make the most of them. Beware of the technological fix – where the technology takes over and stands in for or guides the research process. Hammersley and Atkinson reminds us that the coding of the old code and retrieval system of Ethnograph flattens out the data and although the possibility of re-coding is there, it is extremely time-consuming. The danger, therefore, is that the codes become fixed and the data static. Here we lose the richness and diversity of the qualitative research.

Thus, there are a range of different analytical strategies which you can adopt. Some choices will be already predicted by your research framework and your methods. However, at this stage improvisation and experimentation can continue to open up your research and to pose different kinds of questions. As in all stages in the process of research, the key to making the most of your research material is reflexivity. Most of your decisions will influence, and be influenced by, the process of writing, to which we now turn.

nine

Writing

Writing is the dark secret of social science. (Plummer, 2000: 168)

Imagine an opera singer who spent months learning the words to an opera, the stage moves, the characterisation of their role, but who left singing until the night before the performance. Writing is how researchers communicate their ideas. What craftspeople such as opera singers, musicians, carpenters, journalists, chefs do is to practise their craft regularly and constantly in order to hone their skills, to improve their 'performance' and to find different ways of doing things better or more effectively. How many of us think about writing in this way, I wonder?

There are a number of issues with regard to writing and I want to approach this aspect of research in three rather different ways. The first is a rather pragmatic discussion about finding ways into writing, or how to avoid staring out of the window. The second tackles some of the interesting questions about the ways in which we present, or communicate our research to others, the modes and styles we use and the kinds of meaning which might be produced through these different modes. I quite recognise that for a student or researcher struggling with the blank screen, having difficulty writing anything at all, the latter set of questions and issues might feel like a luxury, self-indulgence or even torture. Finally, I will touch on the need to make our writing accessible to wider readerships than is most usually assumed by the academic monograph. So, let us start with the more pragmatic issues related to writing.

When does 'writing' begin or why didn't I start this earlier?

Just as Wendy Hollway found it difficult to be precise about when she started doing 'actual' research, so researchers working on extended projects should find it retrospectively difficult to establish when 'writing' began. This is certainly not always the case as many of us tend to put off getting down to writing. As a tutor, it is often very difficult to extract drafts from students and this is usually because they don't yet exist. Furthermore, it is indicative of a very familiar attitude to writing which produces fear and anxiety. We can all find a multitude of reasons for thinking we are not yet ready to start writing; there is a new book or article which I should read, or more vague feelings of not being clear about how to approach the task in hand. I find that many mundane tasks become overwhelmingly attractive when I am facing my computer screen. For example, as I write, my kitchen floor has never been cleaner. These 'distraction tactics', while sometimes providing some good thinking time, can eat up your time, causing stress and panic as your deadlines approach. Throughout this book I have suggested that writing should be involved in every phase of research, not left until the last stage where all the data is gathered in and different theoretical texts, related research, etc. have been read. As Michael Green suggests, 'A researcher should write often, whatever the circumstances, as a matter of routine' (1997: 201). A common mistake is to think of writing as a single process, that is expecting to write the finished text at the same time as working through the ideas and the best or most appropriate ways of expressing them. Writing should be provisional until you are in a position to produce a final draft. I agree with Green's observation: 'to be positive, many things happen during writing (connections, insights, metaphors) which are discovered and only happen in and through the writing process' (ibid.: 201). Thus, reaching the final draft will require several stages with time to reflect upon each. You need to work on your written texts several times, getting feedback where you can from your adviser, or anyone who can be persuaded to read and comment on your work. Fortunately, writing, like most other things, gets better with practice and just doing it. For most students writing is occasioned by the demands of assessment, but if you get used to making it part of your work as a routine activity, you will avoid endowing it with some mysterious, magical powers which you must work yourself up to in order to confront. Remember that feeling when you finally get into writing an essay? You think to yourself 'why didn't I start this earlier?', usually when you have run out of time and have a tight deadline to meet. It is worth avoiding this feeling, and being your own worst enemy to boot, certainly with larger projects which simply cannot be achieved in this way.

Writing down and writing up: writing as 'craft'

Referring to ethnographic practices, Paul Atkinson usefully indicates the distinction in writing ethnographic research, usually described as 'writing down' that is your field notes, your observations, descriptive passages, etc. and 'writing up' which Atkinson suggests 'carries stronger connotations of a constructive side to the writing' (1990: 61). Atkinson's point is that while what is written 'down' is treated as 'data' and what is written 'up' is treated as the finished product of the research, both modes are subject to interpretation and should be considered to be matters of 'textual construction'. We can go further and use the distinction to understand some of our own attitudes to the production of texts throughout the research process.

C. Wright Mills suggests that we should develop a file (or notebook) in which we can experiment as writers. Mills, ever the helpful pragmatist, suggests we should write something at least every week. In this way you can 'experiment as a writer and thus ... develop your powers of expression. To maintain [such] a file is to engage in the controlled experience' (1959: 217).

When it comes to producing more finished written material, planning is an essential part of the writing process. Getting a structure clear before you write is an essential part of essay writing. Again, Mills expands this into a more general approach to thinking about your work. Planning should not only take place at the beginning of a project, for example, when applying to do doctoral research or to obtain funding, but rather should be a constant and reflexive process throughout your intellectual life.

Like all aspects of the research process, there are no hard and fast rules for structure and approaches to writing. Clearly, a rough plan and outline is important so that you know what the different elements are of each chapter or section: how the argument is being developed, what your 'moves' are. For PhD students writing seminar papers for presentation, work in progress papers for internal publication, giving papers at conferences and, if possible writing a journal article based on some early research 'statement' are all good strategies for shaping your work.

It is important to practise communicating your thoughts through seminar and conference presentations. This cannot be done most effectively through reading out a paper written for publication. The paper should be re-drafted for oral presentation with the time you have available in mind, your audience and their particular interests, aiming to get across the key points of your argument and your supporting examples in as interesting and engaging a way as possible. How many tedious presentations have you endured at conferences that are delivered in a language constructed for publication rather than for presentation? If you go through this editing progress, it focuses your thoughts, gives you an idea how the material can be handled and what is useful and what is not. A well-presented paper will encourage productive and stimulating questions and debate from which you can learn. Similarly, a well-timed journal article in which you make your first statements about your research can attract interested researchers and academics who are working in similar areas. If you are fortunate, these contacts can enlarge your intellectual community giving much help and encouragement alleviating some of the inevitable feelings of isolation.

Styles and conventions

It is important to be able to consciously select the style which is appropriate to your research material. Just as every stage of our research should be reflexive, this applies also to our writing (and reading) practices. There are a number of useful texts which insist on the textuality of ethnographic research (and other forms of research) and it is no longer acceptable to think about our writing as 'obvious' or a 'neutral' part of the process. It is just as selective and constructive as every other part of the process. Writing seems to be ephemeral, difficult to pin down and it is therefore useful to equip ourselves with modes which deal with more literary genres and texts in order to understand what shape our writing is taking. How we communicate to our ideal reader(s), how we achieve the interplay between the concrete examples and our own discursive and analytic commentary is a matter for decision. How do we present our research subjects? How do we give them a voice? Where am I, the author in the text? These are all questions that will present themselves to you when planning your writing. They require careful, critical and reflexive consideration.

Hammersley and Atkinson (1993) in writing about ethnographic texts and monographs identify major tropes, or figures of speech which inhabit all ethnographic texts. These are: metaphor; synecdoche; metonymy; irony; topos. I have found these useful concepts in thinking about writing practice and they may be helpful in identifying some of our own implicit writing strategies. Again, it is important to emphasise that these are critical tools which we can use to crack open our own and other's texts, not a set of prescriptive ways of writing. They are thinking tools.

Metaphor

Just as in fiction, metaphor can condense and capture a complex set of relations within an image or a symbol. Hammersley and Atkinson remind us that the more traditional social sciences are full of metaphors, e.g. 'social structure', 'the market' to name but two. However, they identify Goffman's use of the metaphors of dramaturgy, theatre and acting as perhaps one of the classic and most insightful uses of metaphor on the social sciences. It illuminates the complexities of social life, of actors within particular settings, of roles and identities, etc. in an elegant and simple way. A useful exercise is to read scholarly texts for the metaphors. Reading examples of good work is, after all, one way in which we can improve our own practice.

Synecdoche

This is where a 'part' is made to stand for the 'whole' as in the use of exemplars, illustrative moments, portraits and vignettes. They provide, through exemplification, an interesting and immediately accessible way in for the reader to the more general analytical framework, or broader issues. Thus, one encounter can form an anecdote; one respondent's story can be told as an exemplar of all other respondents who inhabit the same social position; a story about the researcher's experience, something that happened during her fieldwork, can be used to illustrate the broader questions of research practice.

Metonymy

This deals with causality, sequence, the putting together of events. It is used in moments of 'realist' description' and is about 'telling stories' The researcher collects stories as data and 'recasts' then in sociological or anthropological narratives (Hammersley and Atkinson, 1993: 249). 'The transformation of "the field" into "the text" is partly achieved by means of the narrative construction of everyday life' (ibid.: 250). Indeed, for Mankekar, '[m]y account of viewers' interpretations of television programs, then, is a form of purposeful story-telling, shaped by partial perspectives and accountable positioning' (1999: 68).

Irony

A mode often found in sociological and ethnographic texts. It is found in perspectival or relativist points of view. It points to incongruities, it compares and contrasts the familiar with the strange, the expected with the unexpected and illuminates the unintended consequences of particular courses of action.

Topos

Identified by Hammersley and Atkinson as those points at which the text indicates the already known, the taken-for-granted or common-sense knowledge which is shared between the author and the reader. Citing specific texts, using concepts in particular ways, all indicate a shared knowledge and background which relates to the research at issue.

Portraits

The use of portraits, or synecdoche, was discussed in the chapter on analysis. Obviously your decisions at the interpretation stage will have shaped the kinds of choices you have about constructing the written text. Two authors who have used portraits to good effect are Sean Moores in his study about the use of satellite television in everyday life (Moores, 1996), and Joke Hermes in her study of the readers of women's magazines (Hermes, 1995).

Moores' monograph does not consist entirely of portraits, rather, he presents research material from the three neighbourhoods upon which he based his study in different ways. One chapter only uses the portrait or vignette style. While Moores does not dwell on his reasons too deeply, it seems clear that the portraits are used because they are in direct contrast with each other in relation to the status of satellite television. In this chapter, Moores explores the delicate question, in the UK at least, of the relationship of the appearance of satellite dishes on the exterior of houses to questions of taste. By using vignettes or portraits of specific households he is able to communicate to the reader the intricate and subtle operations of taste cultures within and between the households. This introduces factors of generation, profession, tradition, heritage, etc. in direct and engaging ways. The other two neighbourhoods in his study form a further two chapters of his monograph which deal with his empirical data and are presented in thematic style.

Joke Hermes, in a chapter entitled 'Portrait of Two Readers' departed from the dominant mode in her book in presenting two 'in-depth' portraits that emphasised the significance of life trajectory in magazine reading. While her other interviews had revealed contemporary 'snapshots' of reading practice, in her two extended interviews she was able to explore dimensions of time and memory in relation to the consumption of this popular, and 'easily put down' form.

Connell's (1995) study of changing masculinities, to which I have already made reference in relation to his method of analysis in the previous chapter, chose to present his research material in the form of 'Four Studies of the Dynamics of Masculinity'. In this way, Connell attempts to preserve the individual life story, not in full by any means, but in its essence, within a thematic and comparative structure. The men in his study are grouped within the four studies, which in turn are indicative of critical points in the construction and deconstruction of masculinities. Thus, his 'sample' was strategically selected for exemplification of the 'critical points', e.g. unemployment, encounters with feminism, homosexuality and rationality, and his analysis took him through transcription of the individual stories, the identification of themes and then the construction of the study drawing on the life story accounts. Here he looked for similarities and differences which are identified within the studies. In reading his studies the reader moves in and out of the particular life story and the broader social structural elements of social change. Importantly, however, his individual portraits are not lost within this presentation. His is an inventive way of combining the fragmentation model with the portrait model, the outcome of which goes beyond both and a rich and analytical account of changing masculinities is produced which refers outwards to social reality. It is also makes for a highly readable text.

The author in the text

Many of the projects you have read – and possibly the ones you do yourself – will require the interweaving of respondent's views and voices with your own observations and interpretations within your overall theoretical and interpretive framework. The decisions you make about how you incorporate your research material is indicative of your approach to both your respondents themselves and your epistemological position. We have spoken elsewhere of the status of spoken accounts and especially the necessity to think of them as contingent accounts and responses within the dynamic of the interview, group discussion or observation. How, then, are we to present this material in our research? We can usefully return to our distinction of the life story as that between resource and topic and extend it to our thinking about the status of research material more generally.

If we have gone to the trouble of gathering accounts, conversations and other forms of spoken data, then it is important to find ways of allowing that to be present in the written text. Ken Plummer suggests that this can be thought of as a 'continuum of constructions' (2000: 179-83). He argues that there are 'two major interpreters in any sociological life story: the subject and the social scientist'. The subject, our respondent, is interpreting their lives for our purposes, drawing on 'common-sense' knowledge of the world. The social scientist interprets the material drawing on theoretical and analytical constructs from his or her disciplinary procedures. The issue for analysis and writing is the extent to which the social scientist imposes their view on the material and the extent to which the respondent's more personal accounts are allowed to appear in the text.

Many texts use a method of what Plummer refers to as 'verification by anecdote'. These are a selection of good examples drawn from empirical data in which the author provides no justification for the selection of particular quotes above others. In this way the data is used mainly to support the theoretical hypothesis or framework of the author.

A second, and perhaps more familiar method is to use extracts from interviews under different themes which are linked to sociological or cultural theory. Plummer calls this 'systematic thematic analysis' and, for example, this is the mode I chose for presenting my research into the VCR.

A third mode identified by Plummer is that of presenting the life history document where the sociologist intervenes as little as possible (except for editing). This is an extreme version of life story and, as we have seen, it is possible to present more analytical accounts of life stories, or long conversational interviews, for example, Connell, while remaining respectful of our respondents.

In their study of rock, youth and modernity, Johan Fornas, Ulf Lindberg and Ove Sernhede carried out an ethnography of three different bands. In the written version of their research *In Garageland* (Fornas et al., 1995), they include extracts from interviews and discussions with the bands on the page parallel to their own anthropological discourse. In this way the reader is invited to capture the nature and vocabulary of the exchanges within the bands.

Devault (1990) takes up the importance of writing within feminist work but from a different perspective. She emphasises the importance of finding new terms and forms of speech in order to do justice to the possibly previously unknown or unnamed practices and experiences of women. She insists that feminist scholars should not be constrained by 'scholarly' or 'scientific' language. This should go as far as constructing different expectations in our readers, who should be prepared for different uses of language and styles of writing. For Devault, this is the only way we can be true to our subjects and the complexity of their often hidden lives.

The emphasis throughout this book has been on the importance and significance of lived experience as a rich source for understanding culture and social change. It is then important that respondent's voices should not be lost in our texts, but we must be aware of the impossibility of both 'speaking for others' and 'giving others a voice'. In the end we are the authors of our texts and must take responsibility for the ways in which we choose to present our research. As Les Back states in introducing his study: 'Within this book I use a range of textual devices to narrate the fraught 'contact zones' ... that form its focus. These include extended quotation, description and monologues. All of these devices and the accounts that are made possible through their deployment should be viewed with epistemological suspicion' (1996: 6).

Critical and reflexive writing: critiques

If we now move on to thinking about writing in a different way, that is as a text produced through various and different modes. Back refers to the 'literary turn' in feminism, anthropology and sociology which 'offer(s) new insights into the processes that affect the textual production of research-based knowledge' (1998: 292) and which have been the subject of this book as it has dealt with different phases of research, can offer us insights into our research writing. Back quotes Paul Atkinson who concludes:

> The fully mature ethnography requires a reflexive awareness of its own writing, the possibilities and limits of its own language, and a principled exploration of his modes of representation. Not only do we need to cultivate a self-conscious construction of ethnographic texts, but also a readiness to *read* texts from a more 'literary critical' perspective. Sociologists and their students must cultivate the discipline of reading their own and others' arguments for their stylistic and rhetorical properties. (Atkinson, 1990: 180)

Here we have a clear statement about the importance of reflexive writing. We should, as authors of our research, be aware of our position within our writing and conscious of the rhetorical and other strategies which we are using. It is a question of finding a form of writing which is appropriate to your own work, your own research strategies and the kinds of data you wish to present.

Spatial metaphors are extremely useful in thinking through complex practices and making some kinds of practical distinctions especially in how we as authors and researchers move in and out of the texts which we construct, how and in what ways a range of narratives and voices can be introduced, e.g. dialogic writing; polyvocal accounts; vignettes; case studies and portraits.

The distance and presence axis is especially useful in a discussion of ethnographic texts given that, as Clifford observes, there are two textual elements which determine anthropological authority: the use of the first person in the text which claims that 'I was there', putting the anthropologist in the centre of the text; and, the suppression of that voice so that the text's author is rendered absent, establishing the anthropologist's scientific authority.

The first element is that of a presence – here the ethnographer or researcher can claim validity and thus to speak from a position of authority because they have been there, the text is often (quite literally) in the present tense, the ethnographer as eye-witness, producing an experiential account.

The second element is what I would describe as distance. That of the suppression of the researcher's presence, more typical of research where the author is not declared, but maintains an objective distance from the text. Such texts are written in the academic, scientific style of the third person. Feminist critics have suggested that this ultimately denies responsibility for the text, the author is hidden behind the screen of objectivity and implied neutrality in the text. This unreflexive mode produces what Liz Stanley has called ungrounded or unlocated knowledge.

One answer to thinking about authority of the ethnographic text has been to question the ways in which the ethnographer and researcher approaches fieldwork, but another is to break open the texts of ethnography and reveal the rhetoric and textual strategies which they employ.

The anthropologist James Clifford is one of a number who have begun to deconstruct the texts and writing tactics, or rhetorics of the ethnographic monograph (Clifford and Marcus, 1986). He suggests that what he calls the 'poetics of ethnography' have a number of dimensions, as follows: Contextual; Rhetorical; Institutional; Generic; Political; Historical. These, he suggests, can be useful categories for analysis. The body of work of which Clifford was a key instigator reflects on and questions the tradition of representation in anthropology and is often referred to as evidence of a 'crisis of representation in ethnographic writing'. These reflections have led to calls for different forms of writing, for example, a dialogic form of writing where the 'other' is given an equal voice in the text.

However, many are suspicious of this trend. Rabinow (1986), for example, suggests that these metareflections are to be seen as part of the postmodern shift. They take place within and are imbued with the politics of the academy where the anthropologists reflect on themselves. No longer in his tent doing his fieldwork, but in the campus library.

Strathern, too, is critical of the cosy dialogic model and the impetus behind it. The experimentalists, she points out, are almost all male who, in adopting this nurturing and optimistic mode, express a form of sentimentality. Textual radicals such as these seek to work toward establishing relationships, to demonstrate the importance of connection and openness in their work – to advance the possibilities of shared and mutual understanding – thus power and the realities of socio-economic constraints are rather hazy and not tackled. Strathern rather insists on not losing sight of fundamental differences, power relationships, hierarchical domination. Thus, preserving meaningful difference as a distinctive value for social and cultural critique.

Using images in presenting research

The use of photographs has long been an established part of ethnographic research but, as Sarah Pink points out, these have traditionally been used as 'evidence' that the ethnographer was there (Pink, 2001). The images themselves are not problematised in this realist mode and traditionally left in the texts to speak for themselves, or tied into the descriptive sections of the ethnography, simply as illustrations. Pink insists that the use of the visual has a much greater potential for ethnographic research. However, it requires thinking about the intent of the images and how the reader might interpret the image. She also points to examples of texts which, while not traditional ethnographies, use images as photo-essays, or mixed with texts, in ways which invite the reader to interpret the images as images and not as adjuncts to the text. John Berger working with Jan Mohr, has consistently used the visual in his work (Berger and Mohr, 1967, 1982). Photographs can also provide useful data of different kinds and for different purposes. Jo Spence, working with her own identity, explored her history and biography through visual sources in her family album, juxtaposing these with self-portraits (Spence, 1986). In this way she used her family archives and her reflexive photographic work as a source through which to develop social and cultural analysis.

Questions for you to consider in thinking about your text:

- Narrative: how is the story/stories told? What devices are employed in the text?

- Who tells the story? Whose voice(s) do we hear?

- Who are these texts for and who gets to see/read them?

Experimental texts

There is obviously now a wealth of writing on writing! Some of it focuses on more practical questions and problems, but much of it, especially within anthropology, acknowledges the shift from the idea that language (and research texts) are 'reflections' of the research world where language is seen as neutral, to the notion of language and the texts themselves as constitutive, as formative of the research data itself. Form has meaning. However, a note of caution is sounded by Hammersley and Atkinson (1993) when they remind us that we must always be able to argue for our use of particular textual strategies. Thus, experimentation and transgression of the codes and conventions of research writing cannot simply involve throwing them all to the wind, but should be carefully thought through in relation to your topic. For example, we must still be able to support our claims and our writing must not detach itself completely from the external referent from which our research material has emerged. We must be aware of the need to relate our theoretical frameworks to our empirical data and give the reader sufficient material in order that they can assess our work.

Who are we writing for?

Back and Plummer call for a wider dissemination of our research through different kinds of writing, for example, journalism. Indeed, the kind of research I have been talking about in this book deals with issues and topics which are of great interest to people outside of university libraries. However, many cultural studies texts are not addressed to this wider readership. Often there seems to be a wilful exclusion or even elitism in the language of the texts which does not really make sense. There is nothing to stop us trying to find ways of communicating our insights about the complexity of social and cultural processes in a direct and accessible way. There is, after all, a tremendous appetite for 'stories', witness the growth of television programmes based on the lives of 'ordinary people', but also books and magazines which deal with 'real life' are thriving. This is not to say that we should all turn our hands to producing 'blockbuster' texts – but why not? – rather, there is a great deal of public suspicion and misunderstanding about what we do in cultural studies and sociology – some of which is fuelled by people who should know better – and we need to find ways of entering the public discourses on, say, national identity, public broadcasting, consumption and consumer issues, youth cultures, popular texts, etc. in ways which are not defensive and obscure, but that have something useful to say. By the way, if we do not have anything useful to say outside of the academy, then I do think we should question what we are doing with our time!

| ten | **Sources of Knowledge and Ways of Knowing** |

The focus of this book has been on the notion of lived cultures and how we might develop methods for exploring everyday life. There is clearly no possible conclusion to a book like this, rather, a hope that it has inspired and enabled researchers to formulate projects and develop appropriate and reflexive methods for exploration. In this chapter I want to take some of the implications of the developments within and challenges to more conventional approaches to research which we have seen emerging in a variety of disciplinary areas and suggest new ways of approaching empirical research in cultural studies, along with more appropriate evaluative criteria. This would need to recognise the instability of knowledge claims, referenced in the so-called 'crisis of representation' and the moves into post-structural and postmodern modes within research. It is the case that you will be embarking on your studies and research in a period when the certainties of knowledge exemplified within the modernist and pragmatic modes are under assault themselves (Denzin, 1997: 45). These might be thought of as the 'common-sense' approaches to knowledge that posit a knowable world and a researcher who can come to know through the application of particular observational methods. As Denzin suggests, the only certainty is uncertainty and in this way social science and ethnography become one version of 'reality' among many (ibid.: 45). Science and scientific discourses, or discourses which claim scientific truth, are now called into question and no longer hold the position of power and dominance they once did.

These issues internal to the academy are echoed in parallel developments across the globe where certainties and boundaries are being challenged and transgressed. With the rapid developments in global communication flows and movement and migration of people, the boundaries of the nation-state, and geographical locations more usually associated with culture and belonging are shifting and in flux. At a more mundane level, textual proliferation makes it difficult, if not impossible, to separate 'media' from 'reality', thus, our concepts of 'audience' are severely challenged by the saturation of media texts.

In taking the approach I have for this book, by insisting on looking at text and lived cultures, on the self and autobiography, on reflexivity and the crucial concept of experience, I have laid the ground for ways of conceptualising relationships and identities, including that of the researcher, which might more adequately grasp the realities of the contemporary world and McRobbie's notion of 'identities-in-culture'.

In my view, this involves building on our understanding of 'identity' and the process of subjectivity discussed in Chapter 2, and re-visiting the feminist standpoint theories. Also, following Ang, of arguing for the importance of the radical contextualisation of our research (1996: 66-81) and insisting that there must be 'something at stake' in our research practice which she has called 'a cultural politics' (ibid.: 78). Our studies and the 'knowable spaces' they mark out are contingent and we should have an awareness of their historical specificity and that of the subject under study. A 'cultural politics' informs our sense of contingency as to how we frame specific contexts and which questions we foreground through our research. It is the case, however, that this radical contextualisation presents immediate problems for those who demand generalisability and whose criteria of representativeness, validity and reliability are increasingly inappropriate for these kinds of projects.

Let me begin by identifying something of a paradox which the notions of shifting boundaries, loss of rootedness and flow, might present. There is a sense of dislocation, away from the 'people and culture' model posed by more traditional anthropology, which suggests that space and place are problematic and cannot be linked in any assumed way to people and cultures inhabiting those specific locations. However, in calling for a radical contextualisation, Ang argues that our studies must be more modest and contingent than those which might aim to generalise, or produce a large narrative of explanation. The danger in acknowledging that 'globalisation' has created communication links across all aspects of the globe is for the researcher to attempt to see it all, not to be positioned anywhere in particular, and to speak from nowhere. As I have argued throughout this book, we cannot be everywhere, nor can we speak from nowhere, thus we need at the very start to locate ourselves and our subject of study within the specific context of research investigation and production. This is to challenge 'the self-presentation of theory as an articulation of timeless or placeless universality, relocat[ing] it as a reflexive, self-correcting interpretative practice' (Code, 1995: 2, quoted in Skeggs, 1997: 22). But we do need equally rigorous procedures for this radical contextualisation in order that we can claim it as a legitimate research activity and one that can offer broader implications than the specific case.

To take this further I suggest we need a robust theory of identity and subjectivity along with a clear notion of what we understand by 'experience' and the status it is afforded within the project. We need to reveal our own position as researchers, to be clear about the dangers of standpoint theory in its leaning towards essentialism, thinking rather of our position as adopting a particular vantage point from which we can, tentatively, produce 'situated knowledges'. Our methods of gathering research material will be those of engendering narratives, of generating interpretations of texts and of coaxing of stories. Our research product, then, can best be thought of as the construction of a narrative which claims only to be a 'positioned truth' (Ang, 1996: 78) 'our stories cannot just tell "partial truths", they are also, consciously or not, positioned truths' (Abu-Loghod, 1991: 142, quoted in Ang, 1996: 78).

Standpoint theory

In Chapter 2 I made brief reference to work developed by feminists who contested claims being made as to what constitutes knowledge. Scholars argued that knowledge comes from experience and, further, that those who were on the receiving end of oppression had a privileged access to knowledges of the oppressed and the oppressors. This work was important in bringing experience into the development of theory and ways of seeing the world. The notion that experience engenders knowledge is important, but can be seen, as Skeggs suggests, as a product of its time within feminist debates. In this work there was an urgent need to place female experience more centrally and to demonstrate that knowledges of women's everyday lives were systematically subjugated, refused by the categories and methodological orthodoxy of existing social science. However, 'standpoint theory' is problematic on a number of counts:

1   The individual tends to be essentialised as it assumes that identity is somehow 'there' before experience.

2   Certain accounts of experience can be privileged over others.

3   In aiming and claiming to produce a better truth it remains within the 'scientific' endeavour.

However, what we can draw from the important work which these debates produced from subjugated groups, is that knowledge is at least partial – that there is no 'one place' from which to objectively view the world and claim to 'know'. Feminists also revealed the profoundly political nature of knowledge production and insisted that its processes and its relations of production be revealed. Through the debates which 'standpoint theory' engendered, the category of experience and how it was being used was brought into question. Problematic as it is, it is clear that experience remains a crucial category in our critical understanding of lived cultures. Skeggs' formulation of experience is useful here. She sees it not as the source of authentic knowledge, nor as necessarily coming before standpoint knowledge, rather, it 'informs our take-up and production of positions but it does not fix us either in time or place'

(Skeggs, 1997: 27). We could go further and see experience as articulation, the site upon which subjectivity is constructed, thus 'experience [is] central to the construction of subjectivity and theory' (Skeggs, 1997: 27). Haraway (1988) speaks rather of the notion of 'situated knowledges' and this is useful for an understanding of the researcher's position and the claims she makes for her research and, by extension, the accounts given to her by her respondents. We have, then, a number of 'vantage points', which are those of the researcher in different encounters with respondents and of the respondents themselves, within the research process which can never be fixed, but need to be understood in their specific locations.

Subjectivity

This way of formulating the research process itself is to think of it as producing 'subjectivities'. Nikolas Rose, whose work on subjectivity is useful here, stresses the importance of paying attention to the heterogeneity and specificity of the ideals of models of personhood deployed in different practices' (Rose, 1996: 133). Thus, we can think about articulation of different discourses in the practice of making identity and inhabiting subjectivity. Rose's formulation, following Foucault, suggests that people are subjected to a complex mixture of technologies, in shaping the self, but are at one and the same time active subjects engaged in deploying the tactics of the self when inhabiting different sites and concomitant identities. This allows us to envisage the often contradictory nature of different subjectivities, and is useful in understanding the ways in which human beings respond to opportunities through the deployment of human technologies in specific and contingent ways. Human beings, for Rose,

> are not the unified subjects of some coherent regime of domination that produces persons in the form of which it dreams. On the contrary, they live their lives in a constant movement across different practices that address them in different ways. Within these different practices, persons are addressed as different sorts of human being, presupposed to be different sorts of human being, acted upon as if they were different sorts of human being. (Rose, 1996: 140-1)

In taking Rose's formulation, we can open up for analysis the different institutions and practices which human beings encounter and look at what kinds of subjectivities they invite and the ways in which people employ different technologies, of language, speech and narrative, of demeanour and so on. A modest example is my journey through the city of Birmingham, from the main shopping area, its shop windows an enticement to look, to try and buy. I move through the streets, centres and department stores as a consuming subject. When I walk up the hill, away from the brightly lit shops and stores, I reach the 'civic' centre, where art galleries, the museum and library invite the demeanour and the deportment of the responsible citizen with rights and responsibilities. Thus, we are offered positions which invite us to see ourselves differently and further to embody certain subject regimes appropriate to the specific context. We can, of course, refuse this positioning but this is to emphasise most clearly the existence of the 'ideal' form which is suggested. Taking a historical perspective, Rose argues for a 'genealogy of subjectification' which would move 'towards an account of the ways in which [the] modern "regime of the self" emerges ... out of a number of contingent ... practices and processes' (Rose, 1996: 129). Carolyn Steedman's points about 'writing the self', discussed in Chapter 6 would be relevant here. But where is experience in all of this? Rose's work encourages us to think about how humans give meaning to experience and how they produce experience. Humans thus are not produced by experience, but rather through devices of meaning production, and story-telling, vocabularies, repertoires, employment of codes and conventions, etc. themselves produce experience. These techniques are not ready made, but must be activated, often differently in different social and cultural sites. These are what Rose refers to as processes of subjectification, a diverse range of processes and practices 'by means of which human beings come to relate to themselves and others as subjects of a certain type'. Thus for Rose, subjectification has its own history. Importantly, he is not using the term to imply the subject as object of domination and repression, rather he is suggesting that we look at the process through which the subject is 'made up' as a certain type. There is, in Rose's formulations, the possibility of thinking of subjectivity as being both subject to governance, normalisation and domination, and also as something which is made up through the processes of subjectification which are contingent, often contradictory and by no means fixed.

This formulation of the subjectivising process offers the opportunity to think across different forms of activity, more commonly defined as work and leisure, as areas where subjects encounter different social institutions and are addressed differently by these institutions. For example, DuGay notes how companies and corporate organisations are seeking to cultivate 'enterprising subjects' which are autonomous, self-regulating, productive individuals (Miller and Rose, 1990: 1-31). In the changing working environments of the West, enterprise and entrepreneurial activity are encouraged by large and small organisations alike in the working world. Thus, 'self-management' is the key - 'how to handle yourself to your own best advantage'. The advice to all workers is to 'make a project of themselves' that is, to work on their relations with employment, and on all other areas of their lives, in order to develop a 'lifestyle' which will 'maximise the worth of their existence to themselves' (DuGay, 1991: 55). In my own current research, I am exploring new forms of subjectivity through looking at the ways in which female/feminine subjectivities are being produced and taken up through the discourses of both consumer and enterprise cultures. This is a study of women located within particular social and historical sets of circumstances, of life-worlds, of work and, arguably, of global capital which will explore how forms of feminine subjectivity can be produced within the dynamics of the 'market'.

Moving through the everyday

In Chapter 7, we looked at attempts to understand the relationship between 'audience' and 'text' or, more broadly popular culture and everyday life. In Chapter 3, we noted the move towards the shifting and dispersed identity of the fan and Fiske's provocative suggestion that people in their everyday lives, take from popular culture what they want. 'Everyday life is constituted by the practices of popular culture, and is characterized by the creativity of the weak in using the resources provided by a disempowering system while refusing to submit to that power' (Fiske, 1989: 47). This highly utopian notion of the power of popular culture seems to discount any notion of determination or constraint which shape our lives. Clearly, what I have been arguing suggests that in our everyday lives and in our consumption and use of culture we are constantly being produced and producing ourselves as subjects and identities. But, because we are actively engaged in these tactics of the everyday, this is not to say that, in 'refusing to submit to that power' we become powerful. Roger Silverstone understands this tension to be at the heart of much thinking about popular forms (for him, especially television) and their use. He argues that this paradox of '... the imposed meanings and the selected meanings – the controlled behaviour and the free – the meaningless and the meaningful – the passive and the active – are in constant tension' (Silverstone, 1994: 164). Silverstone further suggests that these tensions can be traced through ethnographic work, but insists that these studies '... must be firmly grounded in the mutuality of empirical and theoretical understanding. For it is in the dynamics of the particular that we will be able to identify, if not fully comprehend, the forces of structure: the forces both of domination and resistance' (ibid.). There are, in the modern world, many poignant examples of 'the dynamics of the particular' set within 'forces of domination and resistance' to which I will now turn.

Diasporic studies

Studies of diaspora or displacement are mobilising this problematic and bringing together scholars from cultural studies, anthropology, sociology and geography. For anthropologists this means questioning the implicit relationship between place and culture as rooted in a particular national or geographic context. Diasporas and displacements are a fact of modern life within all cultures, but there are some poignant examples as refugees flee oppressive regimes, seeking asylum in different locations. Arguably modernity has been built on displacement of populations as rural workers moved into developing cities and industrial bases to seek work. Recent studies of the (re)constructions of community in different parts of the globe by diasporic groups have expanded the notion of identity, community and space and place

Liisa Malkki, an anthropologist, argues that what these studies require is a new 'sociology of displacement' or 'nomadology'. This is not to deny, she insists, the importance of place in the construction of identities, rather to acknowledge that place, space and identity are non-essential, and that the often assumed source, or roots of identity are in themselves changing. She quotes Hebdige in his study of Caribbean music and cultural identity 'Rather than tracing back to the roots ... to their source, I've tried to show how the roots themselves are in a state of constant flux and change. The roots don't stay in one place ... There is no such thing as a pure point of origin ... but that doesn't mean that there isn't history' (Hebdige, 1987: 10). Malkki further argues that deterritorialisation and identity are intimately connected, 'Diasporas always leave a trail of collective memory about another place and time and create new maps of desire and attachment' (Breckenridge and Appadurai, 1989: quoted in Malkki in Gupta and Ferguson, 1997: 72).

Malkki insists that we attend to 'the multiplicy of attachments that people form to places through living in, remembering them and imagining them.' (Malkki, 1997: 72) This rethinking within anthropology both insists on attention to place and space, but as contingent, and the groups which inhabit those spaces as those of identities in process.

Aspects of media use are often central to a sense of identity and community and is reflected in a number of studies. We have already looked at Marie Gillespie's study of young Punjabis now resident in Southall, a suburb of west London.

Such studies are demanding new ways of thinking, especially in relation to communication, representation and media flows across transnational boundaries spaces within the context of 'globalisation'. Naficy's (1993) study of the cultural production of Iranian television in Los Angeles in *The Making of Exile Cultures* emphasised the importance of a business infrastructure which enabled diverse media activity. The construction of imaginary homelands through television and film images available to diasporic communities in their new locations can often have dislocating consequences. Gillespie notes that on visiting their 'homeland' Delhi, some of the young people in her study found it to be more like London than their own home area of Southall. Evidence of the construction of a diasporic community based on memories of an 'imagined' home. Other more recent studies are by Kosnick, Aksoy and Robins on the proliferation of Turkish television channels in Europe, giving the Turkish diasporic communities access to programmes from 'home'. (Kosnick, 2000; Aksoy and Robins, 2000). Robins and Aksoy ask what are the implications of these media cultures for 'questions of identity, particularly of having access to programming 'from home?' (ibid.: 351). Cunningham and Sinclair's edited collection *Floating Lives: The Media and Asian Diasporas* (2000) suggests that the media and cultural activities of diasporic communities construct what they describe as 'public sphericules' but also that these communities do not necessarily exist in relation to 'texts of and from "home"', for example, the Fiji Indian diaspora around the Pacific Rim have, in Sydney, 'fashioned a vibrant popular culture based on consumption and celebration of Hindi filmdom and its associated music, dance and fashion cultures' (Cunningham 2001: 144). These studies above all indicate the complexity of diasporic communities, but do so by addressing media texts, consumption and everyday life within these specific located media cultures. Questions of identity-in-culture are clearly crucial to an understanding of these lived cultures. They also combine an understanding of the 'macro' - the possibilities of trans-border and trans-national communities and identities with the located practices of individuals and groups.

We require innovative methodological strategies in order to continue with the exploration of the experience of modernity, which for many is about mobility, movement, shifting identities and displacement. This means that we need to look within and beyond national boundaries, at the complexity of trans-global communications which collide with and influence those produced within the national networks and the resultant diversity of the cultural/public sphere. Malkki's insistence on separating culture from place within anthropology is to indicate that established disciplinary procedures require continuous re-examination if they are to have any purchase on 'realities' of the very lives and cultures under study. Methodology, and methods, then, must be conscious of the changes in the social world, alert to experience and especially to those which question conceptual assumptions.

Critical understanding

I now want to return to questions of validity and to develop this further suggesting, following Denzin, that we require new criteria for assessing research practices which 'flow from the qualitative project'. The criteria of internal validity, external validity, reliability and objectivity, Denzin argues, are applicable to work which employs a normative epistemology. That is in work that assumes that 'the normal is what is most representative in a larger population, and it is to that "normal" population that generalizations are directed' (Denzin, 1997: 7). As he points out, this approach ignores or renders absent difference, contestation and more marginal formations within populations.

Denzin notes that postmodern ethnographies produce particular understandings of specific cultural processes within particular settings. 'Any given practice that is studied is significant because it is an instance of a cultural practice that happened in a particular time and place' (ibid.: 8). It goes without saying that these practices cannot be generalised, but what they can do is to suggest that these practices instantiate cultural practice. This is rather like the 'tapping in' argument that Richard Johnson advocates and was discussed in Chapter 3.

As research has developed and especially under the influence of feminist work, stress has been placed on the importance of subjectivity, emotionality, feeling, meaning, desire and fantasy in ethnographic research. Authors have been aware of the need for forms of empowerment through the development of dialogic texts and the level of trustworthiness established with respondents. Some of these characteristics would be present in cultural studies research and echo and develop Richard Johnson's call for more politically informed criteria for judgement. Likewise, Denzin suggests that for these kinds of ethnographic, qualitative studies, the evaluative term 'validity' is no longer appropriate and, following Lather (1993), suggests using the terms 'authority' and 'legitimation'. He puts forward some criteria which are political and which are more appropriate to post-structural studies.

Politics

Here our questions would be about how the text, the written research report or monograph, lays its claims to authority. This would also be to look for an understanding of how power and ideology are at work through systems of discourse. Asking in what ways the text exposes how, for example, race, class, gender, ethnicity, ability, age, etc. are woven through discourses and are embedded within the daily lives of individuals. What, in Stuart Hall's words, is at stake in the study and what, in Ang's terms, are its cultural politics?

Verisimilitude

Denzin uses this term to think about how texts attempt to 'map the real'. It recognises that writing is representation, and that its notion of 'the real' is actively constructed within the text. To what extent then, does the text reveal its truth claims, and does it treat its own 'reality' as multi-perspectival and provisional? This criteria is important in that it recognises that meaning is to be struggled over, both within the textual construction, language, argumentation, etc. but also in the reader's encounter with the text. The important question can then be posed: 'Whose verisimilitude?'

I would also want to add two further useful evaluative criteria, that of respect and methodological yield.

Respect, modesty and reflexivity

Throughout the book I have emphasised the importance of respecting respondents or participants of research. This should be reflected in the account given of methods as well as in the ways in which the individual or collective accounts are dealt with in the text. Is the interpretation sensitive to the stories being told and to what extent are they allowed in the tex? Are the theoretical frameworks used modestly and tentatively or do they, as in my example of Hilary's portrait, threaten to evacuate the respondents through heavy-handed or arrogant analysis? And, to what extent is the researcher able to acknowledge their own position, to reflect on that and to recognise the limitations of their project?

Methodological yield

This returns us to more conventionally academic criteria. Hermes, Connell and Back would argue that their work has a wider theoretical relevance, not in terms of generalisation, i.e. that this set of circumstances is applicable to the wider population, but in terms of the critical understanding which can be brought to bear on the practices and processes of, in Hermes' case, the consumption of magazines, in Connell's case, the shifting conditions for the constructions of masculinities and for Back, the struggles over ethnic identities within urban cultures (Back, 1996; Connell, 1995; Hermes, 1995) This methodological yield is useful to future researchers who while engaging with their arguments critically, can draw on the frank accounts of their research practice in thinking through their own approach.

These suggested criteria are more appropriate for the evaluation of the kinds of small-scale ethnographically informed, politically motivated, and theoretically and methodologically innovative studies of which I have given many examples in this book. Their starting point is acknowledging what kinds of questions are being asked through the research, its exploratory and provisional nature and its modest epistemology. These criteria are not easily satisfied, but I hope that this book will be a small contribution to studies which will make brave attempts to fulfil them.

References

Aksoy, A. and Robins, K. (2000) 'Thinking across spaces: transnational television from Turkey', *European Journal of Cultural Studies*, 3 (3): 343-65.

Alasuutari, P. (1995) *Researching Culture: Qualitative Method and Cultural Studies*. London: Sage.

Alasuutari, P. (ed.) (1999) *Rethinking the Media Audience*. London: Sage.

Alexander, C.E. (2000) *The Asian Gang: Ethnicity, Identity, Masculinity*. Oxford: Berg.

Ang, I. (1985) *Watching Dallas: Soap Opera and the Melodramatic Imagination*. London: Methuen.

Ang, I. (1996) *Living Room Wars*. London: Routledge.

Atkinson, P. (1990) *The Ethnographic Imagination: Textual Constructions of Reality*. London: Routledge.

Atkinson, P. (1992) 'The ethnography of a medical setting: reading, writing and rhetoric', *Qualitative Health Research*, 2 (4): 451-74.

Back, L. (1993) 'Gendered participation: masculinity and fieldwork in a south London adolescent community', in D. Bell, P. Caplan and W.J. Karim (eds), *Gendered Fields. Women, Men and Ethnography*. London: Routledge.

Back, L. (1996) *New Ethnicities and Urban Culture: Racisms and Multiculture in Young Lives*. London: UCL Press.

Back, L. (1998) 'Reading and writing research', in C. Seale (ed.), *Researching Society and Culture*. London: Sage. pp. 285-96.

Barthes, R. (1972) *Mythologies*. London: Jonathan Cape.

Barthes, R. (1977) *Image-Music-Text*. Glasgow: Collins.

Bell, D., Caplan, P. and Karim, W.J. (eds) (1993) *Gendered Fields: Women, Men and Ethnography*. London: Routledge.

Benjamin, W. (1973) *Illuminations*. Glasgow: Collins.

Berger, J. and Mohr, J. (1967) *A Fortunate Man*. Cambridge: Granta Books.

Berger, J. and Mohr, J. (1982) *Another Way of Telling*. Cambridge: Granta Books.

Born, G. (2000) 'Inside television: television studies and the sociology of culture', *Screen*, 41 (4): 404-24.

Bourne, G. (2000) 'Inside television: television studies and the sociology of culture', *Screen*, 41 (4), 404-24.

Breckenridge, C. and Appadurai, A. (1989) 'On moving targets', *Public Culture*, 2 (1) i-iv.

Bruno, G. (1989) untitled article. *Camera obscura*, 20/21, 28-40.

Brunsdon, C. (1981) '*Crossroads*: notes on soap opera', *Screen*, 22 (4): 52-7.

Brunsdon, C. (1989) 'Text and audience', in E. Seiter, H. Borchers, G. Kreutzner and E. Warth, *Remote Control*. London: Routledge.

Brunsdon, C. (1993) 'Identity in feminist television criticism', *Media, Culture and Society*, 15 (2): 309-20.

Brunsdon, C. (1996) 'A thief in the night. Stories of feminism in the 1970s at CCCS', in D. Morley and K-H. Chen (eds) *Stuart Hall: Critical Dialogues in Cultural Studies*. London: Routledge.

Brunsdon, C. (2000) *The Feminist, the Housewife, and the Soap Opera*. Oxford: Oxford University Press.

Brunsdon, C. and Morley, D. (1978) *Everyday Television: 'Nationwide'*. London: British Film Institute.

Buckingham, D. (1987) *Public Secrets: 'EastEnders' and its Audience*. London: British Film Institute.

Buckingham, D. (1993) *Children Talking Television: The Making of Television Literacy*. London: Falmer.

Burgos-Debray, E. (1984) 'Introduction', in R. Menchu, *I Rigoberta Menchu*. London: Verso.

Butler, J. and Scott, J.W. (eds) (1992) *Feminists Theorize the Political*. New York: Routledge.

Canclini, N.G. (1995) *Hybrid Cultures*. Minneapolis: University of Minnesota Press.

Canning, K. (1994) 'Feminist history after the linguistic turn: historicizing discourse and experience', *Signs: Journal of Women in Culture and Society*, 19 (2): 368-404.

Cheesman, T. (1994) *The Shocking Ballad Picture Show: German Popular Literature and Cultural History*. Oxford: Berg.

Chen, K.-H. (ed.) (1998) *Trajectories: Inter-Asia Cultural Studies*. London: Routledge.

Clifford, J. and Marcus, G.E. (eds) (1986) *Writing Culture: The Poetics and Politics of Ethnography*. Berkeley, CA: University of California Press.

Code, L. (1995) *Rhetorical Spaces: Essays on Gendered Locations*. London: Routledge.

Cohen, S. (1997) 'Symbols of trouble', in K. Gelder and S. Thornton (eds), *The Subcultures Reader*. London: Routledge.

Coles, R. (1997) *Doing Documentary Work*. Oxford: Oxford University Press.

Comer, L. (1984) *Wedlocked Women*. Leeds: Feminist Books.

Connell, R.W. (1995) *Masculinities*. Cambridge: Polity Press.

Couldry, N. (2000) *The Place of Media Power: Pilgrims and Witnesses of the Media Age*. London: Routledge.

Cruz, J. and Lewis, J. (1994) 'Reflections on the encoding/decoding model: an interview with Stuart Hall', in J. Cruz and J. Lewis (eds), *Viewing, Reading, Listening: Audiences and Cultural Reception*. Boulder, CO: Westview Press.

Cruz, J. and Lewis, J. (eds) (1994) *Viewing, Reading, Listening: Audiences and Cultural Reception*. Boulder, CO: Westview Press.

Cunningham, S. and Sinclair, J. (eds) (2000) *Floating Lives: The Media and Asian Diasporas*. St Lucia: University of Queensland Press (and Boulder, CO: Rowman and Littlefield, 2001).

Cunningham, S. (2001) 'Popular media as public "sphericules" for diasporic communities', *International Journal of Cultural Studies*, 4 (2): 131-48.

Curran, J., Morley, D. and Walkerdine, V. (1996) *Cultural Studies and Communications*. London: Arnold.

Dawson, G. (1994) *Soldier Heroes: British Adventure, Empire and the Imagining of Masculinities*. London: Routledge.

De Certeau, M. (1984) *The Practice of Everyday Life*. Berkeley, CA: University of California Press.

Deem, R. (1986) *All Work and No Play? A Study of Women and Leisure*. Milton Keynes: Open University Press.

De Lauretis, T. (1984) *Alice Doesn't: Feminism, Semiotics, Cinema*. London: Routledge.

Denzin, N.K. (1992) *Symbolic Interactionism and Cultural Studies*. Cambridge, MA: Blackwell.

Denzin, N.K. (1997) *Interpretive Ethnography: Ethnographic Practices for the 21st Century*. Thousand Oaks, CA: Sage.

Devault, M.L. (1990) 'Talking and listening from women's standpoint: feminist strategies for interviewing and analysis', *Social Problems*, 37: 1.

Doane, M.A. (1989) untitled article. *Camera obscura*, 20/21, 142-7.

DuGay, P. (1991) 'Enterprise culture and the ideology of excellence', *New Formations*, 13: 45-61.

DuGay, P. (1996) *Consumption and Identity at Work*. London: Sage.

DuGay, P., Hall, S., Janes, L., Mackay, H. and Negus, K. (1997) *Doing Cultural Studies: The Story of the Walkman*. London: Sage/Open University.

During, S. (1993) *The Cultural Studies Reader*. London: Routledge.

Dyer, R. (1977) '*Victim*: hermeneutic project', in *Film Form*, 1 (2) Autumn.

Dyer, R. (1997) *White*. London: Routledge.

Dyer, R., Geraghty, C., Jordan, J., Lovell, T., Paterson, R. and Stewart, J. (eds) (1981) *Coronation Street*. London: British Film Institute.

Fischer, M.D. (1994) *Applications in Computing for Social Anthropologists*. London: Routledge.

Fiske, J. (1989) 'Moments of television: neither the text nor the audience', in E. Seiter, H. Borchers, G. Kreutzner and E. Warth (eds), *Remote Control: Television, Audiences and Cultural Power*. London: Routledge. pp. 56-68.

Fiske, J. (1996) 'Down under cultural studies', *Cultural Studies*, 10 (2): 369-74.

Fornas, J., Lindberg, U. and Sernhede, O. (1995) In *Garageland: Rock, Youth and Modernity*. London: Routledge.

Frankenberg, R. (1993) *White Women, Race Matters: The Social Construction of Whiteness*. London: Routledge.

Gavron, H. (1968) *The Captive Wife: Conflicts of Housebound Mothers*. Harmondsworth: Penguin.

Geertz. C. (1973) *The Interpretation of Cultures*. New York: Basic Books.

Gelder, K. and Thornton, S. (eds) (1997) *The Subcultures Reader*. London: Routledge.

Gill, R. (2000) 'Discourse analysis: practical implementation', in J.T.E. Richardson (ed.), *Handbook of Qualitative Research Methods for Psychology and the Social Sciences*. Leicester: BPS Books.

Gillespie, M. (1989) 'Technology and tradition - audio-visual culture among south Asian families in west London', *Cultural Studies*, 3: 2.

Gillespie, M. (1995) *Television, Ethnicity and Cultural Change*. London: Routledge.

Gilroy, P. (1996) 'British cultural studies and the pitfalls of identity', in J. Curran, D. Morley. and V. Walkerdine, *Cultural Studies and Communications*. London: Arnold. pp. 35-49.

Glaser, B.G. and Strauss, A.L. (1967) *The Discovery of Grounded Theory*. Chicago: Aldine.

Goffman, E. (1972) *Encounters: Two Studies in the Sociology of Interaction*. London: Allen Lane.

Graham, H. (1984) *Women, Health and the Family*. Brighton: Wheatsheaf.

Gray, A. (1992) *Video Playtime: The Gendering of a Leisure Technology*. London: Routledge.

Gray, A. (1995) 'I want to tell you a story: the narratives of *Video Playtime*', in B. Skeggs (ed.), *Feminist Cultural Theory: Process and Production*. Manchester: Manchester University Press.

Gray, A. (1997) 'Learning from experience: cultural studies and feminism', in J. McGuigan (ed.), *Cultural Methodologies*. London: Sage.

Gray, A. (2001) 'Jobs for the girls: women, consumption and the enterprising self', Anglo-*Saxonica* Serie II 14/15, Lisbon: University of Lisbon. pp. 123-42.

Gray, A. and McGuigan, J. (1993 and 1995) *Studying Culture: An Introductory Reader*. London: Edward Arnold.

Green, M. (1997) 'Working practices', in J. McGuigan (ed.), *Cultural Methodologies*. London: Sage.

Grossberg, L., Nelson, C. and Treichler, P. (eds) (1992) *Cultural Studies*. New York: Routledge.

Guba, E.G. (1990) *The Paradigm Dialogue*.

Gupta, A. and Ferguson, J. (eds) (1997) *Culture, Power, Place: Explorations in Critical Anthropology*. Durham, NC: Duke University Press.

Hall, S. (1980) 'Encoding/decoding', in S. Hall, D. Hobson, A. Lowe and P. Willis (eds), *Culture, Media, Language*. London: Hutchinson.

Hall, S. (1987) 'Minimal selves', in *The Real Me: Post-modernism and the Question of Identity*. ICA Documents 6. London: ICA.

Hall, S. (1992) 'Cultural studies and its theoretical legacies', in L. Grossberg, C. Nelson, and P. Treichler (eds), *Cultural Studies*. New York: Routledge.

Hall, S., Critcher, C., Jefferson, T., Clarke, J. and Roberts. B. (1978) *Policing the Crisis*. London: Macmillan.

Hall, S. and DuGay, P. (eds) (1996) *Questions of Cultural Identity*. London: Sage.

Hall, S., Hobson, D., Lowe, A. and Willis, P. (eds) (1980) *Culture, Media, Language*. London: Hutchinson.

Hammersley, M. and Atkinson, P. (1993) *Ethnography: Principles in Practice*. 2nd edition. London: Routledge.

Hanson, S., Bhattacharyya, G. and Gray, A. (2000) *Placing Yourself in the Community: Workbook 3*. Birmingham: CoBaLT 2000, University of Birmingham.

Haraway, D. (1988) 'Situated knowledge: the science question in feminism and the privilege of partial perspective', *Feminist Studies*, 14: 575-99.

Haraway, D. (1990) 'A manifesto for cyborgs: science, technology and socialist feminism in the 1980s', in L. Nicholson (ed.), *Feminism/Postmodernism*. London: Routledge. pp. 190-233.

Harding, S. (1986) *The Science Question in Feminism*. Milton Keynes: Open University Press.

Harding, S. (ed.) (1987) *Feminism and Methodology*. Milton Keynes: Open University Press.

Harding, S. (1991) *Whose Science, Whose Knowledge? Thinking from Women's Lives*. Milton Keynes: Open University Press.

Hebdige, D. (1979) *Subculture: The Meaning of Style*. London: Routledge.

Hebdige, D. (1987) *Cut'n'Mix*. London: Methuen.

Hermes, J. (1995) *Reading Women's Magazines*. Cambridge: Polity Press.

Hill-Collins, P. (1990) *Black Feminist Thought: Knowledge, Consciousness and the Politics of Empowerment*. London: Routledge.

Hobson, D. (1978) 'Housewives: isolation as oppression', in Women's Studies Group CCCS, *Women Take Issue: Aspects of Women's Subordination*. London: Hutchinson.

Hobson, D. (1980) 'Housewives and the mass media', in S. Hall, D. Hobson, A. Lowe, and P. Willis (eds), *Culture, Media, Language*. London: Hutchinson.

Hobson, D. (1982) *Crossroads: The Drama of a Soap Opera*. London: Methuen.

Hodkinson, P. (2001) 'Subculture as substance: the identities, values, practices and infrastructure of the goth scene'. Unpublished PhD thesis, University of Birmingham.

Hodkinson, P. (2002) *Goth: Identity, Style and Subculture*. Oxford: Berg.

Hoggart, R. (1957) *The Uses of Literacy*. London: Chatto and Windus.

Hollway, W. (1989) *Subjectivity and Method in Psychology: Gender, Meaning and Science*. London: Sage.

Holstein, J.A. and Gubrium, J.F. (1997) 'Active interviewing', in D. Silverman (ed.), *Qualitative Research: Theory, Method and Practice*. London: Sage.

Hunt, J. (1989) *Psychoanalytic Aspects of Fieldwork*. Newbury Park, CA: Sage.

Jefferson, T. (ed.) (1976) *Resistance through Rituals*. London: Hutchinson.

Jenkins, H. (1992) *Textual Poachers: Television Fans and Participatory Culture*. New York: Routledge.

Johnson, R. (1997) 'Reinventing cultural studies: remembering for the best version', in E. Long, *From Sociology to Cultural Studies: New Perspectives*. Malden, MA: Blackwell.

Jones, S. (1988) *Black Culture, White Youth: The Reggae Tradition from JA to UK*. London: Macmillan.

Junker, B. (1960) *Field Work*. Chicago: University of Chicago Press.

Kauffman, B.J. (1992) 'Feminist facts: interview strategies and political subjects in ethnography', *Communication Theory*, 2 (3): 187-206.

Knorr-Cetina, K.D. (1981) 'The micro-sociological challenge of macro-sociology: toward a reconstruction of social theory and methodology', in K. Knorr-Cetina and A.V. Cicourel (eds), *Advances in Social Theory and Methodology: Toward an Integration of Micro- and Macro-sociologies*. Boston: Routledge and Kegan Paul.

Kosnick, K. (2000) Building bridges: media for migrants and the public service mission in Germany', *European Journal of Cultural Studies*, 3 (3): 319-42.

Kuhn, A. (1995) *Family Secrets: Acts of Memory and Imagination*. London: Verso.

Lather, P. (1993) 'Fertile obsession: validity after poststructuralism', *Sociological Quarterly*, 34: 673-94.

Leal, O.F. (1990) 'Popular taste and erudite repertoire: the place and space of television in Brazil', *Cultural Studies*, 4 (1): 19-28.

Lefebvre, H. (1990) *Everyday Life in the Modern World*. New Brunswick, NJ: Transaction.

Lewis, L.A. (ed.) (1992) *The Adoring Audience: Fan Culture and Popular Media*. London: Routledge.

Liebes, T. and Katz, E. (1993) *The Export of Meaning: Cross-cultural Readings of 'Dallas'*. Cambridge: Polity Press.

Lofland, J. (1971) *Analysing Social Settings: A Guide to Qualitative Observation and Analysis*. Belmont, CA: Wadsworth.

Long, E. (ed.) (1997) *From Sociology to Cultural Studies: New Perspectives*. Malden, MA: Blackwell.

Lull, J. (1990) *Inside Family Viewing: Ethnographic Research on Television's Audiences*. London: Routledge.

Malkki, L. (1997) 'National Geographic: the rooting of peoples and the territorialization of national identity among scholars and refugees', in A. Gupta and J. Ferguson (eds), *Culture, Power, Place: Explorations in Critical Anthropology*. Durham, NC: Duke University Press.

Mankekar, P. (1999) *Screening Culture, Viewing Politics: An Ethnography of Television, Womanhood, and Nation in Postcolonial India*. Durham, NC: Duke University Press.

Marcus, G.E. and Fisher, M.M.J. (1986) *Anthropology as Cultural Critique: An Experimental Moment in the Human Sciences*. Chicago: University of Chicago Press.

Martin-Barbero, J. (1993) *Communication, Culture and Hegemony*. London: Sage.

Maynard, M. and Purvis, J. (eds) (1994) *Researching Lives from a Feminist Perspective*. London: Taylor and Francis.

McGuigan, J. (ed.) (1997) *Cultural Methodologies*. London: Sage.

McRobbie, A. (1978) 'Working class girls and the culture of femininity', in Women's Studies Group CCCS, *Women Take Issue: Aspects of Women's Subordination*. London: Hutchinson.

McRobbie, A. (1982) 'The politics of feminist research: between talk, text and action', *Feminist Review*, 12, 46-57.

McRobbie, A. (1992) 'Post-Marxism and cultural studies: a post-script', in L. Grossberg, C. Nelson and P. Treichler (eds), *Cultural Studies*. New York: Routledge.

McRobbie, A. (ed.) (1997) *Back to Reality? Social Experience and Cultural Studies*. Manchester: Manchester University Press.

McRobbie, A. (1998) *British Fashion Design: Rag Trade or Image Industry?* London: Routledge.

Meijer, I.C. (2001) 'The colour of soap opera: an analysis of professional speech on the representation of ethnicity', *European Journal of Cultural Studies*, 4 (2): 207-30.

Menchu, R. (1984) *I Rigoberta Menchu*. London: Verso.

Miller, P. and Rose, N. (1990) 'Governing economic life', *Economy and Society*, 19: 1-31.

Mills, C.W. (1959) *The Sociological Imagination*. Harmondsworth: Penguin.

Modleski, T. (1982) *Loving with a Vengeance: Mass-Produced Fantasies for Women*. Hamden, CT: Shoestring Press.

Modleski, T. (1983) 'The rhythm of reception: daytime television and women's work', in E.A. Kaplan (ed.), *Regarding Television: Critical Approaches - An Anthology*. Los Angeles: American Film Institute.

Moores, S. (1996) *Satellite Television and Everyday Life: Articulating Technology*. Luton: University of Luton Press.

Morley, D. (1980) *The Nationwide Audience*. London: British Film Institute.

Morley, D. (1986) *Family Television: Cultural Power and Domestic Leisure*. London: Comedia.

Morley, D. (1992) *Television, Audiences and Cultural Studies*. London: Routledge.

Morley, D. (2000) *Home Territories. Media, Mobility and Identity*. London: Routledge.

Morley, D. and Chen, K.-H. (eds) (1996) *Stuart Hall: Critical Dialogues in Cultural Studies*. London: Routledge.

Morris, M. (1997) 'A question of cultural studies', in A. McRobbie (ed.), *Back to Reality? Social Experience and Cultural Studies*. Manchester: Manchester University Press.

Myerhoff, B. (1988) 'Surviving stories: reflections on number our days', in J. Kugelmas, (ed.), *Between Two Worlds: Ethnographic Essays on American Jewry*. Ithaca, NY: Cornell University

Press.

Myrdal, G. (1969) *Objectivity and Social Research*. London: Duckworth.

Naficy, H. (1993) *The Making of Exile Cultures: Iranian Television in Los Angeles*. Minneapolis: University of Minnesota Press.

Neale, S. (1981) 'Genre and cinema', in T. Bennett, S. Boyd Bowman, C. Mercer and J. Woollacott (eds) *Culture, Ideology and Social Process*. London: British Film Institute.

Nixon, S. (1996) *Hard Looks: Masculinities, Spectatorship and Contemporary Consumption*. London: UCL Press.

Paget, M.A. (1983) 'Experience and knowledge', *Human Studies*, 6: 67-90.

Penacchioni, I. (1984) 'The reception of popular television in Northeast Brazil', *Media, Culture and Society*, 6: 337-41.

Pink, S. (2000) *Doing Visual Ethnography*. London: Sage.

Plummer, K. (1995) *Telling Sexual Stories: Power, Change and Social Worlds*. London: Routledge.

Plummer, K. (2001) *Documents of Life 2: An Invitation to a Critical Humanism*. London: Sage.

Potter, J. (2000) 'Discourse analysis and constructionist approaches: theoretical background', in Richardson, J.T.E. (ed.), *Handbook of Qualitative Research Methods for Psychology and the Social Sciences*. Leicester: BPS Books.

Probyn, E. (1993) *Sexing the Self: Gendered Positions in Cultural Studies*. London: Routledge.

Propp, V. (1968) *Morphology of the Folk Tale*. Austin, TX: University of Texas Press.

Pursehouse, M. (1989) 'Reading the *Sun*: conflicts in the popular', unpublished MPhil thesis, University of Birmingham.

Rabinow, P. (1986) 'Representations are social facts: modernity and post-modernity in anthropology', in J. Clifford and G.E. Marcuse (eds) *Writing Culture*. Berkeley, CA: University of California Press.

Radway, J. (1988) 'The Book-of-the-Month Club and the general reader: on the uses of "serious" fiction', *Critical Inquiry*, 14 (Spring), 516-38.

Radway, J. (1989) 'Ethnography among elites: comparing discourses of power', *Journal of Communication Inquiry*, 13 (2): 3-11.

Radway, J.A. (1984) *Reading the Romance: Women, Patriarchy, and Popular Literature*. Chapel Hill, NC: University of North Carolina Press.

Radway, J.A. (1987) *Reading the Romance*. London: Verso.

Richardson, J.T.E. (ed.) (2000) *Handbook of Qualitative Research Methods for Psychology and the Social Sciences*. Leicester: BPS Books.

Riis, J.A. (1971) *How the Other Half Lives*. New York: Dover (first published 1890).

Roberts, H. (ed.) (1981) *Doing Feminist Research*. London: Routledge and Kegan Paul.

Rose, G. (2001) *Visual Methodologies: An Introduction to the Interpretation of Visual Materials*. London: Sage.

Rose, N. (1996) 'Identity, genealogy, history', in S. Hall and P. du Gay, *Questions of Cultural Identity*. London: Sage.

Said, E.W. (1978) *Orientalism: Western Conceptions of the Orient*. London: Routledge and Kegan Paul.

Schlesinger, P. (1978) *Putting Reality Together: BBC News*. London: Constable.

Scott, J.W. (1992) 'Experience', in J. Butler and J.W. Scott (eds), *Feminists Theorize the Political*. New York: Routledge.

Seal, C. (ed) (1998) *Researching Society and Culture*. London: Sage.

Seiter, E. (1990) 'Making distinctions in audience research', *Cultural Studies*, 4 (1): 61-84.

Seiter, E., Borchers, H., Kreutzner, G. and Warth, E. (eds) (1989) *Remote Control: Television, Audiences and Cultural Power*. London: Routledge.

Silverman, D. (ed.) (1997) *Qualitative Research: Theory, Method and Practice*. London: Sage.

Silverstone, R. (1994) *Television and Everyday Life*. London and New York: Routledge.

Skeggs, B. (1994) 'Situating the production of feminist ethnography'. In M. Maynard and J. Purvis (eds) *Researching Lives from a Feminist Perspective*. London: Taylor and Francis.

Skeggs, B. (ed.) (1995) *Feminist Cultural Theory: Process and Production*. Manchester: Manchester University Press.

Skeggs, B. (1997) *Formations of Class and Gender*. London: Sage..

Slack, J.D. (1996) 'The theory and method of articulation in cultural studies', in D. Morley and K-H. Chen (eds) *Stuart Hall: Critical Dialogues in Cultural Studies*. London: Routledge.

Song, M. and Parker, D. (1995) 'Commonality, difference and the dynamics of disclosure in in-depth interviewing', *Sociology*, 29 (2), 241-56.

Spence, J. (1986) *Putting Myself in the Picture: A Political, Personal and Photographic Autobiography*. London: Camden Press.

Spivak, G. (1987) *In Other Worlds: Essays in Cultural Politics*. New York: Routledge.

Stacey, J. (1994) *Star Gazing; Hollywood Cinema and Female Spectatorship*. London: Routledge.

Stake, R.E. (1995) *The Art of Case Study Research*. Thousand Oaks, CA: Sage.

Stanley, L. (ed.) (1990) *Feminist Praxis: Research, Theory and Epistemology in Feminist Sociology*. London: Routledge.

Stanley, L. and Wise, S. (1993) *Breaking Out Again: Feminist Ontology and Epistemology*. London: Routledge.

Steedman, C. (1986) *Landscape for a Good Woman: A Story of Two Lives*. London: Virago.

Steedman, C. (1997) 'Writing the self: the end of the scholarship girl', in J. McGuigan (ed.) *Cultural Methodologies*. London: Sage.

Strathern, M. (1999)*Property, Substance and Effect: Anthropological Essays on Persons and Things*. London: The Athlone Press.

Summerfield, P. (1998) *Reconstructing Women's Wartime Lives*. Manchester: Manchester University Press.

Tagg, J. (1988) *The Burden of Representation: Essays on Photographies and Histories*. Basingstoke: Macmillan.

Terkel, S. (1978) *Talking to Myself: A Memoir of My Times*. New York: Pocket Books.

Tesch, R. (1990) *Qualitative Research: Analysis, Types and Software Tools*. London: Falmer.

Thomas, W.I. and Znaniecki, F. (1958) *The Polish Peasant in Europe and America*. New York: Dover Publications.

Thornton, S. (1995) *Club Cultures: Music, Media and Subcultural Capital*. Cambridge: Polity Press.

Ticknell, E. and Raghuram. P. (2002) *Big Brother*: reconfiguring the ''active'' audience of cultural studies', *European Journal of Cultural Studies*, 5 (2).

Tolson, A. (1990) 'Social surveillance and subjectification: the emergence of ''subculture'' in the work of Henry Mayhew', in *Cultural Studies*, 4 : 2. 113-27.

Tudor, A. (1999) *Decoding Culture Theory and Method in Cultural Studies*. London: Sage.

Tufte, T. (2000) *Living with the Rubbish Queen: Telenovelas, Culture and Modernity in Brazil*. Luton: University of Luton Press..

Turkle, S. (1995) *Life on the Screen: Identity in the Age of the Internet*. London: Phoenix.

Van Zoonen, L. (1998) 'A professional, unreliable, heroic marionette (m/f): structure, agency and subjectivity in contemporary journalisms', *European Journal of Cultural Studies*, 1 (1) 123-45.

Walkerdine, V. (1986) 'Video replay: families, films and fantasy', in V. Burgin, J. Donal and C. Kaplen (eds) *Formations of Fantasy*. London: Methuen.

Walkerdine, V. (1997) *Daddy's Girl: Young Girls and Popular Culture*. London: Macmillan.

Walkerdine, V. and Lucey, H. (1989) *Democracy in the Kitchen: Regulating Mothers and Socialising Daughters*. London: Virago.

Whyte, W.F. (1943) *Street Corner Society*. Chicago: University of Chicago Press.

Williams, R. (1958) *Culture and Society, 1780-1950*. London: Chatto and Windus.

Williams, R. (1961) *The Long Revolution*. London: Chatto and Windus.

Williams, R. (1979) *Politics and Letters*. London: Verso.

Williams. R. (1981) *Culture*. Glasgow: Collins.

Williamson, J. (1978) *Decoding Advertisements*. London: Marion Boyars.

Willis, P. (1980) 'Notes on method', in S. Hall, D. Hobson, A. Lowe and P. Willis (eds), *Culture, Media, Language*. London: Hutchinson.

Willis, P.E. (1977) *Learning to Labour: How Working Class Kids Get Working Class Jobs*. Aldershot: Gower.

Willis, P.E. (1981) *Learning to Labour: How Working Class Kids Get Working Class Jobs*. New York: Columbia University Press.

Willis, P.E. (1997) 'Theoretical confessions and reflexive method', in K. Gelder and S. Thornton (eds), *The Subcultures Reader*. London: Routledge

Winship, J. (1987) *Inside Women's Magazines*. London: Pandora.

Women's Studies Group CCCS (1978) *Women Take Issue: Aspects of Women's Subordination*. London: Hutchinson.

Znaniecki, F. (1934) *The Method of Sociology*. New York: Farrar and Rinehart.

Index